1000 Ninja Cookbook 2021#

Your Complete Guide to Pressure Cook, Slow Cook, Air Fry, Dehydrate, and More, 1000 Ninja Foodi Recipes to Help You Live Healthily and Happily

Dr. Jenny Grace

Copyright@2020 by Dr. Jenny Grace

All rights reserved worldwide.

No part of this book may be reproduced or transmitted in any form or by any means, electronic or mechanical, including photocopying, recording or by any information storage and retrieval system, without written permission from the publisher, except for the inclusion of brief quotations in a review.

Contents

Introduction...- 13 -

Chapter 1: Ninja Foodi Cooking...- 14 -

What exactly is the Ninja Foodi?...- 14 -

Understanding the "TenderCrisp Technology".......................................- 14 -

What to expect inside the box..- 15 -

Understanding the basics of the control panel.......................................- 16 -

The Core Functionalities of the Foodi...- 17 -

Looking at the different Core parts of the Ninja Foodi............................- 18 -

Why is the Ninja Foodi so amazing?..- 19 -

Amazing tips for the perfect "TenderCrisp"..- 20 -

Awesome general tips about the appliance..- 21 -

Chapter 2: Delightful Beef Dishes..- 22 -

Tantalizing Beef Jerky...- 22 -

Beefed Up Spaghetti Squash...- 22 -

Adobo Cubed Steak...- 22 -

Cool Beef Bourguignon..- 23 -

A Keto-Friendly Philly Willy Steak And Cheese...................................- 23 -

Beef Stew...- 23 -

Juiciest Keto Bacon Strips..- 24 -

Quick Picadillo Dish..- 24 -

Simple/Aromatic Meatballs...- 24 -

Generous Shepherd's Pie..- 24 -

Hybrid Beef Prime Roast..- 25 -

The Epic Carne Guisada...- 25 -

No-Noodle Pure Lasagna..- 25 -

The Wisdom Worthy Corned Beef...- 26 -

Hearty Korean Ribs...- 26 -

Traditional Beef Sirloin Steak...- 27 -

Beef And Broccoli Platter...- 27 -

Alternative Corned Cabbage And Beef...- 27 -

Marked Beef Goulash...- 28 -

Lemon Delicious Pork Chop..- 28 -

Meat Dredged Loaf..- 28 -

The Chipotle Copycat Dish...- 29 -

All-Buttered Up Beef...- 29 -

Beef And Broccoli Delight..- 29 -

Rich Beef Rendang..- 30 -

Spiritual Indian Beef Dish..- 30 -

Premium Mexican Beef Dish..- 31 -

All-Tim Favorite Beef Chili...- 31 -

Ingenious Bo Kho...- 31 -

Sesame Beef Ribs..- 32 -

Balsamic Pot Roast Of Beef...- 32 -

Extremely Satisfying Beef Curry...- 32 -

Braised Up Bone Short Ribs...- 33 -

The Authentic Beef Casserole...- 33 -

The Great Pepper Steak...- 33 -

The Ground Beef Root Chili...- 34 -

Ground Beef With Green Beans...- 34 -

Delicious Tomatillo Beef And Pork Chili...- 34 -

Chapter 3: High-Quality Seafood Dishes..**- 36 -**

Hearty Swordfish Meal..- 36 -

Gentle And Simple Fish Stew...- 36 -

Cool Shrimp Zoodles..- 36 -

Heartfelt Sesame Fish..- 37 -

Awesome Sock-Eye Salmon..- 37 -

Buttered Up Scallops...- 37 -

NAwesome Cherry Tomato Mackerel...- 37 -

Lovely Air Fried Scallops...- 38 -

Packets Of Lemon And Dill Cod...- 38 -

Adventurous Sweet And Sour Fish..- 38 -

Garlic And Lemon Prawn Delight..- 39 -

Lovely Carb Soup...- 39 -

The Rich Guy Lobster And Butter...- 39 -

Lovely Panko Cod...- 40 -

Salmon Paprika..- 40 -

Heartfelt Air Fried Scampi...- 40 -

Ranch Warm Fillets...- 40 -

Alaskan Cod Divine...- 41 -

Kale And Salmon Delight...- 41 -

Breathtaking Cod Fillets..- 41 -

Lemon And Pepper Salmon Delight...- 42 -

Fresh Steamed Salmon..- 42 -

Spiced Up Cajun Style Tilapia..- 42 -

Delightful Salmon Fillets...- 43 -

A Pot Full Of Shellfish..- 43 -

Orange Sauce And Salmon.. - 44 -

Cucumber And Salmon Mix... - 44 -

The Ginger Flavored Tilapia.. - 44 -

Favorite Salmon Stew.. - 45 -

Tilapia And Asparagus Delight.. - 45 -

Asian Salmon And Veggie Meal.. - 45 -

All-Time Favorite Codes.. - 46 -

The Great Poached Salmon.. - 46 -

Great Seafood Stew.. - 46 -

Garlic Sauce And Mussels... - 47 -

Shrimp And Tomato Delight.. - 47 -

Juicy Mediterranean Cod... - 48 -

Medi-Bass Stew.. - 48 -

Delicious Smoked Salmon And Spinach Frittata.. - 48 -

Dijon Flavored Lemon Whitefish.. - 49 -

Very Low Carb Clam Chowder... - 49 -

Chapter 4: Mouthwatering Poultry Recipes.......................................**- 50 -**

Lemon And Chicken Extravaganza.. - 50 -

Bruschetta Chicken Meal.. - 50 -

The Great Hainanese Chicken.. - 50 -

A Genuine Hassel Back Chicken.. - 51 -

Shredded Up Salsa Chicken.. - 51 -

Mexico's Favorite Chicken Soup... - 51 -

Taiwanese Chicken Delight.. - 52 -

Cabbage And Chicken Meatballs.. - 52 -

Poached Chicken With Coconut Lime Cream Sauce................................... - 52 -

Hot And Spicy Paprika Chicken... - 53 -

Inspiring Turkey Cutlets... - 53 -

Lemongrass And Tamarind Chicken.. - 53 -

Fluffy Whole Chicken Dish.. - 54 -

Sensible Chettinad Chicken.. - 54 -

Hawaiian Pinna Colada Chicken Meal... - 54 -

Garlic And Butter Chicken Dish.. - 55 -

Creamy Chicken Curry... - 55 -

Lemon And Artichoke Medley... - 55 -

Awesome Sesame Ginger Chicken... - 56 -

Chicken Korma... - 56 -

Turkey With Garlic Sauce.. - 57 -

Awesome Ligurian Chicken... - 57 -

Creative French Chicken..- 57 -
Daring Salted Baked Chicken...- 58 -
Worthy Ghee-Licious Chicken..- 58 -
Hearty Duck Breast Meal...- 59 -
Fancy Chicken Chile Verde..- 59 -
Mushroom And Chicken Bowl...- 60 -
Chicken And Broccoli Platter...- 60 -
Complex Garlic And Lemon Chicken...- 60 -
Chicken Puttanesca..- 61 -
Awesome Ligurian Chicken..- 61 -
Garlic And Lemon Chicken Dish..- 62 -
The Hungarian Chicken Meal...- 62 -
Lime And Cilantro Chicken Meal...- 62 -
The Original Mexican Chicken Cacciatore...- 63 -
Magnificent Chicken Curry Soup...- 63 -
Summer Time Chicken Salad..- 63 -
Ham And Stuffed Turkey Rolls..- 64 -
High-Quality Belizean Chicken Stew...- 64 -
The Great Poblano Chicken Curry..- 65 -
Hearty Chicken Yum..- 65 -
The Turkey Pizza Casserole...- 65 -
Heartfelt Chicken Curry Soup..- 66 -
Your's Truly Lime Chicken Chili..- 66 -
Hungry Man's Indian Chicken Keema..- 66 -
The Borderline Crack Chicken...- 67 -
The Decisive Red Curry Chicken...- 67 -
Spinach And Chicken Curry...- 68 -
Cheese Dredged Lemon Chicken..- 68 -
Best Chicken Wings..- 68 -
Simple And Juicy Chicken Stock..- 69 -
Keto-Friendly Chicken Tortilla..- 69 -

Chapter 5: Heart-Warming Pork Recipes...**- 70 -**
Awesome Korean Pork Lettuce Wraps...- 70 -
Spicy "Faux" Pork Belly...- 70 -
Spiced Up Chipotle Pork Roast..- 70 -
Happy Burrito Bowl Pork...- 71 -
Awesome Sauerkraut Pork..- 71 -
Spice Lover's Jalapeno Hash..- 71 -
The Premium Red Pork...- 72 -

Cool Spicy Pork Salad Bowl...- 72 -

Dill And Butter Pork Chops...- 72 -

Cranberry Pork BBQ Dish...- 73 -

Definitive Pork Carnita...- 73 -

Technical Keto Pork Belly...- 74 -

Jamaican Pork Pot...- 74 -

The Mexican Pulled Pork Ala Lettuce...- 74 -

Pork With Cranberries And Pecan...- 75 -

Cuban And Garlic Pork Meal...- 75 -

Mean Cream Mushroom Garlic Chicken...- 76 -

Pork Roast And Cauliflower Gravy...- 76 -

Premium Pork Chili Colorado...- 77 -

Advanced Smothered Pork Chops...- 77 -

The Big Deal Bone-y Pork Chops...- 77 -

Coconut And Ginger Pork Dish...- 78 -

Bacon Kale And Winning Delight...- 78 -

Rosemary Pork Roast...- 78 -

Apple And Sauerkraut Loin...- 79 -

Bacon And Brussels Platter...- 79 -

Healthy Oxtail Ragout...- 79 -

Lemon And Pork Chops Artichokes...- 80 -

Simple Pressure Cooked Lamb Meat...- 80 -

Sassy Evergreen Pork Chops...- 80 -

The Pork "Loin" With Pear...- 81 -

Creative Garlic And Butter Pork...- 81 -

Elegant Lamb Spare Ribs...- 81 -

Cool Lamb Tajine...- 82 -

Pork And Cauliflower Dish...- 82 -

Lime And Ginger Low Carb Pork...- 83 -

Generous Indian Lamb Shanks...- 83 -

Greek Lamb Gyros...- 84 -

Pork Dish With Coconut Added In...- 84 -

Tastiest Pork Cheek Stew...- 84 -

Veal And Rosemary Stew...- 85 -

Keto – Suitable Steamed Pork...- 85 -

Refined Carrot And Bacon Soup...- 85 -

Lovely Pulled Pork Ragu...- 86 -

The Calabacita Squash meal...- 86 -

Chapter 6: Healthy Vegan/Vegetarian Ninja Foodi Recipes...- 87 -

Comfortable Mushroom Soup..- 87 -
Chives And Radishes Platter..- 87 -
Garlic And Swiss Chard Garlic..- 87 -
Healthy Rosemary And Celery Dish...- 88 -
Awesome Veggie Hash...- 88 -
Thyme And Carrot Dish With Dill..- 88 -
Creative Coconut Cabbage..- 88 -
Complete Cauliflower Zoodles..- 89 -
Simple Mushroom Hats And Eggs..- 89 -
Ginger And Butternut Bisque Yum...- 89 -
Hearty Cheesy Cauliflower..- 90 -
Mesmerizing Spinach Quiche..- 90 -
Running Away Broccoli Casserole..- 90 -
Spaghetti Squash Fancy Noodles..- 91 -
Dill And Garlic Fiesta Platter..- 91 -
Quick Red Cabbage...- 91 -
Simple Rice Cauliflower..- 92 -
Very Spicy Cauliflower Steak...- 92 -
Authentic Indian Palak Paneer...- 92 -
All-Time Mixed Vegetable Curry...- 93 -
Worthy Caramelized ONion..- 93 -
A Very Greeny Green Beans Platter...- 93 -
A Mishmash Cauliflower Mash...- 94 -
Zucchini And Artichoke Platter..- 94 -
Winning Broccoli Casserole..- 94 -
Spaghetti Squash Drizzled With Sage Butter Sauce.................- 95 -
Uber-Keto Caper And Beet Salad...- 95 -
The Greeny And Beany Horseradish Mix.................................- 95 -
Fully Stuffed Whole Chicken..- 96 -
Rosemary Dredged Green Beans...- 96 -
Italian Turkey Breast...- 96 -
Crazy Fresh Onion Soup...- 97 -
Elegant Zero Crust Kale And Mushroom Quiche.....................- 97 -
Delicious Beet Borscht..- 97 -
Pepper Jack Cauliflower Meal..- 98 -
Slow-Cooked Brussels..- 98 -
Slowly Cooked Lemon Artichokes...- 98 -
Well Dressed Brussels...- 99 -
Cheddar Cauliflower Bowl..- 99 -

A Prosciutto And Thyme Eggs...- 99 -
The Authentic Zucchini Pesto Meal...- 99 -
Supreme Cauliflower Soup...- 100 -
Very Rich And Creamy Asparagus Soup..- 100 -
Summertime Vegetable Platter..- 101 -
The Creative Mushroom Stroganoff..- 101 -
Garlic And Ginger Red Cabbage Platter..- 101 -
The Veggie Lover's Onion And Tofu Platter...- 102 -
Feisty Maple Dredged Carrots..- 102 -
The Original Sicilian Cauliflower Roast..- 102 -

Chapter 7: Holiday And Weekend Ninja Recipes............................**- 104 -**
Simple Weeknight Vanilla Yogurt...- 104 -
The Great Family Lemon Mousse..- 104 -
Tangy Berry Slices...- 104 -
Over The Weekend Apple And Sprouts..- 104 -
Generous Gluten Free Pancakes..- 105 -
Fancy Holiday Lemon Custard..- 105 -
Gentle Peanut Butter Cheesecake...- 105 -
Decisive Crème Brulee...- 106 -
The Cool Pot-De-Crème..- 106 -
Humming Key Lime Curd..- 106 -
Runny Eggs In A Cup...- 107 -
Simple Party Week Poached Pears..- 107 -
A Wedding Worthy Coconut Cake..- 107 -
Uniform Dark Chocolate Cake...- 108 -
Party Night Lamb Gyros...- 108 -
Extreme Choco Fudge Eatery For The Party...- 108 -
The Delightful Cauliflower And Cheese "Cake".....................................- 109 -
Fan-Favorite Aunt's Coconut Custard..- 109 -
The Christmas Strawberry Shortcake...- 109 -
Kid-Friendly Peanut Butter Cheesecake...- 110 -
Quick Lava Molten Cake For Keto Lovers..- 110 -
Grandmother's Pumpkin Carrot Cake..- 110 -
Spiced Up Jack Cheese Muffin...- 111 -
Early Morning Vegetable Stock..- 111 -
Grandmother's Carrot Halwa..- 111 -
Lemon And Ricotta Party-Friendly Cheesecake......................................- 112 -
Highly Sough-After Egg Devils..- 112 -
Hearty Mushroom Stock..- 112 -

A Christmas-y Pot De Crème..- 113 -

Creative Almond And Carrot Cake..- 113 -

Heavenly Zucchini Bread...- 113 -

Heart Melting Choco-Mousse...- 114 -

Chapter 8: 5 Ingredients Or Less Ninja Foodi Recipes................................- 115 -

The Coolest New York Strip Steak...- 115 -

French Onion Pork Chops..- 115 -

Hearty Apple Infused Water...- 115 -

Simple And Easy Chicken Breast..- 115 -

Italian Dark Kale Crisps..- 116 -

Quick Ginger And Sesame Chicken...- 116 -

Butter Melted Broccoli Florets...- 116 -

The Epic Fried Eggs...- 116 -

Gentle Keto Butter Fish..- 117 -

Sensational Carrot Puree...- 117 -

Simple Broccoli Florets...- 117 -

Awesome Magical 5 Ingredient Shrimp..- 118 -

Romantic Mustard Pork..- 118 -

Creative And Easy Lamb Roast...- 118 -

Crispy Tofu And Mushrooms..- 118 -

A Hearty Sausage Meal...- 119 -

Deserving Mushroom Saute..- 119 -

Slightly Zesty Lamb Chops..- 119 -

Bacon And Scrambled Egg...- 119 -

Delicious Creamy Crepes...- 120 -

Egg Stuffed Avocado Dish..- 120 -

Lovely Asparagus Bites...- 120 -

Easy to Make Mustard Pork Chops..- 121 -

Generous Lemon Mousse...- 121 -

Terrific Baked Spinach Quiche..- 121 -

Juicy Keto Lamb Roast..- 121 -

Warm Avocado Chips..- 122 -

Nutty Assorted Collection..- 122 -

Exquisite Mediterranean Cheese Spinach...- 122 -

English Green Peas And Asparagus...- 122 -

The Pecan Delight..- 123 -

Favorite Peanut Butter Cups..- 123 -

Crispy Mixed Up Nuts...- 123 -

Quick And Simple Pork Carnitas...- 123 -

Simple Teriyaki Chicken .... - 124 -

Lovely Yet "Stinky" Garlic .... - 124 -

Simple Veggie And Bacon Platter .... - 124 -

Cream Cheese And Zucchini Fries .... - 124 -

Creamy Beef And Garlic Steak .... - 125 -

Delicious Bacon Swiss Pork Chops .... - 125 -

Hearty Baked Brisket .... - 125 -

Nice Beef Fajitas .... - 126 -

Divine Keto Nut Porridge .... - 126 -

Delicious Prosciutto Cane Wraps .... - 126 -

Green Bean Mix .... - 126 -

5 Ingredients Keto Choco Cheese Cake .... - 127 -

Helpful Raspberry And Peach Aid .... - 127 -

The Eldar Shrub .... - 127 -

Cool "Cooked" Ice Tea .... - 127 -

Chapter 9: 20 Minutes Ninja Foodi Recipes .... - 129 -

Quick And Easy Buttery Pancake .... - 129 -

Decisive Asian Brussels .... - 129 -

Busy Man's Bacon Jalapeno .... - 129 -

Lovely Bok Choy Soup .... - 130 -

Mushroom Hats Stuffed With Cheese .... - 130 -

A King's Favorite Egg Salad .... - 130 -

Come-Back Cauliflower And Parm .... - 130 -

The Chorizo Flavored Casserole .... - 131 -

Sensible Chinese Salad .... - 131 -

Mushroom And Bok Choy Health Bite .... - 131 -

Cool Cabbage Soup .... - 132 -

Sensible Steamed Keto Salad .... - 132 -

Okra And Bacon Delight .... - 132 -

Awesome Luncheon Green Beans .... - 132 -

Powerful Keto Tuscan Soup .... - 133 -

Turnip Greens And Sausage .... - 133 -

Easy And Cheesy Asparagus .... - 133 -

Crisped Up Sweet Fish .... - 134 -

Flimsy Buffalo Fish .... - 134 -

Tomato And Zucchini Rosemary .... - 134 -

Herbed Up 13 Minutes Cod .... - 134 -

New Broccoli Pops .... - 135 -

Great Salmon Stew .... - 135 -

Creative Srilankan Coconut Dish..- 135 -
Baked Paprika Delight...- 136 -
The Good Eggs De Provence...- 136 -
Spiced Up Brussels...- 136 -
The Epic French Egg...- 137 -
Quick Avocado And Coconut Pudding...- 137 -
Juicy Glazed Carrots...- 137 -
All-Round Pumpkin Puree...- 137 -
Broccoli And Scrambled Egg Ala Gusto..- 138 -
Onion And Tofu Scramble...- 138 -
Quick Gouda Sauce..- 138 -
Quick And Easy Garlic Turkey Breasts..- 139 -
Creamy 5 Ingredients Chicken Breasts..- 139 -
Tasty Pepperoni Omelette...- 139 -
The Cool Scrambled Eggs...- 140 -
Decisive Eggplant And Olive Keto Spread...- 140 -
A Ballet Of Roasted Ham And Spinach...- 140 -
Secret Indian Fish Curry...- 141 -
Magnificent Cauliflower Alfredo Zoodles..- 141 -
Chicken Coriander Soup..- 141 -
Garlic And Mushroom Chicken Stew...- 142 -
Spaghetti Squash In Sage And Butter Sauce...- 142 -
Ham And Hollandaise Delight...- 143 -
Delicious Ghee Carrots...- 143 -
Simple Cheese Casserole...- 143 -

Chapter 10: Awesome Snacks And Appetizers...**- 144 -**
Inspiring Cauliflower Hash Browns...- 144 -
Everybody's Favorite Cauliflower Patties..- 144 -
Kale And Almonds Mix...- 144 -
Simple Treat Of Garlic..- 145 -
Buttered Up Garlic And Fennel..- 145 -
Obvious Paprika And Cabbage...- 145 -
Authentic Western Omelet...- 145 -
Bowl Full Of Broccoli Salad...- 146 -
Rise And Shine Breakfast Casserole..- 146 -
Cauliflower And Egg Dish...- 146 -
Just A Simple Egg Frittata...- 147 -
Ultimate Cheese Dredged Cauliflower Snack...- 147 -
The Great Mediterranean Spinach..- 147 -

Quick Turkey Cutlets .... - 147 -

Veggies Dredged In Cheese .... - 148 -

Egg Dredged Casserole .... - 148 -

Excellent Bacon And Cheddar Frittata .... - 148 -

Pork Packed Jalapeno .... - 149 -

Juicy Garlic Chicken Livers .... - 149 -

The Original Zucchini Gratin .... - 149 -

Quick Bite Zucchini Fries .... - 150 -

Pickled Up Green Chili .... - 150 -

Spaghetti Squash And Chicken Parmesan .... - 150 -

Spice Lover's Jar Of Chili .... - 150 -

Easy To Swallow Beet Chips .... - 151 -

Bacon Samba Bok Choy .... - 151 -

Sour Cream Mushroom Appetizer .... - 151 -

Tasty Brussels .... - 152 -

Visible Citrus And Cauli Salad .... - 152 -

Faithful Roasted Garlic .... - 152 -

Feisty Chicken Thighs .... - 153 -

Garlic And Tomato "Herbed" Chicken Thighs .... - 153 -

The Kool Poblano Cheese Frittata .... - 153 -

The Divine Fudge Meal .... - 154 -

The Original Braised Kale And Carrot Salad .... - 154 -

Delicious Bacon- Wrapped Drumsticks .... - 154 -

Stuffed Chicken Mushrooms .... - 154 -

A Hot Buffalo Wing Platter .... - 155 -

Garlic And Mushroom Crunchies .... - 155 -

Delicious Cocoa Almond Bites .... - 155 -

Chicken Crescent Wraps .... - 156 -

Diced And Spiced Up Paprika Eggs .... - 156 -

Faux Daikon Noodles .... - 156 -

Simple Vegetable Stock .... - 157 -

Conclusion .... **- 158 -**

Appendix: Measurement Conversion Table .... **- 159 -**

Introduction

Throughout the 1000 absolutely amazing Ninja Foodi recipes found in this book, you will notice that I have tried to cover every single type of recipe possible. You will get easy to make recipes, meat, poultry, seafood, holiday recipes, and even simple 5 ingredient recipes, the list goes on!

And if you are daring and want to take on more of a challenge, then a good number of slightly complicated recipes are also there to challenge your inner chef!

Welcome, to the amazing world of Ninja Foodi Cooking!

Chapter 1: Ninja Foodi Cooking

What exactly is the Ninja Foodi?

Well, Ninja Foodi is possibly the latest and one of the most versatile and revolutionary multi-cooker to date that every chef and budding enthusiast should have! At its heart, the Ninja Foodi is an electric pressure cooker, but behind its seemingly innocent façade, it's much more than that.

This fine kitchen gadget is an appliance that not only combines all the features of a modern electric pressure cooker such as an Instant Pot but also adds the added benefit of being able to Air Fryer using the same device! And does so by utilizing it's patented "Tender Crisp" technology which we will talk about in a bit.

But asides from the built-in features of being an electric pressure cooker and an Air Fryer, the Ninja Foodi also has the capacity to be used as a steamer, slow cooker, browning pan, air crisper, roaster, broiler, and even a dehydrator!

This basically means that using the Ninja Foodi, you will be able to make your favorite Keto-Friendly dish ranging from stews, meat, snacks, and even desserts!

Using the dehydrator feature, the Ninja Foodi will also allow you to preserve and fruits and vegetables.

And the best part? Despite having a myriad of amazing features, the Ninja is still a very accessible and user-friendly device that anyone can use!

Understanding the "TenderCrisp Technology"

The TenderCrisp Technology is possibly the core feature that makes the Ninja Foodi so unique and interesting.

Before moving forward, it is crucial that you have a good understanding of what this technology actually means and how it will influence your cooking style using the Foodi.

So, consider this.

Whenever you are using a pressure cooker to cook hardy ingredients similar to poultry meat or any other tough meat, you usually get food that is very juicy and great to eat. However, you simply the act of pressure cooking won't be able to produce meat that is both tenders on the inside and crispy on the outside.

And this is why appliances such as the "Air Fryers" were created so that an individual can produce deliciously tender and juicy meals, with a fine crispy finish.

The Ninja Foodi incorporates this amazing cooking method of Air Fryers and infuses the art of Pressure Cooking and Air Frying into one complete package.

So essentially, using the Ninja Foodi, at first you will be able to pressure cook your meat to a very juicy and tender finish, and end it with a nice crispy exterior.

The crispiness is achieved in the Ninja Foodi using the installed Crisping Lid alongside the Crisping Basket, included with the appliance.

A function known as the "AirCrisp" mode initiates the crisping action.

This whole process of first pressure cooking and then crisping the meals in a single pot using their crisping basket and Air Crisper is known as their patented "TenderCrisp" technology.

The inclusion of this amazing tech instantly makes this appliance one of a kind and completely separates itself from the rest of the crowd.

What to expect inside the box

Assuming that you are going to buy a new Ninja Foodi or have purchased one but haven't open it yet, below is a summary of what you might expect when you open up a box for the first time.

- ➢ The Pressure Lid
- ➢ The Crisping Lid
- ➢ A 1,400 Watt Housing Unit
- ➢ A 6 and ½ quart ceramic coated pot
- ➢ A Stainless-Steel reversible Steam/Broil rack
- ➢ 4-quart Ceramic Coated Cook/Crisping Basket
- ➢ Cook and Crisp Layered Insert
- ➢ An included recipe book that covers 45 recipes

However, if you want to completely unleash the full potential of the appliance, you should consider purchasing these additional components as they will help you in the long run. Keep in mind that none of these are included in the pot itself and if you want them, you have to purchase them separately.

- ➢ Multi-Purpose Pan
- ➢ Crisper Pan
- ➢ Loaf Pan
- ➢ Dehydrating Pan

➤ Roasting Pan Insert

Understanding the basics of the control panel

If you want to quickly master the art of using your Ninja Foodi, the first thing that you should know about is how the various buttons on the control panel work. Each button has its own purpose and having a good understanding of all them will allow you to create amazing recipes in no time!

At first, let me talk about the core buttons, after which I will discuss a little bit about the various functions.

Standby

This is self-explanatory, if the Ninja Foodi stays idle for 10 minutes, it will automatically go into Standby mode until further command.

Power

This button allows you to turn your appliance on or off.

Keep Warm

This button allows you Ninja Foodi to keep the food at a food-safe temperature for a prolonged period of time.

Start/Stop

Once the cooking temperature has been set, you can use the start/stop button to stop or initiate the cooking process.

Time Arrow

The time arrows allow you to set the timer for your cooking mode.

Temp Arrow

The temp arrow allows you to set the temperature for your appliance.

Preset Cooking

The Pre-Set cooking button allows you to choose one of the 8 built-in cooking modes and choose the best one suitable for your meal. The different functions are broken down in the next section.

The Core Functionalities of the Foodi

With the TenderCrisp tech out of the way, let me talk a little bit about the different buttons and features found in the Foodi.

The following guide should help you understand what each of the buttons does and how you can use them to their fullest extent.

Pressure

The Pressure Button will allow you to simply Pressure Cook your foods using the Ninja Foodi. This will allow you to cook meals almost 70% faster than other traditional methods. Keep in mind that if you use the Pressure Button, you will also get the option to release the pressure naturally or perform a quick release pressure in the end.

Releasing the pressure naturally is often recommended for tough meats while the quick release is often suited for tender cuts like fish or even vegetables.

Steam

This particular button allows you to use the "Steam" function of the Ninja Foodi. Using steam, you will be able to cook very delicate food at high temperatures. Just make sure to use at least a cup of liquid when steaming your food. While using this feature, make sure to use the Pressure Lid.

Slow Cooker

This particular button will allow you to utilize the Slow Cooker mode that allows you to use the Ninja Foodi as a traditional Slow Cooker. Through this method, your cooks will be cooked at a very low temperature over a prolonged period of time. The time can be adjusted from 12-4 hours, and once the cooking is done, the appliance will automatically switch to "KEEP WARM" function where the meal stays hot until you open it up.

Sear/Saute

This particular button allows you to use your Ninja Foodi to brown meat. This feature is excellent when you need searing or browning meat/ Sautéing spices. This same function can also be used to simmer sauces. Similar to Broil mode, this does not come with a temperature setting, rather, once you are done browning, you simply need to press the "START/STOP" button to initiate or stop the process.

Air Crisp

This is possibly the most unique feature of the Ninja Foodi. Using the Air Crisp feature, you will be able to use your Ninja Foodi as an Air Fryer, that allows you to add a nice crispy and crunchy texture with little to almost no oil. This particular setting cooks the food at extremely high temperatures of 300F to 400F. As a general tip, it is advised that you pre-heat the appliance before adding your ingredients for best results. Needless to say, this feature uses the Crisping lid.

Bake/Roast

This particular function is for those who like to bake! The Bake/Roast function is an awesome mode that allows users to seamlessly use their Foodi as a regular oven (thanks to crisping lid) that allows them to create inspiring baked goods.

Broil

The Broil feature is used in conjunction with the Crisping Lid in order to slightly brown or caramelizes the surface of your food. It cooks food at a higher temperature to create the required brown surface. Keep in mind that this feature has no temperature adjustment.

Dehydrate

The Dehydrate function allows you to dehydrate food between 105 degrees F and 195 degrees F, and this feature will allow you to make healthy dried snacks out of meat, vegetables, and fruits. However, if you want to use this device, it is advised that you purchase a dehydrating rack for maximum efficiency.

Looking at the different Core parts of the Ninja Foodi

Now that you are familiar with the basics of the Ninja Foodi, let me walk you through the core parts of your Ninja Foodi to help you to further familiarize yourself with the appliance itself.

In short, there are 5 core components of your Ninja Foodi that you should know about.

Pressure Lid

The pressure lid turns your Ninja Foodi into a fine electric pressure that allows you to cook your food efficiently and quickly using the power of pressure.

Crisping Lid

The Crisping lid adapts the fan and temperature of the Ninja Foodi so that you use the Air Crisp feature, alongside bake/Roast, broil and dehydrate mode.

The powerful fan present rotates at 2500 rpm and distributes heat all around your meal. Temperatures up to 450 degrees F can be reached using this method. On the other side of the spectrum, you can set the temperature to as low as 100 degrees F as well, this allows you to dehydrate vegetables, fruits, meats etc.

Cooking Pot

The Ninja Foodie's cooking pot is carefully designed with the extra-wide diameter to ensure that you are able to use to not only pressure cook your meals, but Saute and sear vegetables and meat when needed. The Nano ceramic coating of the pot ensures that you can cook anything you want! However, always make sure to use wooden or silicone utensils with the appliance.

Cook and Crisp Basket

This particular basket is specifically designed to ensure that you are able to efficiently Air Crisp your goodies when needed and get the perfect brown and crispy finish.

Reversible Rack

In the lower position, the provided Reversible Rack will actually allow you to steam vegetables and fish rapidly. On the other hand, if you flip the rack and in a higher position, you can use it broil goodies and give them a nice crispy finish.

Now that the basics of the Ninja Foodi are covered, let me share some other information that should be helpful to you.

Why is the Ninja Foodi so amazing?

Wholesome 360 Meals

The Ninja Foodi actually allows you to make a wide variety of healthy meals with various different components using just a single pot. You can quickly cook your desired meat on the bottom while adding veggies on top using the reversible rack. Each individual part of your meal will get an even and fine texture in the end that will provide a fine and satisfying meal.

One Pot that does it all

I cannot stress this enough, the versatility of the Ninja Foodi is what makes them so unique. Using the TenderCrisp tech, you will be able to turn simple recipes like soups and stews into amazing Wonders! Alternatively, using the pressure cooking feature, you will simply cook stews, chilis, casseroles, and even desserts! The list goes on. As a matter of fact, the crisping lid also allows you to bake biscuits too!

Defrost-Be Gone

The Ninja Foodi is one of that rare appliance that actually allows you to directly cook frozen meals, saving a lot of time. The pressure method can easily defrost and tenderize frozen meat, while the Crisping Lid will allow you to get a fine crispy finish.

Restaurant Quality Dish At Home

Yes, you read that right! Using the Ninja Foodi and its patented Air Crisping technology, you can even create restaurant style BBQ meals in an instant! A fine 5-pound chicken, beef brisket, pork belly! Nothing is off limits when you have the power of the Ninja Foodi with you.

Saves space in Kitchen

The versatility of the Ninja Foodi and its capacity act as multiple appliances allow you to get rid of the steamer, Saute pan, slow cooker, pressure cooker and a myriad of different appliances and use the Ninja Foodi for everything.

High-Pressure kills microbes

The excellent way in which the Ninja Foodi cook, ensure that the temperature inside is able to reach sufficiently high enough levels during pressure cooking to ensure that 99% of harmful microbes are killed during the process. In fact, the Ninja Foodi is even able to kill significantly more resistant microbes as well.

Amazing tips for the perfect "TenderCrisp"

Using the TenderCrisp technology to create mouthwatering crispy meals might seem a little bit intimated at first. The following tips should help you during your early days and make things easier:

> ➢ Always make sure to pre-heat your Ninja Foodi before using the Sear/Saute, Air Crips or Broil functions. A general method would be to pre-heat your Foodi for at least 5 minutes before adding food.

> ➢ It is highly recommended that you sometimes shake up your ingredients when trying to Air Fry using the Ninja Foodi. This allows for even cooking on all side. The general idea is to shake it once or twice during the whole crisping session.

> ➢ If you are crisping large protein or veggies, try to drizzle a little bit of oil on top/or use a brush to slather a bit of oil on top to ensure that it is well coated.

> ➢ When crisping, it is highly advised that you try to keep the ingredients at the same size. This will allow for even cooking as well.

➤ In Ketogenic Diet, we are not using rice, so this tip won't be applicable in your case. But as a general rule, it is advised that you rinse your rice thoroughly under water before adding them to the Foodi.

➤ If you are making an all-in-one-pot meal, then you may add a layer of meat to the base of the pot, place your reversible rack and place veggies/or whatever you require on the rack. This will not only help to build more flavor but will make it more convenient for you to crisp all the ingredients in one go.

Awesome general tips about the appliance

While the previous one covered tips specifically are given to improve your Tender Crisping experience, the following should help you in general.

➤ Always make sure to remember that the provided "Timer" button is not necessarily included to only work as a time setting button. This button can also be used as a "Delay Timer'. Meaning, you will be able to set a specific time after which the appliance will automatically start up and cook the food.

➤ When using "Unfrozen" meat, always try to ensure that you are using the same amount of water as you would've used when cooking with frozen meat.

➤ If you find yourself in a hurry, you may skip the natural pressure release method and opt for a quick release. For this, all you have to do is simply move the pressure valve to "Open" position. However, keep in mind that release the pressure in such a way might be a little hazardous as a lot of pressure gets released at once. So be cautious

➤ You should know that the proper sealing of the lid is crucial to efficient cooking in the Ninja Foodi. So, always make sure to check and be sure that the silicon ring is firmly placed all around the groove of the Ninja Foodi.

➤ Before pressure cooking, make sure that your pressure valve is set in the position labeled "Locked", otherwise your Ninja Foodi won't be able to build up the pressure.

➤ If you are completely new to using a Ninja Foodi, you might find yourself a little bit confused by the term "Release pressure naturally". Well, all you have to do to release pressure naturally is just let your appliance release pressure on its own after the timer reaches "0". It would take around 10-15 minutes for the pressure to come down to safe levels.

Chapter 2: Delightful Beef Dishes

Tantalizing Beef Jerky
(Prepping time: 10 minutes\ Cooking time: 20 minutes |For 4 servings)

Ingredients

- ½ pound beef, sliced into 1/8 inch thick strips
- ½ cup of soy sauce
- 2 tablespoons Worcestershire sauce
- 2 teaspoons ground black pepper
- 1 teaspoon onion powder
- ½ teaspoon garlic powder
- 1 teaspoon salt

Directions

1. Add listed ingredient to a large-sized Ziploc bag, seal it shut
2. Shake well, leave it in the fridge overnight
3. Lay strips on dehydrator trays, making sure not to overlap them
4. Lock Air Crisping Lid and set the temperature to 135 degrees F, cook for 7 hours
5. Store in airtight container, enjoy!

Beefed Up Spaghetti Squash
(Prepping time: 5 minutes\ Cooking time: 10-15 minutes |For 4 servings)

Ingredients

- 2 pounds ground beef
- 1 medium spaghetti squash
- 32 ounces marinara sauce
- 3 tablespoons olive oil

Directions

1. Slice squash in half lengthwise and dispose of seeds
2. Add trivet to your Ninja Foodi. Add 1 cup water
3. Arrange squash on the rack and lock lid, cook on HIGH pressure for 8 minutes
4. Quick release pressure.Remove from pot. Clean pot and set your Ninja Foodi to Saute mode
5. Add ground beef and add olive oil, let it heat up
6. Add ground beef and cook until slightly browned and cooked
7. Separate strands from cooked squash and transfer to a bowl
8. Add cooked beef, and mix with marinara sauce. Serve and enjoy!

Adobo Cubed Steak
(Prepping time: 5 minutes\ Cooking time: 25 minutes |For 4 servings)

Ingredients

- 2 cups of water
- 8 steaks, cubed, 28 ounces pack
- Pepper to taste
- 1 and ¾ teaspoons adobo seasoning
- 1 can (8 ounces) tomato sauce
- 1/3 cup green pitted olives
- 2 tablespoons brine
- 1 small red pepper
- ½ a medium onion, sliced

Directions

1. Chop peppers, onions into ¼ inch strips
2. Prepare beef by seasoning with adobo and pepper . Add into Ninja Foodi
3. Add remaining ingredients and Lock lid, cook on HIGH pressure for 25 minutes
4. Release pressure naturally. Serve and enjoy!

Cool Beef Bourguignon

(Prepping time: 10 minutes\ Cooking time: 30 minutes |For 4 servings)

Ingredients

- 1 pound stewing steak
- ½ pound bacon
- 5 medium carrots, diced
- 1 large red onion, peeled and sliced
- 2 garlic cloves, minced
- 2 teaspoons salt

- 2 tablespoons fresh thyme
- 2 tablespoons fresh parsley
- 2 teaspoons ground pepper
- ½ cup beef broth
- 1 tablespoon olive oil
- 1 tablespoon sugar-free maple syrup (Keto friendly)

Directions

1. Set your Ninja Foodi to Saute mode and add 1 tablespoon of oil, allow the oil to heat up
2. Pat your beef dry and season it well
3. Add beef into the Ninja Foodi (in batches) and Saute them until nicely browned up
4. Slice up the cooked bacon into strips and add the strips to the pot
5. Add onions as well and brown them. Add the rest of the listed ingredients and lock up the lid
6. Cook for 30 minutes on HIGH pressure
7. Allow the pressure to release naturally over 10 minutes . Enjoy!

A Keto-Friendly Philly Willy Steak And Cheese

(Prepping time: 10 minutes\ Cooking time: 40 minutes |For 4 servings)

Ingredients

- 2 tablespoons olive oil
- 2 large onion, sliced
- 8 ounces mushrooms, sliced
- 1-2 teaspoons Keto friendly steak seasoning

- 1 tablespoon butter
- 2 pounds beef chuck roast
- 12 cup beef stock

Directions

1. Set your Ninja Foodi to Saute mode and add oil, let it heat up
2. Rub seasoning over roast and Saute for 1-2 minutes per side
3. Remove and add butter, onion. Add mushrooms, pepper, stock, and roast
4. Lock lid and cook on HIGH pressure for 35 minutes. Naturally, release pressure over 10 minutes
5. Shred meat and sprinkle cheese if using, enjoy!

Beef Stew

(Prepping time: 10 minutes\ Cooking time: 10 minutes |For 4 servings)

Ingredients

- 1 pound beef roast
- 4 cups beef broth
- 3 garlic cloves, chopped
- 1 carrot, chopped
- 2 celery stalks, chopped

- 2 tomatoes, chopped
- ½ white onion, chopped
- ¼ teaspoon salt
- 1/8 teaspoon ground black pepper

Directions

1. Add listed ingredients to your Ninja Foodi and lock lid, cook on HIGH pressure for 10 minutes
2. Quick release pressure. Open the lid and shred the bee using forks, serve and enjoy!

Juiciest Keto Bacon Strips
(Prepping time: 5 minutes\ Cooking time: 7 minutes |For 2 servings)

Ingredients

- 10 bacon strips
- ¼ teaspoon chili flakes
- 1/3 teaspoon salt
- ¼ teaspoon basil, dried

Directions

1. Rub the bacon strips with chili flakes, dried basil, and salt
2. Turn on your air fryer and place the bacon on the rack
3. Lower the air fryer lid. Cook the bacon at 400F for 5 minutes
4. Cook for 3 minutes more if the bacon is not fully cooked. Serve and enjoy!

Quick Picadillo Dish
(Prepping time: 10 minutes\ Cooking time: 15-20 minutes |For 4 servings)

Ingredients

- ½ pound lean ground beef
- 2 garlic cloves, minced
- ½ large onion, chopped
- 1 teaspoon salt
- 1 tomato, chopped
- ½ red bell pepper, chopped
- 1 tablespoon cilantro
- ½ can (4 ounces) tomato sauce
- 1 teaspoon ground cumin
- 1-2 bay leaves
- 2 tablespoons green olives, capers
- 2 tablespoons brine
- 3 tablespoons water

Directions

1. Set your Ninja Foodi to Saute mode and add meat, salt, and pepper, slightly brown
2. Add garlic, tomato, onion, cilantro and Saute for 1 minute
3. Add olives, brine, leaf, cumin, and mix. Pour in sauce, water, and stir
4. Lock lid and cook on HIGH pressure for 15 minutes. Quick release pressure

Simple/Aromatic Meatballs
(Prepping time: 8 minutes\ Cooking time: 11 minutes |For 4 servings)

Ingredients

- 2 cups ground beef
- 1 egg, beaten
- 1 teaspoon Taco seasoning
- 1tablespoon sugar-free marinara sauce
- 1 teaspoon garlic, minced
- ½ teaspoon salt

Directions

1. Take a big mixing bowl and place all the ingredients into the bowl
2. Add all the ingredients into the bowl. Mix together all the ingredients by using a spoon or fingertips. Then make the small size meatballs and put them in a layer in the air fryer rack
3. Lower the air fryer lid. Cook the meatballs for 11 minutes at 350 F. Serve immediately and enjoy!

Generous Shepherd's Pie
(Prepping time: 10 minutes\ Cooking time: 10-15 minutes |For 4 servings)

Ingredients

- 2 cups of water
- 4 tablespoons butter
- 4 ounces cream cheese
- 1 cup mozzarella

- 1 whole egg
- Salt and pepper to taste
- 1 tablespoon garlic powder
- 2-3 pounds ground beef
- 1 cup frozen carrots
- 8 ounces mushrooms, sliced
- 1 cup beef broth

Directions

1. Add water to Ninja Foodi, arrange cauliflower on top, lock lid and cook for 5 minutes on HIGH pressure
2. Quick release and transfer to a blender, add cream cheese, butter, mozzarella cheese, egg, pepper, and salt. Blend well. Drain water from Ninja Foodi and add beef
3. Add carrots, garlic powder, broth and pepper, and salt
4. Add in cauliflower mix and lock lid, cook for 10 minutes on HIGH pressure
5. Release pressure naturally over 10 minutes. Serve and enjoy!

Hybrid Beef Prime Roast

(Prepping time: 10 minutes\ Cooking time: 45 minutes |For 4 servings)

Ingredients

- 2 pounds chuck roast
- 1 tablespoon olive oil
- 1 teaspoon salt
- 1 teaspoon ground black pepper
- 1 teaspoon onion powder
- 1 teaspoon garlic powder
- 4 cups beef stock

Directions

1. Place roast in Ninja Food pot and season it well with salt and pepper
2. Add oil and set the pot to Saute mode, sear each side of roast for 3 minutes until slightly browned . Add beef broth, onion powder, garlic powder, and stir
3. Lock lid and cook on HIGH pressure for 40 minutes
4. Once the timer goes off, naturally release pressure over 10 minutes
5. Open the lid and serve hot. Enjoy!

The Epic Carne Guisada

(Prepping time: 10 minutes\ Cooking time: 45 minutes |For 4 servings)

Ingredients

- 3 pounds beef stew
- 3 tablespoon seasoned salt
- 1 tablespoon oregano chili powder
- 1 tablespoon organic cumin
- 1 pinch crushed red pepper
- 2 tablespoons olive oil
- ½ medium lime, juiced
- 1 cup beef bone broth
- 3 ounces tomato paste
- 1 large onion, sliced

Directions

1. Trim the beef stew as needed into small bite-sized portions
2. Toss the beef stew pieces with dry seasoning
3. Set your Ninja Foodi to Saute mode and add oil, allow the oil to heat up
4. Add seasoned beef pieces and brown them
5. Combine the browned beef pieces with rest of the ingredients
6. Lock up the lid and cook on HIGH pressure for 3 minutes. Release the pressure naturally . Enjoy!

No-Noodle Pure Lasagna

(Prepping time: 10 minutes\ Cooking time: 10-15 minutes |For 4 servings)

Ingredients

- 2 small onions
- 2 garlic cloves, minced

- 1 pound ground beef
- 1 large egg
- 1 and ½ cups ricotta cheese
- ½ cup parmesan cheese
- 1 jar (25 ounces0 marinara sauce
- 8 ounces mozzarella cheese, sliced

Directions

1. Set your Ninja Foodi to Saute mode add beef, brown the beef
2. Add onion and garlic
3. Add parmesan, ricotta, egg in a small dish and keep it on the side
4. Add sauce to browned meat, reserve half for later
5. Sprinkle mozzarella and half of ricotta cheese to the browned meat
6. Top with remaining meat sauce
7. For the final layer, add more mozzarella cheese and remaining ricotta
8. Stir well . Cover with foil transfer to Ninja Foodi
9. Lock lid and cook on HIGH pressure for 8-10 minutes
10. Quick release pressure. Drizzle parmesan cheese on top. Enjoy!

The Wisdom Worthy Corned Beef

(Prepping time: 10 minutes\ Cooking time: 60 minutes |For 4 servings)

Ingredients

- 4 pounds beef brisket
- 2 garlic cloves, peeled and minced
- 2 yellow onions, peeled and sliced
- 11 ounces celery, thinly sliced
- 1 tablespoon dried dill
- 3 bay leaves
- 4 cinnamon sticks, cut into halves
- Salt and pepper to taste
- 17 ounces of water

Directions

1. Take a bowl and add beef, add water and cover, let it soak for 2-3 hours
2. Drain and transfer to the Ninja Foodi
3. Add celery, onions, garlic, bay leaves, dill, cinnamon, dill, salt, pepper and rest of the water to the Ninja Foodi
4. Stir and combine it well. Lock lid and cook on HIGH pressure for 50 minutes
5. Release pressure naturally over 10 minutes
6. Transfer meat to cutting board and slice, divide amongst plates and pour the cooking liquid (alongside veggies) over the servings. Enjoy!

Hearty Korean Ribs

(Prepping time: 10 minutes\ Cooking time: 45 minutes |For 6 servings)

Ingredients

- 1 teaspoon olive oil
- 2 green onions, cut into 1-inch length
- 3 garlic cloves, smashed
- 3 quarter sized ginger slices
- 4 pounds beef short ribs, 3 inches thick, cut into 3 rib portions
- ½ cup of water
- ½ cup coconut aminos
- ¼ cup dry white wine
- 2 teaspoons sesame oil
- Mince green onions for serving

Directions

1. Set your Ninja Foodi to "SAUTE" mode and add oil, let it shimmer
2. Add green onions, garlic, ginger, Saute for 1 minute
3. Add short ribs, water, amines, wine, sesame oil, and stir until the ribs are coated well
4. Lock lid and cook on HIGH pressure for 45 minutes . Release pressure naturally over 10 minutes
5. Remove short ribs from pot and serve with the cooking liquid. Enjoy!

Traditional Beef Sirloin Steak

(Prepping time: 5 minutes\ Cooking time: 17 minutes |For 4 servings)

Ingredients

- 3 tablespoons butter
- ½ teaspoon garlic powder
- 1-2 pounds beef sirloin steaks
- Salt and pepper to taste
- 1 garlic clove, minced

Directions

1. Set your Ninja Foodi to sauté mode and add butter, let the butter melt
2. Add beef sirloin steaks . Saute for 2 minutes on each side
3. Add garlic powder, garlic clove, salt, and pepper
4. Lock lid and cook on Medium-HIGH pressure for 15 minutes
5. Release pressure naturally over 10 minutes
6. Transfer prepare Steaks to a serving platter, enjoy!

Beef And Broccoli Platter

(Prepping time: 10 minutes\ Cooking time: 20 minutes |For 4 servings)

Ingredients

- 3 pounds beef chuck roast, cut into thin strips
- 1 tablespoon olive oil
- 1 yellow onion, peeled and chopped
- ½ cup beef stock
- 1 pound broccoli florets
- 2 teaspoons toasted sesame oil
- 2 tablespoons arrowroot

For Marinade

- 1 cup coconut aminos
- 1 tablespoon sesame oil
- 2 tablespoons fish sauce
- 5 garlic cloves, peeled and minced
- 3 red peppers, dried and crushed
- ½ teaspoon Chinese five spice powder
- Toasted sesame seeds, for serving

Directions

1. Take a bowl and mix in coconut aminos, fish sauce, 1 tablespoon sesame oil, garlic, five spice powder, crushed red pepper and stir
2. Add beef strips to the bowl and toss to coat. Keep it on the side for 10 minutes
3. Set your Ninja Foodi to "Saute" mode and add oil, let it heat up, add onion and stir cook for 4 minutes. Add beef and marinade, stir cook for 2 minutes. Add stock and stir
4. Lock the pressure lid of Ninja Foodi and cook on HIGH pressure for 5 minutes
5. Release pressure naturally over 10 minutes
6. Mix arrowroot with ¼ cup liquid from the pot and gently pour the mixture back to the pot and stir
7. Place a steamer basket in the pot and add broccoli to the steamer rack, lock lid and cook on HIGH pressure for 3 minutes more, quick release pressure
8. Divide the dish between plates and serve with broccoli, toasted sesame seeds and enjoy!

Alternative Corned Cabbage And Beef

(Prepping time: 10 minutes\ Cooking time: 100 minutes |For 4 servings)

Ingredients

- 1 corned beef brisket
- 4 cups of water
- 1 small onion, peeled and quartered
- 3 garlic cloves, smashed and peeled
- 2 bay leaves
- 3 whole black peppercorns
- ½ teaspoon allspice berries
- 1 teaspoon dried thyme

- 5 medium carrots
- 1 cabbage, cut into wedges

Directions

1. Add corned beef, onion, garlic cloves, water, allspice, peppercorn, thymes to the Ninja Foodi
2. Lock up the lid and cook for about 90 minutes at HIGH pressure
3. Allow the pressure to release naturally once done . Open up and transfer the meat to your serving plate. Cover it with tin foil and allow it to cool for 15 minutes
4. Add carrots and cabbage to the lid and let them cook for 10 minutes at HIGH pressure
5. Once done, do a quick release . Take out the prepped veggies and serve with your corned beef

Marked Beef Goulash
(Prepping time: 10 minutes\ Cooking time: 15-20 minutes |For 4 servings)

Ingredients

- 1-2 pounds extra lean beef, ground
- 2 teaspoons olive oil + 11 teaspoons extra
- 1 large red bell pepper, stemmed and seeded
- 1 large onion, cut into short strips
- 1 tablespoon garlic, minced
- 2 tablespoons sweet paprika
- ½ teaspoon hot paprika
- 4 cups beef stock
- 2 cans tomatoes, diced and petite

Directions

1. Set your Ninja Foodi to Saute mode and add 2 teaspoons of olive oil
2. Add ground beef to the pot and cook, making sure to stir it until it breaks apart
3. Once the beef is browned, transfer it to a bowl. Cut the steam off the pepper and deseed them and cut into strips. Cut the onion into short strips as well
4. Add a teaspoon of olive oil to the pot alongside pepper and onion
5. Saute for 3-4 minutes.Add minced garlic, sweet paprika, hot paprika and cook for 2-3 minutes
6. Add beef stock alongside the tomatoes. Add ground beef
7. Allow it to cook for about 15 minutes on Soup mode over the low pressure
8. Once done, quick release the pressure and have fun!

Lemon Delicious Pork Chop
(Prepping time: 10 minutes\ Cooking time: 5 minutes |For 4 servings)

Ingredients

- ½ cup hot sauce
- ½ cup of water
- 2 tablespoons butter
- 1/3 cup lemon juice
- 1 pound pork cutlets
- ½ teaspoon paprika

Directions

1. Add listed ingredients to your Ninja Foodi cook and crisp basket, place the basket inside
2. Lock lid and cook on HIGH pressure for 5 minutes, release pressure naturally over 10 minutes
3. Gently stir and serve, enjoy!

Meat Dredged Loaf
(Prepping time: 10 minutes\ Cooking time: 1 hour 10 minutes |For 6 servings)

Ingredients

- ½ cup onion, chopped
- 2 garlic cloves, minced
- ¼ cup sugar-free ketchup
- 1 pound grass fed lean ground beef
- ½ cup green bell pepper, seeded and chopped
- 1 cup cheddar cheese, grated
- 2 organic eggs, beaten
- 1 teaspoon dried thyme, crushed

- 3 cups fresh spinach, chopped
- 6 cups mozzarella cheese, freshly grated
- Black pepper to taste

Directions

1. Take a bowl and add all of the listed ingredients except cheese and spinach
2. Place a wax paper on a smooth surface and arrange the meat over it
3. Top with spinach, cheese and roll the paper around the paper to form a nice meatloaf
4. Remove wax paper and transfer loaf to your Ninja Foodi
5. Lock lid and select "Bake/Roast" mode, setting the timer to 70 minutes and temperature to 380 degrees F. Let it bake and take the dish out once done. Serve and enjoy!

The Chipotle Copycat Dish
(Prepping time: 5 minutes\ Cooking time: 90 minutes |For 6 servings)

Ingredients

- 3 pounds grass-fed chuck roast, large chunks
- 1 large onion, peeled and sliced
- 6 garlic cloves
- 2 cans (14.5 ounces) green chilies
- 1 tablespoon oregano
- 1 teaspoon salt and pepper
- 3 dried chipotle pepper, stems removed, broken into small pieces
- Juice of 3 limes
- 3 tablespoons coconut vinegar
- 1 tablespoon cumin
- ½ cup of water

Directions

1. Add the listed ingredients to your Ninja Foodi
2. Stir and lock up the lid, cook on HIGH pressure for 60 minutes
3. Release the pressure naturally over 10 minutes . Remove the lid and shred using a fork
4. Set your pot to Saute mode and reduce for 30 minutes . Enjoy once ready!

All-Buttered Up Beef
(Prepping time: 5 minutes\ Cooking time: 60 minutes |For 6 servings)

Ingredients

- 3 pounds beef roast
- 1 tablespoon olive oil
- 2 tablespoons Keto-Friendly ranch dressing
- 1 jar pepper rings, with juices
- 8 tablespoons butter
- 1 cup of water

Directions

1. Set your Ninja Foodi to Saute mode and add 1 tablespoon of oil
2. Once the oil is hot, add roast and sear both sides
3. Set the Saute off and add water, seasoning mix, reserved juice, and pepper rings on top of your beef. Lock up the lid and cook on HIGH pressure for 60 minutes
4. Release the pressure naturally over 10 minutes. Cut the beef with salad sheers and serve with pureed cauliflower. Enjoy!

Beef And Broccoli Delight
(Prepping time: 5 minutes\ Cooking time:6-8 hours |For 6 servings)

Ingredients

- 1 and ½ pounds beef round steak, cut into 2 inches by 1/8 inch strips
- 1 cup broccoli, diced
- ½ teaspoon red pepper flakes

- 2 teaspoon garlic, minced
- 2 teaspoons olive oil
- 2 tablespoons apple cider vinegar
- 2 tablespoons coconut aminos
- 2 tablespoons white wine vinegar
- 1 tablespoons arrowroot
- ¼ cup beef broth

Directions

1. Take a large sized bowl and make the sauce by mixing in red pepper flakes, olive oil, coconut aminos, garlic, white wine vinegar, apple cider vinegar, broth and arrowroot
2. Mix well. Add the mix to your Ninja Foodi. Add beef and place a lid
3. Cook on SLOW COOK MODE (LOW) for 6-8 hours
4. Uncover just 30 minutes before end time and add broccoli, lock lid again and let it finish
5. Serve and enjoy!

Rich Beef Rendang
(Prepping time: 5 minutes\ Cooking time: 25 minutes |For 6 servings)

Ingredients

- 1 cup onion, chopped
- 1 tablespoon ginger, chopped
- 1 tablespoon garlic, minced
- 1 small jalapeno pepper
- 2 tablespoons olive oil
- 1 pack rendang curry paste
- 1 pound skirt steak, cut into 2 inch chunks
- ½ cup of water
- 1 cup coconut milk (full fat)
- 2 tablespoons coconut, shredded

Directions

1. Mince the onion, garlic, and ginger. Set your Ninja Foodi to Saute mode and add oil
2. Allow the oil to heat up and add veggies and stir them well. Add rending paste and stir for 3-4 minutes. Add skirt steak and stir to coat with the spices for about 2 minutes
3. Pour ¼ cup of water and deglazed. Lock up the lid and cook on HIGH pressure for 25 minutes
4. Release the pressure naturally over 10 minutes . Add ½ a cup of coconut milk and stir
5. Garnish with shredded coconut and serve!

Spiritual Indian Beef Dish
(Prepping time: 15 minutes\ Cooking time: 20 minutes |For 4 servings)

Ingredients

- ½ yellow onion, chopped
- 1 tablespoon olive oil
- 2 garlic cloves, minced
- 1 jalapeno pepper, chopped
- 1 cup cherry tomatoes, quartered
- 1 teaspoon fresh lemon juice
- 1-2 pounds grass-fed ground beef
- 1-2 pounds fresh collard greens, trimmed and chopped

Spices

- 1 teaspoon cumin, ground
- ½ teaspoon ginger, ground
- 1 teaspoon coriander, ground
- ½ teaspoon fennel seeds, ground
- ½ teaspoon cinnamon, ground
- Salt and pepper to taste
- ½ teaspoon turmeric, ground

Directions

1. Set your Ninja Foodi to sauté mode and add garlic, onions
2. sauté for 3 minutes. Add jalapeno pepper, beef, and spices
3. Lock lid and cook on Medium-HIGH pressure for 15 minutes
4. Release pressure naturally over 10 minutes, open lid

5. Add tomatoes, collard greens and sauté for 3 minutes
6. Stir in lemon juice, salt, and pepper. Stir well
7. Once the dish is ready, transfer the dish to your serving bowl and enjoy!

Premium Mexican Beef Dish
(Prepping time: 5 minutes\ Cooking time: 12 minutes |For 4 servings)

Ingredients

- 2 and ½ pounds boneless beef short ribs
- 1 tablespoon chili powder
- 1 and ½ teaspoons salt
- 1 tablespoon fat
- 1 medium onion, thinly sliced
- 1 tablespoon tomato sauce
- 6 garlic cloves, peeled and smashed
- ½ cup roasted tomato salsa
- ½ cup bone broth
- Fresh ground black pepper
- ½ cup cilantro, minced
- 2 radishes, sliced

Directions

1. Take a large sized bowl and add the cubed beef, salt, and chili powder, give it a nice mix
2. Set your Ninja Foodi to Saute mode and add butter, allow it to melt
3. Add garlic and tomato paste and Saute for 30 seconds. Add seasoned beef, stock and fish sauce
4. Lock up the lid and cook on HIGH pressure for 35 minutes on MEAT/STEW mode
5. Release the pressure naturally over 10 minutes . Season with some salt and pepper and enjoy!

All-Tim Favorite Beef Chili
(Prepping time: 10 minutes\ Cooking time: 40 minutes |For 4 servings)

Ingredients

- 1 and ½ pounds ground beef
- 1 sweet onion, peeled and chopped
- Salt and pepper to taste
- 28 ounces canned tomatoes, diced
- 17 ounces beef stock
- 6 garlic clove, peeled and chopped
- 7 jalapeno peppers, diced
- 2 tablespoons olive oil
- 4 carrots, peeled and chopped
- 3 tablespoons chili powder
- 1 bay leaf
- 1 teaspoon chili powder

Directions

1. Set your Ninja Foodi to "Saute" mode and add half of the oil, let it heat up
2. Add beef and stir brown for 8 minutes, transfer to a bowl
3. Add remaining oil to the pot and let it heat up, add carrots, onion, jalapenos, garlic and stir Saute for 4 minutes. Add tomatoes and stir
4. Add bay leaf, stock, chili powder, chili powder, salt, pepper, and beef, stir and lock lid
5. Cook on HIGH pressure for 25 minutes . Release pressure naturally over 10 minutes
6. Stir the chili and serve. Enjoy!

Ingenious Bo Kho
(Prepping time: 5 minutes\ Cooking time: 45 minutes |For 6 servings)

Ingredients

- ½ teaspoon ghee
- 2 and ½ pounds grass-fed beef brisket
- 1 yellow onion, peeled and diced
- 1 and ½ teaspoon curry powder
- 2 and ½ tablespoons fresh ginger, peeled
- 2 cups tomatoes, drained and crushed
- 3 tablespoons red boat fish sauce
- 1 large stalk lemongrass
- 2 whole star anise
- 1 bay leaf
- 1 cup bone broth

- 31 -

Directions

1. Set your Ninja Foodi to Saute mode and add ghee
2. Allow it to melt. Add briskets. Keep frying them until they have a nice brown texture
3. Remove the brisket and add onion and Saute them
4. Add curry powder, ginger, seared beef, fish sauce, star anise, diced tomatoes
5. Stir well and add bay leaf and lemongrass. Pour broth and lock up the lid
6. Cook for 35 minutes at HIGH pressure. Allow the pressure to release naturally
7. Add carrots . Cook for another 7 minutes at HIGH pressure
8. Release the pressure naturally. Serve hot!

Sesame Beef Ribs
(Prepping time: 10 minutes\ Cooking time: 60 minutes |For 6 servings)

Ingredients

- 1 tablespoon sesame oil
- 2 garlic cloves, peeled and smashed
- Knob fresh ginger, peeled and finely chopped
- 1 pinch red pepper flakes
- ¼ cup white wine vinegar

- 2/3 cup coconut aminos
- 2/3 cup beef stock
- 4 pounds beef ribs, chopped in half
- 2 tablespoons arrowroot
- 1-2 tablespoons water

Directions

1. Set your Ninja Foodi to Saute mode and add sesame oil, garlic, ginger, red pepper flakes and Saute for 1 minute. Deglaze pot with vinegar and mix in coconut aminos and beef stock
2. Add ribs to the pot and coat them well. Lock lid and cook on HIGH pressure for 60 minutes
3. Release pressure naturally over 10 minutes . Remove the ribs and keep them on the side
4. Take a small bowl and mix in arrowroot and water, stir and mix in the liquid into the pot, set the pot to Saute mode and cook until the liquid reaches your desired consistency
5. Put the ribs under a broiler to brown them slightly (also possible to do this in the Ninja Foodi using the Air Crisping lid) . Serve ribs with the cooking liquid. Enjoy!

Balsamic Pot Roast Of Beef
(Prepping time: 10 minutes\ Cooking time: 55 minutes |For 4 servings)

Ingredients

- 1 teaspoon of each pepper and garlic powder
- 1 tablespoon kosher salt
- 1 (3 pounds) boneless chuck roast
- ¼ cup balsamic vinegar

- ½ cup onion, chopped
- 2 cups of water
- ¼ teaspoon xanthan game
- For garnish, chopped parsley

Directions

1. Slice roast in half and season with garlic powder, salt, and pepper
2. Set your Ninja Foodi to Saute mode and add meat, brown the meat
3. Add onion and pour water and vinegar. Lock lid and cook on HIGH pressure for 35 minutes
4. Release pressure naturally over 10 minutes. Transfer meat to a container and break it apart, discard fat. Set your pot to Saute mode and simmer the cooking liquid
5. Whisk in xanthan gum to the Pot and transfer back the chicken. Stir
6. Cancel Saute mode. Garnish and enjoy!

Extremely Satisfying Beef Curry
(Prepping time: 10 minutes\ Cooking time: 20 minutes |For 4 servings)

Ingredients

- 2 pounds beef steak, cubed
- 2 tablespoons extra virgin olive oil
- 1 tablespoon Dijon mustard
- 2 and ½ tablespoons curry powder
- 2 yellow onions, peeled and chopped
- 2 garlic cloves, peeled and minced
- 10 ounces canned coconut milk
- 2 tablespoons tomato sauce
- Salt and pepper to taste

Directions

1. Set your Ninja Foodi to "Saute" mode and add oil, let it heat up
2. Add onions, garlic, stir cook for 4 minutes. Add mustard, stir and cook for 1 minute
3. Add beef and stir until all sides are browned
4. Add curry powder, salt, and pepper, stir cook for 2 minutes
5. Add coconut milk and tomato sauce, stir, and cove
6. Lock lid and cook on HIGH pressure for 10 minutes
7. Release pressure naturally over 10 minutes. Serve and enjoy!

Braised Up Bone Short Ribs
(Prepping time: 10 minutes\ Cooking time: 35 minutes |For 4 servings)

Ingredients

- 4 pounds beef short ribs
- A generous amount of kosher salt
- 1 tablespoon beef fat
- 1 onion, skin on, quartered
- 3 garlic cloves
- Water as needed

Directions

1. Season the ribs generously with salt
2. Take a skillet and heat up the beef oil over medium-high. Toss in the ribs and gently cook them until browned. Once browned, toss in the garlic, onion and about 2 inches of water.
3. Once mixed, transfer the mixture to the instant pot
4. Lock lid and cook on HIGH pressure for 35 minutes . Release pressure naturally over 10 minutes
5. Once the ribs complete, serve the dish with the dish on the bone
6. Alternatively, you can also pull the meat from the bones and braise the liquid and skim the fat. Store them in a jar and serve the ribs with the broth making sure to season them well.

The Authentic Beef Casserole
(Prepping time: 10 minutes\ Cooking time: 8 hours |For 4 servings)

Ingredients

- ½ cabbage, roughly sliced
- 1 onion, diced
- 3 cloves garlic, chopped
- 1 and ½ pounds ground beef
- 2 cups cauliflower rice
- 4 tablespoons Ghee
- 1 heaping tablespoon Italian seasoning
- ½ teaspoon crushed red pepper
- Salt and pepper to taste
- ½ cup fresh parsley, chopped

Directions

1. Add the listed ingredients to your Ninja Foodi (except parsley) and give it a nice stir
2. Place lid and cook on SLOW COOK MODE (LOW) for 7-8 hours until the beef is cooked
3. Stir in parsley and serve. Enjoy!

The Great Pepper Steak
(Prepping time: 5 minutes\ Cooking time: 20 minutes |For 6 servings)

Ingredients

- 1 pound boneless Beef Eye, Round Steak
- 80 ounces mushrooms, sliced
- 1 red pepper, sliced
- 1 tablespoon garlic, minced
- 1 pack onion soup mix
- 1 tablespoon sesame oil
- 1 cup of water

Directions

1. Add the listed ingredients to your Ninja Foodi
2. Lock up the lid and cook on HIGH pressure for 20 minutes
3. Release the pressure naturally over 10 minutes
4. Serve the pepper steak and enjoy!

The Ground Beef Root Chili
(Prepping time: 5 minutes\ Cooking time: 10 minutes |For 6 servings)

Ingredients

- 10 ounce of sliced beets
- 1 cup of cooked ground beef
- 1 and a 1/3 cup of diced carrot
- 1 and 1/3 cups of peeled and diced sweet potato
- 10 and a 2/3 ounce of pumpkin
- 1 teaspoon of dried rosemary
- 1 teaspoon of sea salt
- 2 teaspoon of dried basil
- 2/3 teaspoon of cinnamon
- 13 and a 1/3 of beef bone broth
- 1 and a 1/3 tablespoon of Apple Cider Vinegar

Directions

1. Add beets to a food processor and puree.Transfer the beets to your Ninja Foodi
2. Add the rest of the ingredients . Lock up the lid and cook on HIGH pressure for 10 minutes
3. Release the pressure naturally over 10 minutes. Enjoy!

Ground Beef With Green Beans
(Prepping time: 5 minutes\ Cooking time: 30 minutes |For 6 servings)

Ingredients

- 1 teaspoon olive oil
- 1 pound lean ground beef
- 1 medium onion, chopped
- 1 tablespoon garlic, minced
- 1 teaspoon thyme
- 1 teaspoon oregano
- ½ pound green beans, ends trimmed and cut into 1-inch pieces
- 2 cans (14.5 ounces) diced tomatoes, with juice
- Salt and pepper to taste
- Fresh parmesan for serving

Directions

1. Set your Ninja Foodi to Saute mode and add oil, allow the oil to heat up
2. Add ground beef and stir well as it cooks
3. Once the beef is browned up, add chopped onion, dried thyme, minced garlic, dried oregano and cook for 3 minutes. Add petite-dice tomatoes alongside the juice and beef broth
4. Allow them to heat for a while.Trim the beans on both ends and cut into 1-inch pieces
5. Add beans to your pot. Lock up the lid and cook on SLOW COOK (LOW) mode for 30 minutes
6. Perform a quick release . Season with salt and pepper
7. Serve freshly with a grating of parmesan. Enjoy!

Delicious Tomatillo Beef And Pork Chili
(Prepping time: 5 minutes\ Cooking time: 35 minutes |For 6 servings)

Ingredients

- 1 pound ground beef
- 1 pound ground pork
- 3 tomatillos, chopped
- 1 teaspoon garlic powder
- 1 jalapeno pepper
- 1 tablespoon ground cumin
- 1 tablespoon chili powder
- Salt as needed

Directions

1. Set your Ninja Foodi to Saute mode and add beef and pork, brown them slightly
2. Add the rest of the ingredients to the pot onion, tomatillo, garlic, tomato paste, jalapeno, cumin, water, chili powder . Mix well
3. Lock up the lid and cook on HIGH pressure for 35 minutes and release the pressure naturally
4. Serve and enjoy!

Chapter 3: High-Quality Seafood Dishes

Hearty Swordfish Meal

(Prepping time: 5 minutes\ Cooking time: 150 minutes |For 4 servings)

Ingredients

- 5 swordfish fillets
- ½ a cup of melted clarified butter
- 6 garlic cloves, chopped
- 1 tablespoon black pepper

Directions

1. Take a mixing bowl and add garlic, clarified butter, black pepper
2. Take a parchment paper and add the fillet. Cover and wrap the fish
3. Keep repeating until the fillets are wrapped up
4. Transfer wrapped fish to Ninja Foodi pot and lock lid
5. Allow them to cook for 2 and a ½ hour at high pressure. Release the pressure naturally
6. Serve and enjoy!

Gentle And Simple Fish Stew

(Prepping time: 5 minutes\ Cooking time: 20 minutes |For 4 servings)

Ingredients

- 3 cups fish stock
- 1 onion, diced
- 1 cup broccoli, chopped
- 2 cups celery stalks, chopped
- 1 and ½ cups cauliflower, diced
- 1 carrot, sliced
- 1 pound white fish fillets, chopped
- 1 cup heavy cream
- 1 bay leaf
- 2 tablespoons butter
- ¼ teaspoon pepper
- ½ teaspoon salt
- ¼ teaspoon garlic powder

Directions

1. Set your Ninja Foodi to Saute mode and add butter, let it melt
2. Add onion and carrots, cook for 3 minutes. Stir in remaining ingredients
3. Lock lid and cook on HIGH pressure for 4 minutes.Naturally, release pressure over 10 minutes
4. Discard bay leaf . Serve and enjoy!

Cool Shrimp Zoodles

(Prepping time: 5 minutes\ Cooking time: 3 minutes |For 4 servings)

Ingredients

- 4 cups zoodles
- 1 tablespoon basil, chopped
- 2 tablespoons Ghee
- 1 cup vegetable stock
- 2 garlic cloves, minced
- 2 tablespoons olive oil
- ½ lemon
- ½ teaspoon paprika

Directions

1. Set your Ninja Foodi to Saute mode and add ghee, let it heat up
2. Add olive oil as well. Add garlic and cook for 1 minute
3. Add lemon juice, shrimp and cook for 1 minute
4. Stir in rest of the ingredients and lock lid, cook on LOW pressure for 5 minutes
5. Quick release pressure and serve . Enjoy!

Heartfelt Sesame Fish
(Prepping time: 8 minutes\ Cooking time: 8 minutes |For 4 servings)

Ingredients

- 1 and ½ pound salmon fillet
- 1 teaspoon sesame seeds
- 1 teaspoon butter, melted
- ½ teaspoon salt
- 1 tablespoon apple cider vinegar
- ¼ teaspoon rosemary, dried

Directions

1. Take apple cider vinegar and spray it to the salmon fillets
2. Then add dried rosemary, sesame seeds, butter and salt
3. Mix them well. Take butter sauce and brush the salmon properly
4. Place the salmon on the rack and lower the air fryer lid. Set the air fryer mode
5. Cook the fish for 8 minutes at 360 F.Serve hot and enjoy!

Awesome Sock-Eye Salmon
(Prepping time: 5 minutes\ Cooking time: 5 minutes |For 4 servings)

Ingredients

- 4 sockeye salmon fillets
- 1 teaspoon Dijon mustard
- ¼ teaspoon garlic, minced
- ¼ teaspoon onion powder
- ¼ teaspoon lemon pepper
- ½ teaspoon garlic powder
- ¼ teaspoon salt
- 2 tablespoons olive oil
- 1 and ½ cup of water

Directions

1. Take a bowl and add mustard, lemon juice, onion powder, lemon pepper, garlic powder, salt, olive oil. Brush spice mix over salmon
2. Add water to Instant Pot. Place rack and place salmon fillets on rack
3. Lock lid and cook on LOW pressure for 7 minutes
4. Quick release pressure .Serve and enjoy!

Buttered Up Scallops
(Prepping time: 10 minutes\ Cooking time: 5 minutes |For 4 servings)

Ingredients

- 4 garlic cloves, minced
- 4 tablespoons rosemary. chopped
- 2 pounds sea scallops
- 12 cup butter
- Salt and pepper to taste

Directions

1. Set your Ninja Foodi to Saute mode and add butter, rosemary, and garlic
2. Saute for 1 minute. Add scallops, salt, and pepper
3. Saute for 2 minutes. Lock Crisping lid and Crisp for 3 minutes at 350 degrees F. Serve and enjoy!

NAwesome Cherry Tomato Mackerel
(Prepping time: 5 minutes\ Cooking time: 7 minutes |For 4 servings)

Ingredients

- 4 Mackerel fillets
- ¼ teaspoon onion powder
- ¼ teaspoon lemon powder
- ¼ teaspoon garlic powder

- ½ teaspoon salt
- 2 cups cherry tomatoes
- 3 tablespoons melted butter
- 1 and ½ cups of water
- 1 tablespoon black olives

Directions

1. Grease baking dish and arrange cherry tomatoes at the bottom of the dish
2. Top with fillets sprinkle all spices. Drizzle melted butter over
3. Add water to your Ninja Foodi
4. Lower rack in Ninja Foodi and place baking dish on top of the rack
5. Lock lid and cook on LOW pressure for 7 minutes . Quick release pressure. Serve and enjoy!

Lovely Air Fried Scallops

(Prepping time: 5 minutes\ Cooking time: 5 minutes |For 4 servings)

Ingredients

- 12 scallops
- 3 tablespoons olive oil
- Salt and pepper to taste

Directions

1. Gently rub scallops with salt, pepper, and oil
2. Transfer to your Ninja Foodie's insert, and place the insert in your Foodi
3. Lock Air Crisping lid and cook for 4 minutes at 390 degrees F
4. Half through, make sure to give them a nice flip and keep cooking. Serve warm and enjoy!

Packets Of Lemon And Dill Cod

(Prepping time: 10 minutes\ Cooking time: 5-10 minutes |For 4 servings)

Ingredients

- 2 tilapia cod fillets
- Salt, pepper and garlic powder to taste
- 2 sprigs fresh dill
- 4 slices lemon
- 2 tablespoons butter

Directions

1. Layout 2 large squares of parchment paper
2. Place fillet in center of each parchment square and season with salt, pepper and garlic powder
3. On each fillet, place 1 sprig of dill, 2 lemon slices, 1 tablespoon butter
4. Place trivet at the bottom of your Ninja Foodi. Add 1 cup water into the pot
5. Close parchment paper around fillets and fold to make a nice seal
6. Place both packets in your pot . Lock lid and cook on HIGH pressure for 5 minutes
7. Quick release pressure . Serve and enjoy!

Adventurous Sweet And Sour Fish

(Prepping time: 10 minutes\ Cooking time: 6 minutes |For 4 servings)

Ingredients

- 2 drops liquid stevia
- ¼ cup butter
- 1 pound fish chunks
- 1 tablespoon vinegar
- Salt and pepper to taste

Directions

1. Set your Ninja Foodi to Saute mode and add butter, let it melt
2. Add fish chunks and Saute for 3 minutes. Add stevia, salt, and pepper, stir
3. Lock Crisping Lid and cook on "Air Crisp" mode for 3 minutes at 360 degrees F
4. Serve once done and enjoy!

Garlic And Lemon Prawn Delight

(Prepping time: 5 minutes\ Cooking time: 5 minutes |For 4 servings)

Ingredients

- 2 tablespoons olive oil
- 1 pound prawns
- 2 tablespoons garlic, minced
- 2/3 cup fish stock
- 1 tablespoon butter
- 2 tablespoons lemon juice
- 1 tablespoon lemon zest
- Salt and pepper to taste

Directions

1. Set your Ninja Foodi to Saute mode and add butter and oil, let it heat up
2. Stir in remaining ingredients. Lock lid and cook on LOW pressure for 5 minutes
3. Quick release pressure. Serve and enjoy!

Lovely Carb Soup

(Prepping time: 5 minutes\ Cooking time: 6-7 hours |For 4 servings)

Ingredients

- 1 cup crab meat, cubed
- 1 tablespoon garlic, minced
- Salt as needed
- Red chili flakes as needed
- 3 cups vegetable broth
- 1 teaspoon salt

Directions

1. Coat the crab cubes in lime juice and let them sit for a while
2. Add the all ingredients (including marinated crab meat) to your Ninja Foodi and lock lid
3. Cook on SLOW COOK MODE (MEDIUM) for 3 hours
4. Let it sit for a while
5. Unlock lid and set to Saute mode, simmer the soup for 5 minutes more on LOW
6. Stir and check to season. Enjoy!

The Rich Guy Lobster And Butter

(Prepping time: 15 minutes\ Cooking time: 20 minutes |For 4 servings)

Ingredients

- 6 Lobster Tails
- 4 garlic cloves,
- ¼ cup butter

Directions

1. Preheat the Ninja Foodi to 400 degrees F at first
2. Open the lobster tails gently by using kitchen scissors
3. Remove the lobster meat gently from the shells but keep it inside the shells
4. Take a plate and place it
5. Add some butter in a pan and allow it melt
6. Put some garlic cloves in it and heat it over medium-low heat
7. Pour the garlic butter mixture all over the lobster tail meat
8. Let the fryer to broil the lobster at 130 degrees F
9. Remove the lobster meat from Ninja Foodi and set aside
10. Use a fork to pull out the lobster meat from the shells entirely
11. Pour some garlic butter over it if needed. Serve and enjoy!

Lovely Panko Cod

(Prepping time: 5 minutes\ Cooking time: 15 minutes |For 6 servings)

Ingredients

- 2 uncooked cod fillets, 6 ounces each
- 3 teaspoons kosher salt
- ¾ cup panko bread crumbs
- 2 tablespoons butter, melted
- ¼ cup fresh parsley, minced
- 1 lemon. Zested and juiced

Directions

1. Pre-heat your Ninja Foodi at 390 degrees F and place Air Crisper basket inside
2. Season cod and salt
3. Take a bowl and add bread crumbs, parsley, lemon juice, zest, butter, and mix well
4. Coat fillets with the bread crumbs mixture and place fillets in your Air Crisping basket
5. Lock Air Crisping lid and cook on Air Crisp mode for 15 minutes at 360 degrees F
6. Serve and enjoy!

Salmon Paprika

(Prepping time: 5 minutes\ Cooking time: 7 minutes |For 4 servings)

Ingredients

- 2 wild caught salmon fillets, 1 to 1 and ½ inches thick
- 2 teaspoons avocado oil
- 2 teaspoons paprika
- Salt and pepper to taste
- Green herbs to garnish

Directions

1. Season salmon fillets with salt, pepper, paprika, and olive oil
2. Place Crisping basket in your Ninja Foodi, and pre-heat your Ninja Foodie at 390 degrees F
3. Place insert insider your Foodi and place the fillet in the insert, lock Air Crisping lid and cook for 7 minutes. Once done, serve the fish with herbs on top. Enjoy!

Heartfelt Air Fried Scampi

(Prepping time: 5 minutes\ Cooking time: 5 minutes |For 4 servings)

Ingredients

- 4 tablespoons butter
- 1 tablespoon lemon juice
- 1 tablespoon garlic, minced
- 2 teaspoons red pepper flakes
- 1 tablespoon chives, chopped
- 1 tablespoon basil leaves, minced
- 2 tablespoons chicken stock
- 1 pound defrosted shrimp

Directions

1. Set your Foodi to Saute mode and add butter, let the butter melt and add red pepper flakes and garlic, Saute for 2 minutes
2. Transfer garlic to crisping basket, add remaining ingredients (including shrimp) to the basket
3. Return basket back to the Ninja Foodi and lock the Air Crisping lid, cook for 5 minutes at 390 degrees F. Once done, serve with a garnish of fresh basil

Ranch Warm Fillets

(Prepping time: 5 minutes\ Cooking time: 13 minutes |For 4 servings)

Ingredients

- ¼ cup panko
- ½ packet ranch dressing mix powder
- 1 and ¼ tablespoons vegetable oil
- 1 egg beaten
- 2 tilapia fillets
- A garnish of herbs and chilies

Directions

1. Pre-heat your Ninja Foodi with the Crisping Basket inside at 350 degrees F
2. Take a bowl and mix in ranch dressing and panko
3. Beat eggs in a shallow bowl and keep it on the side
4. Dip fillets in the eggs, then in the panko mix
5. Place fillets in your Ninja Foodie's insert and transfer insert to Ninja Foodi
6. Lock Air Crisping Lid and Air Crisp for 13 minutes at 350 degrees F
7. Garnish with chilies and herbs. Enjoy!

Alaskan Cod Divine

(Prepping time: 10 minutes\ Cooking time: 5-10 minutes |For 4 servings)

Ingredients

- 1 large fillet, Alaskan Cod (Frozen)
- 1 cup cherry tomatoes
- Salt and pepper to taste
- Seasoning as you need
- 2 tablespoons butter
- Olive oil as needed

Directions

1. Take an ovenproof dish small enough to fit inside your pot
2. Add tomatoes to the dish, cut large fish fillet into 2-3 serving pieces and lay them on top of tomatoes. Season with salt, pepper, and your seasoning
3. Top each fillet with 1 tablespoon butter and drizzle olive oil
4. Add 1 cup of water to the pot.Place trivet to the Ninja Foodi and place dish on the trivet
5. Lock lid and cook on HIGH pressure for 9 minutes.Release pressure naturally over 10 minutes
6. Serve and enjoy!

Kale And Salmon Delight

(Prepping time: 10 minutes\ Cooking time: 5 minutes |For 4 servings)

Ingredients

- 1 lemon, juiced
- 2 salmon fillets
- ¼ cup extra virgin olive oil
- 1 teaspoon Dijon mustard
- 4 cups kale, thinly sliced, ribs removed
- 1 teaspoon salt
- 1 avocado, diced
- 1 cup pomegranate seeds
- 1 cup walnuts, toasted
- 1 cup goat parmesan cheese, shredded

Directions

1. Season salmon with salt and keep it on the side. Place a trivet in your Ninja Foodi
2. Place salmon over the trivet. Lock lid and cook on HIGH pressure for 15 minutes
3. Release pressure naturally over 10 minutes. Transfer salmon to a serving platter
4. Take a bowl and add kale, season with salt
5. Take another bowl and make the dressing by adding lemon juice, Dijon mustard, olive oil, and red wine vinegar. Season kale with dressing and add diced avocado, pomegranate seeds, walnuts and cheese. Toss and serve with the fish. Enjoy!

Breathtaking Cod Fillets

(Prepping time: 10 minutes\ Cooking time: 5-10 minutes |For 4 servings)

Ingredients

- 1 pound frozen cod fish fillets
- 2 garlic cloves, halved
- 1 cup chicken broth
- ½ cup packed parsley
- 2 tablespoons oregano
- 2 tablespoons almonds, sliced½ teaspoon paprika

Directions

1. Take the fish out of the freezer and let it defrost
2. Take a food processor and stir in garlic, oregano, parsley, paprika, 1 tablespoon almond and process. Set your Ninja Foodi to "SAUTE" mode and add olive oil, let it heat up
3. Add remaining almonds and toast, transfer to a towel. Pour broth in a pot and add herb mixture
4. Cut fish into 4 pieces and place in a steamer basket, transfer steamer basket to the pot
5. Lock lid and cook on HIGH pressure for 3 minutes. Quick release pressure once has done
6. Serve steamed fish by pouring over the sauce.Enjoy!

Lemon And Pepper Salmon Delight

(Prepping time: 5 minutes\ Cooking time: 6 minutes |For 4 servings)

Ingredients

- ¾ cup of water
- Sprigs of parsley, basil, tarragon
- 1 pound salmon, skin on
- 3 teaspoons ghee
- ¾ teaspoon salt
- ½ teaspoon pepper
- ½ lemon, sliced
- 1 red bell pepper, julienned
- 1 carrot, julienned

Directions

1. Set your Ninja Foodi to Saute mode and add water and herbs
2. Place a steamer rack and add the salmon. Drizzle ghee on top of the salmon
3. Season with pepper and salt. Cover lemon slices on top
4. Lock up the lid and cook on HIGH pressure for 3 minutes
5. Release the pressure naturally over 10 minutes
6. Transfer the salmon to a platter. Add veggies to your pot and set the pot to Saute mode
7. Cook for 1-2 minutes. Serve the cooked vegetables with salmon. Enjoy!

Fresh Steamed Salmon

(Prepping time: 5 minutes\ Cooking time: 5 minutes |For 4 servings)

Ingredients

- 2 salmon fillets
- ¼ cup onion, chopped
- 2 stalks green onion stalks, chopped
- 1 whole egg
- Almond meal
- Salt and pepper to taste
- 2 tablespoons olive oil

Directions

1. Add a cup of water to your Ninja Foodi and place a steamer rack on top
2. Place the fish. Season the fish with salt and pepper and lock up the lid
3. Cook on HIGH pressure for 3 minutes. Once done, quick release the pressure
4. Remove the fish and allow it to cool
5. Break the fillets into a bowl and add egg, yellow and green onions
6. Add ½ a cup of almond meal and mix with your hand. Divide the mixture into patties
7. Take a large skillet and place it over medium heat. Add oil and cook the patties.Enjoy!

Spiced Up Cajun Style Tilapia

(Prepping time: 10 minutes\ Cooking time: 5 minutes |For 4 servings)

Ingredients

- 4 tilapia fillets, 6 ounces each
- 1 cup ghee
- 2 teaspoons cayenne pepper
- 2 tablespoons smoked paprika

- 2 teaspoons garlic powder
- 2 teaspoons onion powder
- Pinch of salt
- 1 teaspoon dried oregano
- 1 teaspoon dried thyme
- 1 cup of water

Directions

1. Take a small bowl and add cayenne pepper, smoked paprika, garlic powder, onion powder, salt, pepper, dried oregano, dried thyme and ghee
2. Dip the fillets into the seasoned ghee mix. Add 1 cup of water to your Ninja Foodi
3. Place steamer rack and place the fillets on the rack
4. Lock lid and cook on HIGH pressure for 5 minutes. Release naturally over 10 minutes
5. Transfer to serving platter and garnish with parsley. Serve and enjoy!

Delightful Salmon Fillets

(Prepping time: 5 minutes\ Cooking time: 5 minutes |For 4 servings)

Ingredients

- 2 salmon fillets
- ¼ cup onion, chopped
- 2 stalks green onion stalks. chopped
- 1 whole egg
- Almond meal as needed
- Salt and pepper to taste
- 2 tablespoons olive oil

Directions

1. Add a cup of water to your Ninja Foodi and place a steamer rack on top
2. Place the fish. Season the fish with salt and pepper and lock up the lid
3. Cook on HIGH pressure for 3 minutes. Once done, quick release the pressure
4. Remove the fish and allow it to cool
5. Break the fillets into a bowl and add egg, yellow and green onions
6. Add ½ a cup of almond meal and mix with your hand. Divide the mixture into patties
7. Take a large skillet and place it over medium heat. Add oil and cook the patties.Enjoy!

A Pot Full Of Shellfish

(Prepping time: 15 minutes \ Cooking time: 1 minute |For 4 servings)

Ingredients

- 3 pounds mussels
- 1 tablespoon extra-virgin olive oil
- 4 garlic cloves, minced
- 1 large roasted bell pepper
- ¾ cup fish stock
- ½ cup white wine vinegar
- 1/8 teaspoon red pepper flakes
- 2 tablespoons cashew cream
- 3 tablespoons parsley, chopped

Directions

1. Clean the mussels well and scrub them, debeard if needed. Make a steaming liquid
2. Set your Ninja Foodi to Saute mode and add olive oil, allow it to heat up
3. Add garlic and cook for 1 minute
4. Add roasted red pepper, vinegar, fish stock, red pepper flakes and stir
5. Add mussels to the Ninja Foodi and lock up the lid
6. Cook on HIGH pressure for 1 minute and quick release the pressure
7. Remove the lid and check the mussels, if they are open then enjoy
8. If not, lock up the lid and steam for 1 minute more.Garnish with a bit of parsley. Enjoy!

Orange Sauce And Salmon

(Prepping time: 30 minutes\ Cooking time: 15 minutes |For 4 servings)

Ingredients

- 1 pound salmon
- 1 tablespoon coconut amino
- 2 teaspoons ginger, minced
- 1 teaspoon garlic, minced
- 1 teaspoon salt
- 2 tablespoons sugar marmalade

Directions

1. Take a zip bag and add the Salmon. Take a bowl and add all of the ingredients and mix well
2. Pour the mixture into the salmon container bag and mix well to ensure that the salmon is coated well. Allow it to marinate for 30 minutes
3. Add 2 cups of water to the Ninja Foodi. Carefully put a steamer rack/trivet on top of your Foodi
4. Add the marinated salmon and sauce on the rack
5. Lock up the lid and cook on LOW pressure for 3 minutes
6. Allow the pressure to release naturally.Serve or broil for 3-4 minutes for a brown texture
7. Alternatively, you may bake the salmon at 350 degrees Fahrenheit for a slightly flaky fish. Enjoy!

Cucumber And Salmon Mix
(Prepping time: 5 minutes\ Cooking time: 5 minutes |For 4 servings)

Ingredients
- 1 pound salmon steaks
- ½ cup plain low-fat Greek yogurt
- ½ cup cucumber, peeled and diced
- 1 tablespoon fresh dill, chopped
- 1 tablespoon olive oil
- ½ teaspoon ground coriander
- 1 teaspoon fresh lemon juice
- 1 cup of water
- Salt and pepper to taste

Directions

1. Mix in low-fat Greek yogurt, dill, cucumber, a pinch of salt and pepper each, mix well and put in the fridge
2. Brush salmon steaks with olive oil, season salmon with salt, pepper and coriander and lemon juice. Add water to Ninja Foodi and place a steamer rack
3. Add fish fillets on rack and lock lid. Cook on HIGH pressure for 3 minutes
4. Release pressure naturally over 10 minutes . Open the lid and serve salmon with cucumber sauce. Enjoy!

The Ginger Flavored Tilapia
(Prepping time: 10 minutes\ Cooking time: 5 minutes |For 4 servings)

Ingredients

- 1 pound Tilapia fish fillets
- 3 tablespoons low-sodium coconut aminos
- 2 tablespoons white vinegar
- 2 fresh garlic cloves, minced
- Pinch of salt and pepper
- 1 tablespoon olive oil
- 2 tablespoons fresh ginger, julienned
- ¼ cup fresh scallions, julienned
- ¼ cup fresh cilantro, chopped

Directions

1. Take a bowl and add coconut aminos, white vinegar, minced garlic, salt, white pepper and mix well. Add tilapia fish and carefully spoon the sauce over and coat it
2. Marinate for 2 hours. Add 2 cups of water to the Ninja Foodi
3. Add steamer rack to the Ninja Foodi and remove fillets from marinade, transfer them to Steamer Rack. Lock lid and cook on LOW pressure for 2 minutes
4. Quick release pressure. Transfer fillets to serving the dish and discard water
5. Set your pot to Saute mode and add olive oil, let it heat up
6. Add julienned ginger and Saute for a few seconds
7. Add scallions, cilantro and Saute for 2 minutes. Stir in remaining marinade and let it heat up
8. Spoon the sauce over fish. Enjoy!

Favorite Salmon Stew

(Prepping time: 5 minutes\ Cooking time: 11 minutes |For 4 servings)

Ingredients

- 1 cup fish broth
- Salt and pepper to taste
- 1 medium onion, chopped
- 1-2 pounds salmon fillets, cubed
- 1 tablespoon butter

Directions

1. Add the listed ingredients to a large-sized bowl and let the shrimp marinate for 30-60 minutes
2. Grease the inner pot of the Ninja Foodi with butter and transfer marinated shrimp to the pot
3. Lock the lid and select "Bake/Roast" mode and bake for 15 minutes at 355 degrees F
4. Once done, serve and enjoy!

Tilapia And Asparagus Delight

(Prepping time: 5 minutes\ Cooking time: 2 hours |For 4 servings)

Ingredients

- 1 bunch asparagus
- 4-6 tilapia fillets
- 8-12 tablespoons lemon juice
- Pepper for seasoning
- Lemon juice for seasoning
- ½ tablespoons for clarified butter, for each fillet

Directions

1. Cut single pieces of foil for the fillets
2. Divide the bundle of asparagus into even number depending on the number of your fillets
3. Lay the fillets on each of the pieces of foil and sprinkle pepper and add a teaspoon of lemon juice. Add clarified butter and top with asparagus
4. Fold the foil over the fish and seal the ends.Repeat with all the fillets and transfer to Ninja Foodi
5. Cook on SLOW COOK MODE (HIGH) for 2 hours. Enjoy!

Asian Salmon And Veggie Meal

(Prepping time: 5 minutes\ Cooking time: 2 hours |For 4 servings)

Ingredients

For Fish

- 2 medium salmon fillets
- 1 garlic cloves, diced
- 2 teaspoons ginger, grated
- ¼ a long red chili, diced
- Salt as needed
- 2 tablespoons coconut aminos
- 1 teaspoon agave nectar

For Veggies

- ½ pound mixed green veggies
- 1 large carrot, sliced
- 1 garlic clove, diced
- ½ lime, juice
- 1 tablespoon tamari sauce
- 1 tablespoon olive oil
- ½ teaspoon sesame oil

Directions

1. Add 1 cup of water to your Ninja Foodi and place a trivet inside
2. Place fish fillets inside a heatproof tin (small enough to fit inside the pot) and sprinkle diced garlic, chili, and ginger on top. Season with salt and pepper

3. Take a small bowl and create a mixture of tamari and agave nectar
4. Pour the mixture over the fillets. Place tin with salmon on top of the trivet
5. Lock up the lid and cook on HIGH pressure for 3 minutes and perform a quick release
6. Cut the vegetables and place the veggies in a steam basket. Sprinkle garlic
7. Place the steamer basket with veggies on top of the salmon tin and drizzle lime juice, olive oil, tamari, sesame oil. Season with salt and pepper
8. Lock up the lid and cook on HIGH pressure for 0 minutes (just the time required for the pressure to build up). Quick release the remove the and basket and tin
9. Transfer the salmon to a plate alongside veggies and pour any remaining sauce over the salmon, enjoy!

All-Time Favorite Codes
(Prepping time: 5 minutes\ Cooking time: 8 minutes |For 4 servings)

Ingredients

- 4 garlic cloves, minced
- 2 teaspoons coconut aminos
- ¼ cup butter
- 6 whole eggs

- 2 small onions, chopped
- 3 (4 ounces each) skinless cod fish fillets, cut into rectangular pieces
- 2 green chilies, chopped
- Salt and pepper to taste

Directions

1. Take a shallow dish and add all ingredients except cod, beat the mixture well
2. Dip each fillet into the mixture and keep it on the side
3. Transfer prepared fillets to your Ninja Foodi Crisping basket and transfer basket to Pot
4. Lock Crisping lid and cook on "Air Crisp" mode for 8 minutes at 330 degrees F.Serve and enjoy!

The Great Poached Salmon
(Prepping time: 10 minutes\ Cooking time: 5 minutes |For 4 servings)

Ingredients

- 16-ounce salmon fillet, skin on
- 4 scallions, chopped
- Zest of 1 lemon
- ½ a teaspoon of fennel seeds
- 1 teaspoon white wine vinegar

- 1 bay leaf
- ½ cup dry white wine
- 2 cups chicken broth
- ¼ cup fresh dill
- Salt and pepper

Directions

1. Add the listed ingredients to your Ninja Foodi, stir well
2. Lock lid and cook on HIGH pressure for 4 minutes. Release pressure naturally over 10 minutes
3. Serve and enjoy!

Great Seafood Stew
(Prepping time: 10 minutes\ Cooking time: 10 minutes |For 4 servings)

Ingredients

- 3 tablespoons extra virgin olive oil
- 2 bay leaves
- 2 teaspoons paprika
- 1 small onion, sliced
- 1 small green bell pepper
- 2 garlic cloves, mashed

- Salt and pepper to taste
- 1 cup fish stock
- 1 and ½ pound meat fish
- 1 pound shrimp, cleaned and deveined
- 12 neck clams
- ¼ cup cilantro, garnish

- 1 tablespoon extra virgin olive oil

Directions

1. Set your Ninja Foodi to Saute mode and add olive oil
2. Add bay leaves and paprika and Saute for 30 seconds
3. Add onion, bell pepper, tomatoes, 2 tablespoons of cilantro, garlic and season with salt and pepper. Stir for a few minutes . Add fish stock
4. Season fish with salt and pepper and Nestle the clams and shrimp among the veggies in the Ninja Foodi. Add fish on top
5. Lock up the lid and cook on HIGH pressure for 10 minutes
6. Release the pressure over 10 minutes
7. Divide the stew amongst bowls and drizzle 1 tablespoon of olive oil
8. Sprinkle 2 tablespoon of cilantro and serve. Enjoy!

Garlic Sauce And Mussels

(Prepping time: 15 minutes \ Cooking time: 1 minute |For 4 servings)

Ingredients

- 3 pounds mussels
- 1 tablespoon extra-virgin olive oil
- 4 garlic cloves, minced
- 1 large roasted bell pepper
- ¾ cup fish stock

- ½ cup white wine vinegar
- 1/8 teaspoon red pepper flakes
- 2 tablespoons cashew cream
- 3 tablespoons parsley, chopped

Directions

9. Clean the mussels well and scrub them, debeard if needed. Make a steaming liquid
10. Set your Ninja Foodi to Saute mode and add olive oil, allow it to heat up
11. Add garlic and cook for 1 minute
12. Add roasted red pepper, vinegar, fish stock, red pepper flakes and stir
13. Add mussels to the Ninja Foodi and lock up the lid
14. Cook on HIGH pressure for 1 minute and quick release the pressure
15. Remove the lid and check the mussels, if they are open then enjoy
16. If not, lock up the lid and steam for 1 minute more. Garnish with a bit of parsley. Enjoy!

Shrimp And Tomato Delight

(Prepping time: 10 minutes\ Cooking time: 5 minutes |For 4 servings)

Ingredients

- 3 tablespoons unsalted butter
- 1 tablespoon garlic
- ½ teaspoon red pepper flakes
- 1 and ½ cup onion, chopped
- 1 can (14 and ½ ounces) tomatoes, diced

- 1 teaspoon dried oregano
- 1 teaspoon salt
- 1 pound frozen shrimp, peeled
- 1 cup crumbled feta cheese
- ½ cup black olives, sliced
- ½ cup parsley, chopped

Directions

1. Pre-heat your Ninja Foodi by setting in in the Saute mode on HIGH settings, add butter and let it melt. Add garlic, pepper flakes, cook for 1 minute
2. Add onion, tomato, oregano, salt and stir well. Add frozen shrimp
3. Lock lid and cook on HIGH pressure for 1 minute. Quick release pressure
4. Mix shrimp with tomato broth, let it cool and serve with a sprinkle of feta, olives, and parsley
5. Enjoy!

Juicy Mediterranean Cod

(Prepping time: 5 minutes\ Cooking time: 15 minutes |For 4 servings)

Ingredients

- 6 Fresh Cod
- 3 tablespoons clarified butter
- 1 lemon, juiced
- 1 onion, sliced
- 1 teaspoon salt
- ½ teaspoon pepper
- 1 teaspoon oregano
- 1 can (28 ounces) tomatoes, diced

Directions

1. Set your pot to Saute mode and add clarified butter
2. Once the butter is hot, add the rest of the ingredients and stir (except fish).Saute for 10 minutes
3. Arrange the fish portions in the sauce and spoon the sauce over the fish to coat it
4. Lock up the lid and cook under HIGH pressure for 5 minutes. Perform a quick release and serve!

Medi-Bass Stew

(Prepping time: 10 minutes\ Cooking time: 28 minutes |For 6 servings)

Ingredients

- 1 pound sea bass fillets, patted dry and cut into 2 inch chunks
- 3 tablespoons Cajun seasoning, divided
- ½ teaspoon salt
- 2 tablespoons extra virgin olive oil
- 2 yellow onion, diced
- 2 bell peppers, diced
- 4 celery stalks, diced
- 1 can (28 ounces) diced tomatoes, drained
- ¼ cup tomato paste
- 1 and ½ cups veggie broth
- 2 pounds large shrimp, peeled and deveined

Directions

1. Set your Pot to Saute mode at a temperature of Medium-HIGH heat, let it pre-heat for 5 minutes
2. Season sea bass on both sides with 1 and ½ tablespoons Cajun seasoning and ¼ teaspoon salt. Put 1 tablespoon oil and sea bass in your pre-heated pot. Saute for 4 minutes
3. Add remaining 1 tablespoon oil and onions to the pot and cook for 3 minutes, add bell peppers, celery, and 1 and ½ tablespoons Cajun seasoning to the pot. Cook for 2 minutes more
4. Add sea bass, diced tomatoes, tomato paste, broth to the pot, place the lid and seal the valves
5. Cook on HIGH pressure for 5 minutes, quick release the pressure once did
6. Set your pot to Saute mode again with the temperature set at Medium-HIGH mode and add shrimp. Place lid and seal the pressure valve, cook for 4 minutes until the shrimp is opaque
7. Season with ¼ teaspoon salt and serve, enjoy!

Delicious Smoked Salmon And Spinach Frittata

(Prepping time: 10 minutes\ Cooking time: 8 hours |For 4 servings)

Ingredients

- 10 whole eggs
- ¼ cup unsweetened almond milk
- 1 teaspoon garlic powder
- 1 teaspoon orange-chili-garlic sauce
- ½ teaspoon of sea salt
- ¼ teaspoon freshly ground black pepper
- 8 ounces smoked salmon, flaked
- 8 ounces shiitake mushrooms, sliced
- 2 cups baby spinach
- Oil for greasing

Direction

1. Take a large sized bowl and add eggs, orange chili garlic sauce, almond milk, garlic powder and season with salt and pepper. Fold in smoked salmon, spinach and mushrooms
2. Mix well. Grease Ninja Foodi with oil. Pour egg mix in Ninja Foodi
3. Close lid and cook on SLOW COOK Mode (LOW) for 8 hours. Serve and enjoy!

Dijon Flavored Lemon Whitefish
(Prepping time: 5 minutes\ Cooking time: 2 minutes |For 4 servings)

Ingredients

- 1 pound whitefish fillets
- 2 tablespoons Dijon mustard
- 1 teaspoon horseradish, grated
- 1 tablespoon fresh lemon juice
- 1 teaspoon fresh ginger, grated
- ½ teaspoon salt and black pepper (each)
- 1 lemon, sliced
- ½ tablespoon olive oil
- 1 cup of water

Directions

1. Mix in Dijon mustard, lemon juice and horseradish in a bowl
2. Season white fish fillets with salt and pepper, add Dijon marinade
3. Let it marinate for 20 minutes. Add water to your Ninja Foodi and place a steamer rack inside
4. Put fillets on the rack and pour marinade on top
5. Lock lid and cook on HIGH pressure for 20 minutes
6. Release pressure naturally over 10 minutes. Enjoy!

Very Low Carb Clam Chowder
(Prepping time: 5 minutes\ Cooking time: 4 hours 20 minutes |For 6 servings)

Ingredients

- 13 slices bacon, thick cut
- 2 cups chicken broth
- 1 cup celery, chopped
- 1 cup onion, chopped
- 6 cups baby clams, with juice
- 2 cups heavy whipping cream
- 1 teaspoon salt
- 1 teaspoon ground thyme
- 1 teaspoon pepper

Directions

1. Take a skillet and place it over medium heat, cook bacon until crispy
2. Drain and crumble the bacon. Chop onion, celery and add them to the pan
3. Once tender add veggies alongside remaining ingredients to your Ninja Foodi
4. Lock lid and cook on SLOW COOK MODE(LOW) for 4-6 hours. Serve and enjoy!

Chapter 4: Mouthwatering Poultry Recipes

Lemon And Chicken Extravaganza
(Prepping time: 5 minutes\ Cooking time: 18 minutes |For 4 servings)

Ingredients

- 4 bone-in, skin on chicken thighs
- Salt and pepper to taste
- 2 tablespoons butter, divided
- 2 teaspoons garlic, minced
- ½ cup herbed chicken stock
- ½ cup heavy whip cream
- ½ a lemon, juiced

Directions

1. Season your chicken thighs generously with salt and pepper
2. Set your Foodi to sauté mode and add oil, let it heat up
3. Add thigh, Sauté both sides for 6 minutes. Remove thigh to a platter and keep it on the side
4. Add garlic, cook for 2 minutes. Whisk in chicken stock, heavy cream, lemon juice and gently stir
5. Bring the mix to a simmer and reintroduce chicken
6. Lock lid and cook for 10 minutes on HIGH pressure
7. Release pressure over 10 minutes. Serve and enjoy!

Bruschetta Chicken Meal
(Prepping time: 5 minutes\ Cooking time: 9 minutes |For 4 servings)

Ingredients

- 2 tablespoons balsamic vinegar
- 1/3 cup olive oil
- 2 teaspoons garlic cloves, minced
- 1 teaspoon black pepper
- ½ teaspoon salt
- ½ cup sun-dried tomatoes, in olive oil
- 2 pounds chicken breasts, quartered, boneless
- 2 tablespoons fresh basil, chopped

Direction

1. Take a bowl and whisk in vinegar, oil, garlic, pepper, salt
2. Fold in tomatoes, basil and add breast, mix well. Transfer to fridge and let it sit for 30 minutes
3. Add everything to Ninja Foodi and lock lid, cook on High Pressure for 9 minutes
4. Quick release pressure. Serve and enjoy!

The Great Hainanese Chicken
(Prepping time: 20 minutes \ Cooking time: 4 hours |For 4 servings)

Ingredients

- 1 ounces ginger, peeled
- 6 garlic cloves, crushed
- 6 bundles cilantro/basil leaves
- 1 teaspoon salt
- 1 tablespoon sesame oil
- 3 (1 and ½ pounds each) chicken meat, ready to cook

For Dip

- 2 tablespoons ginger, minced
- 1 teaspoon garlic, minced
- 1 tablespoon chicken stock
- 1 teaspoon sesame oil
- ½ teaspoon sugar
- Salt to taste

Directions

1. Add chicken, garlic, ginger, leaves, and salt in your Ninja Food
2. Add enough water to fully submerge chicken, lock lid cook on SLOW COOK mode on LOW for 4 hours. Release pressure naturally
3. Take chicken out of pot and chill for 10 minutes
4. Take a bowl and add all the dipping ingredients and blend well in a food processor
5. Take chicken out of ice bath and drain, chop into serving pieces. Arrange onto a serving platter
6. Brush chicken with sesame oil. Serve with ginger dip. Enjoy!

A Genuine Hassel Back Chicken
(Prepping time: 5 minutes\ Cooking time: 60 minutes |For 4 servings)

Ingredients

- 4 tablespoons butter
- Salt and pepper to taste
- 2 cups fresh mozzarella cheese, thinly sliced
- 8 large chicken breasts
- 4 large Roma tomatoes, thinly sliced

Directions

1. Make few deep slits in chicken breasts, season with salt and pepper
2. Stuff mozzarella cheese slices and tomatoes in chicken slits
3. Grease Ninja Foodi pot with butter and arrange stuffed chicken breasts
4. Lock lid and BAKE/ROAST for 1 hour at 365 degrees F. Serve and enjoy!

Shredded Up Salsa Chicken
(Prepping time: 5 minutes\ Cooking time: 20 minutes |For 4 servings)

Ingredients

- 1 pound chicken breast, skin and bones removed
- ¾ teaspoon cumin
- ½ teaspoon salt
- Pinch of oregano
- Pepper to taste
- 1 cup chunky salsa Keto friendly

Directions

1. Season chicken with spices and add to Ninja Foodi
2. Cover with salsa and lock lid, cook on HIGH pressure for 20 minutes
3. Quick release pressure. Add chicken to a platter and shred the chicken. Serve and enjoy!

Mexico's Favorite Chicken Soup
(Prepping time: 5 minutes\ Cooking time: 20 minutes |For 4 servings)

Ingredients

- 2 cups chicken, shredded
- 4 tablespoons olive oil
- ½ cup cilantro, chopped
- 8 cups chicken broth
- 1/3 cup salsa
- 1 teaspoon onion powder
- ½ cup scallions, chopped
- 4 ounces green chilies, chopped
- ½ teaspoon habanero, minced
- 1 cup celery root, chopped
- 1 teaspoon cumin
- 1 teaspoon garlic powder
- Salt and pepper to taste

Directions

1. Add all ingredients to Ninja Foodi. Stir and lock lid, cook on HIGH pressure for 10 minutes
2. Release pressure naturally over 10 minutes. Serve and enjoy!

Taiwanese Chicken Delight

(Prepping time: 5 minutes\ Cooking time: 10 minutes |For 4 servings)

Ingredients

- 6 dried red chilis
- ¼ cup sesame oil
- 2 tablespoons ginger
- ¼ cup garlic, minced
- ¼ cup red wine vinegar
- ¼ cup coconut aminos
- Salt as needed
- 1.2 teaspoon xanthan gum (for the finish)
- ¼ cup Thai basil, chopped

Directions

1. Set your Ninja Foodi to Saute mode and add ginger, chilis, garlic and Saute for 2 minutes
2. Add remaining ingredients. Lock lid and cook on HIGH pressure for 10 minutes
3. Quick release pressure. Serve and enjoy!

Cabbage And Chicken Meatballs

(Prepping time: 10 minutes + 30 minutes\ Cooking time: 4-6 minutes |For 4 servings)

Ingredients

- 1 pound ground chicken
- ¼ cup heavy whip cream
- 2 teaspoons salt
- ½ teaspoon ground caraway seeds
- 1 and ½ teaspoons fresh ground black pepper, divided
- 1/4 teaspoon ground allspice
- 4-6 cups green cabbage, thickly chopped
- ½ cup almond milk
- 2 tablespoons unsalted butter

Directions

1. Transfer meat to a bowl and add cream, 1 teaspoon salt, caraway, ½ teaspoon pepper, allspice and mix it well. Let the mixture chill for 30 minutes
2. Once the mixture is ready, use your hands to scoop the mixture into meatballs
3. Add half of your balls to Ninja Foodi pot and cover with half of the cabbage
4. Add remaining balls and cover with rest of the cabbage
5. Add milk, pats of butter, season with salt and pepper
6. Lock lid and cook on HIGH pressure for 4 minutes. Quick release pressure
7. Unlock lid and serve. Enjoy!

Poached Chicken With Coconut Lime Cream Sauce

(Prepping time: 5 minutes \ Cooking time: 10 minutes |For 4 servings)

Ingredients

- 1-ounce shallot, minced
- 1 ounces ginger, sliced
- 2 medium banana peppers,
- 1 cup of coconut milk
- 1 cup chicken stock
- Juice of 1 lime, and zest
- 2 tablespoons fish sauce
- 3 pieces of 1/3 pounds each chicken breasts, meat

Directions

1. Add listed ingredients to your Ninja Foodi
2. Stir well and lock lid, cook on HIGH pressure for 10 minutes
3. Quick release pressure. Top with fresh cilantro. Serve and enjoy!

Hot And Spicy Paprika Chicken
(Prepping time: 10 minutes\ Cooking time: 20-25 minutes |For 4 servings)

Ingredients

- 4 piece (4 ounces each) chicken breast, skin on
- Salt and pepper to taste
- ½ cup sweet onion, chopped
- ½ cup heavy whip cream
- 2 teaspoons smoked paprika
- ½ cup sour cream
- 2 tablespoons fresh parsley, chopped

Directions

1. Season chicken with salt and pepper
2. Set your Foodi to Saute mode and add oil, let it heat up
3. Add chicken and sear both sides until nicely browned. Should take around 15 minutes
4. Remove chicken and transfer to a plate
5. Take a skillet and place it over medium heat, add onion and Sauté for 4 minutes
6. Stir in cream, paprika, bring the liquid to simmer. Return chicken to skillet and warm
7. Transfer the whole mixture to your Foodi and lock lid, cook on HIGH pressure for 5 minutes
8. Release pressure naturally over 10 minutes. Stir in cream, serve and enjoy!

Inspiring Turkey Cutlets
(Prepping time: 10 minutes\ Cooking time: 20-25 minutes |For 4 servings)

Ingredients

- 1 teaspoon Greek seasoning
- 1 pound turkey cutlets
- 2 tablespoons olive oil
- 1 teaspoon turmeric powder
- ½ cup almond flour

Directions

1. Take a bowl and add Greek seasoning, turmeric powder, almond flour, and mix
2. Dredge turkey cutlets in a bowl and let them sit for 30 minutes
3. Set Ninja Foodi to Sauté mode and add oil, let it heat up. Add cutlets and Sauté for 2 minutes
4. Lock lid and cook on LOW- MEDIUM pressure for 20 minutes
5. Release pressure naturally over 10 minutes. Take it out and serve, enjoy!

Lemongrass And Tamarind Chicken
(Prepping time: 10 minutes \ Cooking time: 4 hours |For 4 servings)

Ingredients

- 3 chicken thighs
- 1 ounce strips fresh turmeric
- 2 shallots, quartered
- Handful of mustard
- 1 stalk lemongrass, bruised and bundled up
- 2 cups chicken stock
- 1 banana pepper
- 4 tablespoons olive oil
- 2 tablespoons tamarind paste
- 2 Roma tomatoes, quartered
- 1 radish, peeled and chopped
- Fish sauce to taste
- Salt and pepper to taste

Directions

1. Add listed ingredients to your Ninja Foodi
2. Stir well and lock lid, cook on HIGH pressure for 10 minutes
3. Quick release pressure. Top with fresh cilantro. Serve and enjoy!

Fluffy Whole Chicken Dish

(Prepping time: 10 minutes\ Cooking time: 8 hours |For 4 servings)

Ingredients

- 1 cup mozzarella cheese
- 4 whole garlic cloves, peeled
- 1 whole chicken (2 pounds), cleaned and pat dried
- Salt and pepper to taste
- 2 tablespoons fresh lemon juice

Directions

1. Stuff chicken cavity with garlic cloves and mozzarella cheese
2. Season chicken generously with salt and pepper
3. Transfer chicken to Ninja Foodi and drizzle lemon juice
4. Lock lid and set to Slow Cooker mode, let it cook on LOW for 8 hours
5. Once done, serve and enjoy!

Sensible Chettinad Chicken

(Prepping time: 10 minutes\ Cooking time: 15 minutes |For 4 servings)

Ingredients

- 1 pound of boneless chicken thigh cut up into pieces
- 1 tablespoon of Ghee
- 1 bay leaf
- 5 curry leaves
- 1 inch Ginger piece
- 5 cloves of Garlic
- ¼ cup of grated coconut (fresh)
- 1 large onion, diced
- 2 medium tomatoes, diced
- 1 teaspoon of salt
- ½ a cup of water
- Cilantro as needed

Whole Spices

- 4 pieces of Red Chili Whole Kashmiri
- 1 teaspoon of black peppercorns
- 1 teaspoon of cumin seeds
- 2 teaspoon of coriander seeds
- 5 pieces of Green coriander
- 1 stick of cinnamon
- 4 pieces of cloves
- 1 tablespoon of cloves
- 1 tablespoon of poppy seeds
- 1 teaspoon of fennel seeds

Directions

1. Set your Ninja Foodi to Saute mode and add whole spices and cook them until dry roasted (for about 30 seconds)
2. Add garlic, ginger, grated coconut and Saute for 30 seconds more
3. Transfer the mixture to a blender and Grind until you have a paste. This is your Chettinad Spice Mix. Clean the Ninja Foodi and set your pot to Saute mode again
4. Add oil and allow it to heat it up. Add bay leaf and curry leaves, Saute for 30 seconds
5. Add diced up onions and Saute for about 30 seconds
6. Add diced up onion and Saute for 3 minutes
7. Add tomatoes, salt and ground spices and Saute for 2 minutes (including the previous blend)
8. Add chicken pieces and Saute for 3 minutes more
9. Add water and lock up the lid, cook for 5 minutes at HIGH pressure
10. Once done, do a quick release and enjoy with a garnish of cilantro. Enjoy!

Hawaiian Pinna Colada Chicken Meal

(Prepping time: 10 minutes\ Cooking time: 15 minutes |For 4 servings)

Ingredients

- 2 pounds organic chicken thigh
- 1 cup fresh pineapple chunks
- ½ cup coconut cream
- 1 teaspoon cinnamon
- 1/8 teaspoon salt
- 2 tablespoons coconut aminos
- ½ cup green onion, chopped
- Arrowroot flout

Directions

1. Add all of the ingredients to your Ninja Foodi except green onion
2. Lock up the lid and cook for 15 minutes at HIGH pressure
3. Once done, allow the pressure to release naturally. Open up the lid and stir well
4. Take a bowl and mix arrowroot flour and a tablespoon of water to make a slurry
5. Add the slurry to your pot and mix well to make a thick mixture
6. Set your pot to Saute mode and wait until the sauce is just thick enough
7. Garnish with some green onion and enjoy!

Garlic And Butter Chicken Dish

(Prepping time: 10 minutes\ Cooking time: 35 minutes |For 4 servings)

Ingredients

- 4 pieces of chicken breasts, chopped up
- ¼ cup of turmeric ghee/ normal ghee
- 1 teaspoon of salt
- 10 cloves of garlic, peeled and diced up

Directions

1. Add chicken breast to the Ninja Foodi
2. Add ghee, salt, diced garlic and lock up the lid
3. Cook on HIGH pressure for 35 minutes
4. Release the pressure naturally and open the lid
5. Serve with extra ghee

Creamy Chicken Curry

(Prepping time: 10 minutes\ Cooking time: 10 hours |For 4 servings)

Ingredients

- 10 bone-in chicken thighs, skinless
- 1 cup sour cream
- 2 tablespoons. Curry powder
- 1 onion, chopped
- 1 jar (16 ounces) chunky salsa sauce

Directions

1. Add chicken thigh to your Ninja Foodi
2. Add onions, salsa, curry powder over chicken, stir and place the lid
3. Cook SLOW COOK MODE (LOW) for 10 hours. Open lid and transfer chicken to a serving platter
4. Pour sour cream into the sauce (cooking liquid) in the Ninja Foodi
5. Stir well and pour the sauce over chicken. Serve!

Lemon And Artichoke Medley

(Prepping time: 10 minutes\ Cooking time: 8 hours |For 6 servings)

Ingredients

- 1 pound boneless and skinless chicken breast
- 1 pound boneless and skinless chicken thigh
- 14 ounces (can) artichoke hearts, packed in water and drained
- 1 onion, diced
- 2 carrots, diced
- 3 garlic cloves, minced

- 1 bay leaf
- ½ teaspoon pepper
- 3 cups turnips, peeled and cubed
- 6 cups chicken broth
- 14 cup fresh lemon juice
- ¼ cup parsley, chopped

Directions

1. Add the above mentioned ingredients to your Ninja Foodi except for lemon juice and parsley
2. Cook on Slow Cooker (LOW) for 8 hours. Remove the chicken and shred it up
3. Return it back to the Ninja Foodi. Season with some pepper and salt!
4. Stir in parsley and lemon juice and serve!

Awesome Sesame Ginger Chicken
(Prepping time: 10 minutes\ Cooking time: 10 minutes |For 4 servings)

Ingredients

- 1 tablespoon rice vinegar
- 1 tablespoon Truvia
- 1 tablespoon garlic, minced
- 1 tablespoon fresh ginger, minced
- 1 tablespoon sesame oil
- 2 tablespoons soy sauce
- 1 and ½ pound boneless, skinless chicken thigh, cut into large pieces

Directions

1. Take a heatproof bowl and add soy sauce, ginger, sesame oil, garlic, Truvia and vinegar
2. Stir well to coat it. Cover bowl with foil. Add 2 cups of water to Ninja Foodie's inner pot
3. Place a trivet and place the bowl with chicken on the trivet
4. Lock lid and cook for 10 minutes on HIGH pressure. Release pressure naturally over 10 minutes
5. Remove chicken and shred it, mix it back into the bowl. Serve and enjoy!

Chicken Korma
(Prepping time: 10 minutes\ Cooking time: 20 minutes |For 6 servings)

Ingredients

- 1 pound of chicken

For Sauce

- 1 ounce of cashews
- 1 small chopped onion
- ½ a cup of diced tomatoes
- ½ of green Serrano pepper
- 5 cloves of garlic
- 1 teaspoon of minced ginger
- 1 teaspoon of turmeric
- 1 teaspoon of Garam masala
- 1 teaspoon of cumin-coriander powder
- ½ a teaspoon of cayenne pepper
- ½ a cup of water

For topping

- 1 teaspoon of Garam masala
- ½ a cup of coconut milk
- ¼ cup of chopped cilantro

Directions

1. Add the sauce ingredients to a blender and blend them well
2. Pour the sauce to your Ninja Foodi. Place the chicken on top
3. Lock up the lid and cook on HIGH pressure for 10 minutes
4. Release the pressure naturally. Take the chicken out and cut into bite-sized portions
5. Add coconut milk, Garam masala to the pot
6. Transfer the chicken back and garnish with cilantro. Enjoy!

Turkey With Garlic Sauce

(Prepping time: 10 minutes\ Cooking time: 8 hours |For 6 servings)

Ingredients

- 5 large onions, thinly sliced
- 4 garlic cloves, minced
- ¼ cup white wine vinegar
- ½ teaspoon salt
- ¼ teaspoon ground black pepper
- ¼ teaspoon cayenne pepper
- 4 large skinless turkey thighs

Directions

1. Gently lay the garlic and onions into the bottom of your Ninja Foodi
2. Pour in some wine with a sprinkle of salt, cayenne pepper, and black pepper.
3. Add turkey thighs and cover it up. Let it cook SLOW COOKER MODE (low) for about 8 hours.
4. Remove the turkey from the crock pot and clean up the flesh from the bones.
5. Keep the lid open and keep cooking until the liquid has completely evaporated, making sure to stir from time to time. Return the turkey to the pot.
6. Nestle the turkey into the mix. Serve hot. Enjoy!

Awesome Ligurian Chicken

(Prepping time: 10 minutes\ Cooking time: 15 minutes |For 4 servings)

Ingredients

- 2 garlic cloves, chopped
- 3 sprigs fresh rosemary
- 2 sprigs fresh sage
- ½ bunch parsley
- 3 lemon, juiced
- 4 tablespoons extra virgin olive oil
- 1 teaspoon salt
- ¼ teaspoon pepper
- 1 and ½ cup of water
- 1 whole chicken, cut into parts
- 3 and ½ ounces black gourmet salt-cured olives
- 1 fresh lemon

Directions

1. Take a bowl and add chopped up garlic, parsley, sage, and rosemary
2. Pour lemon juice, olive oil to a bowl and season with salt and pepper
3. Remove the chicken skin and from the chicken pieces and carefully transfer them to a dish
4. Pour the marinade on top of the chicken pieces and allow them to chill for 2-4 hours
5. Set your Ninja Foodi to Saute mode and add olive oil, allow it to heat up
6. Add chicken and browned on all sides
7. Measure out the marinade and add to the pot (it should cover the chicken, add a bit of water if needed). Lock up the lid and cook on HIGH pressure for 10 minutes
8. Release the pressure naturally. The chicken out and transfer to a platter
9. Cover with a foil and allow them to cool. Set your pot in Saute mode and reduce the liquid to ¼
10. Add the chicken pieces again to the pot and allow them to warm
11. Sprinkle a bit of olive, lemon slices, and rosemary. Enjoy!

Creative French Chicken

(Prepping time: 10 minutes\ Cooking time: 15 minutes |For 4 servings)

Ingredients

For Marinade

- 2 teaspoon of Herbes De Provence
- 2 tablespoon of olive oil
- 1 tablespoon of prepped Dijon mustard
- 1 tablespoon of cider vinegar

- ½ a teaspoon of salt
- 1 teaspoon of pepper
- 1 tablespoon of minced garlic
- 1 pound of boneless and skinless chicken thigh

For Cooking

- 2 tablespoon of butter
- 8 cloves of garlic, chopped
- ¼ cup of water
- ¼ cup of cream

Directions

1. Take a bowl and add all of the marinade ingredients and whisk well
2. Add chicken thigh and the chicken to marinate for 30 minutes at room temperature
3. Set your Ninja Foodi to Saute mode and add butter, allow the butter to heat up
4. Add chopped garlic and sauté for 2-3 minutes
5. Add chicken and Saute for 3-5 minutes until slightly browned
6. Add the marinade from the chicken bowl alongside a ¼ cup of water
7. Lock up the lid and cook on HIGH pressure for 5 minutes. Release the pressure naturally over 10 minutes. Remove the chicken and transfer to a platter
11. Add ¼ cup of cream to the pot and stir. Once the sauce thickens, transfer the chicken thigh to the pot and serve!

Daring Salted Baked Chicken

(Prepping time: 10 minutes\ Cooking time: 30 minutes |For 6 servings)

Ingredients

- 2 teaspoons ginger, minced
- 1 and ¼ teaspoons salt
- ¼ teaspoons five spice powder
- Dash of white pepper
- 5-6 chicken legs

Directions

1. Season the chicken legs by placing them in a large mixing bowl
2. Pour 2 teaspoon of ginger, 1 and a ¼ teaspoon of kosher salt, ¼ teaspoon of five spice powder and mix
3. Transfer them to a parchment paper
4. Wrap up tightly and place them to a shallow dish
5. Place a steamer rack in your Ninja Foodi and add 1 cup of water
6. Place the chicken dish onto the rack
7. Lock up the lid and cook on HIGH pressure for 18-26 minutes
8. Release the pressure naturally
9. Open the lid and unwrap the paper
10. Pour the juice into a small bowl
11. Transfer the chicken on a wire rack and broil for a while
12. Serve immediately with the cooking liquid used as a dipping sauce

Worthy Ghee-Licious Chicken

(Prepping time: 10 minutes\ Cooking time: 8 minutes |For 6 servings)

Ingredients

- 2-3 pounds boneless chicken thigh
- 1 tablespoon ghee
- 1 and a ½ large onion, chopped
- 3 and ½ teaspoons salt
- 2 teaspoons garlic powder
- 2 teaspoons ginger powder
- 2 heaping teaspoons turmeric
- 1 and ½ teaspoon cayenne powder
- 1 and ½ cup stewed tomatoes
- 1 cup stewed tomatoes
- 2 cans of coconut milk
- 2 heaping teaspoons Garam masala
- ½ cup almond, sliced
- ½ cup cilantro

Directions

1. Set your Ninja Foodi to Saute mode and add ghee, allow it to melt
2. Add 2 teaspoon of salt alongside onion and cook well
3. Add ginger, garlic, turmeric, paprika, cayenne pepper and mix well
4. Add your canned tomatoes alongside coconut milk and mix
5. Add chicken and give it a nice stir
6. Lock up the lid and cook on HIGH pressure for about 8 minutes
7. Once done, pour coconut cream, tomato paste, and Garam Masala
8. Garnish with some cilantro and serve with a sprinkle of sliced up almonds. Enjoy!

Hearty Duck Breast Meal
(Prepping time: 120 minutes\ Cooking time: 30 minutes |For 4 servings)

Ingredients

- 2 duck breast halves, boneless and skin on
- 1 teaspoon salt
- 2 teaspoons fresh garlic, minced
- ½ teaspoon black pepper

- 1/3 teaspoon thyme
- 1/3 teaspoon peppercorn
- 1 tablespoon olive oil
- 1 tablespoon apricot, peeled and cored
- 2 teaspoons date paste

Directions

1. Clean the duck breast and rub the spices all over. Cover and allow it to chill for 2 hours
2. Rinse the spices off and place the breast in a zip bag, seal it up making sure to remove as much air as possible. (look on the internet for immersion sealing method for best results)
3. Add 5 cups of water to your Ninja Foodi
4. Set your Ninja Foodi to Saute mode and allow the water to heat up for about 20 minutes
5. Place the bag in the water bath and keep it for 35-40 minutes
6. Remove the bag from water and pat the breasts dry
7. Sear the skin side of the duck breast in a nonstick frying pan with about 1 tablespoon of oil over medium-high heat. Turn the breast over and cook for 20 seconds more
8. Prepare the apricot sauce by mixing apricot and date paste in a small pot and bringing the mix to a boil, followed by a simmer for 5 minutes at low heat
9. Slice the duck breast and serve with apricot sauce. Serve the duck breast with the sauce. Enjoy!

Fancy Chicken Chile Verde
(Prepping time: 120 minutes\ Cooking time: 25 minutes |For 4 servings)

Ingredients

- 1/3 cup water
- 3 pounds chicken breasts, skinless
- ¾ pound quartered tomatillos
- ¾ pound poblano peppers, seeds and stems discarded
- ½ pound Anaheim pepper, seeds and stems discarded
- 4-5 jalapeno pepper stems removed and halved

- 1 white onion, quartered
- 4-6 medium garlic clove, peeled
- 1 tablespoon ground cumin
- ½ tablespoon paprika
- 1 tablespoon salt
- 1 tablespoon pepper
- 1 tablespoon ground cinnamon
- 1 tablespoon red boat fish sauce

Directions

1. Add Anaheim, tomatillos, pepper, poblano pepper, jalapeno pepper, onion, cumin, garlic, paprika, salt and chicken to your Ninja Foodi. Add water to cover them
2. Lock up the lid and cook on HIGH pressure for 25 minutes

3. Release the pressure naturally over 10 minutes
4. Add the red boat fish sauce to a blender and puree the sauce
5. Take the chicken out from your Instant Pot and shred it using a fork, return it back to the pot
6. Add puree and stir. Serve over lettuce wraps and enjoy!

Mushroom And Chicken Bowl

(Prepping time: 10 minutes\ Cooking time: 25 minutes |For 4 servings)

Ingredients

- 1 and ½ cups unsweetened coconut milk
- 1 pound chicken thigh, skinless
- 3-4 garlic cloves, crushed
- ½ an onion, finely diced
- 2-inch knob ginger, minced
- 1 cup mushrooms, sliced
- 4 ounces baby spinach
- ½ teaspoon of cayenne pepper
- ½ teaspoon turmeric
- 1 teaspoon salt
- 1 teaspoon Garam Masala
- ¼ cup cilantro, chopped

Directions

1. Add the listed ingredients to your Ninja Foodi
2. Lock lid and cook on HIGH pressure for 15 minutes
3. Release pressure naturally over 10 minutes
4. Remove chicken and roughly puree the veggies using an immersion blender
5. Shred chicken and add it back to the pot. Add cream and stir. Serve and enjoy!

Chicken And Broccoli Platter

(Prepping time: 10 minutes\ Cooking time: 15 minutes |For 4 servings)

Ingredients

- 1 tablespoon olive oil
- 1 tablespoon butter
- 2 large chicken breasts, boneless
- ½ cup onion, chopped
- 14 ounces chicken broth
- ½ teaspoon salt
- ½ teaspoon pepper
- 1/8 teaspoon red pepper flakes
- 1 tablespoon parsley
- 1 tablespoon arrowroot
- 2 tablespoons water
- 4 ounces light cream cheese, cubed
- 1 cup cheddar cheese, shredded
- 3 cups steamed broccoli, chopped

Directions

1. Season the chicken breast with pepper and salt
2. Set your Ninja Foodi to Saute mode and add butter and vegetable oil
3. Allow it to melt and transfer the seasoned chicken to the pot. Allow it to brown
4. Remove the chicken and add the onions to the pot, Saute them for 5 minutes
5. Add chicken broth, pepper, red pepper and salt, parsley. Add the browned breast
6. Lock up the lid and cook for about 5 minutes at high pressure
7. Once done, quick release the pressure. Remove the chicken and shred it up into small portions
8. Take a bowl and add 2 tablespoons of water and dissolve cornstarch \
9. Select the simmer mode and add the mixture to the Ninja Foodi
10. Toss in the cubed and shredded cheese. Stir completely until everything is melted
11. Toss in the diced chicken again and the steamed broccoli and cook for 5 minutes
12. Once done, sever with white rice and shredded cheese as garnish

Complex Garlic And Lemon Chicken

(Prepping time: 10 minutes\ Cooking time: 30 minutes |For 6 servings)

Ingredients

- 1-2 pounds chicken breast
- 1 teaspoon salt
- 1 onion, diced
- 1 tablespoon ghee
- 5 garlic cloves, minced
- ½ cup organic chicken broth
- 1 teaspoon dried parsley
- 1 large lemon juice
- 3-4 teaspoon arrowroot flour

Directions

1. Set your Ninja Foodi to Saute mode. Add diced up onion and cooking fat
2. Allow the onions to cook for 5 -10 minutes
3. Add the rest of the ingredients except arrowroot flour
4. Lock up the lid and set the pot to poultry mode. Cook until the timer runs out
5. Allow the pressure to release naturally
6. Once done, remove ¼ cup of the sauce from the pot and add arrowroot to make a slurry
7. Add the slurry to the pot to make the gravy thick. Keep stirring well. Serve!

Chicken Puttanesca

(Prepping time: 10 minutes\ Cooking time: 50 minutes |For 6 servings)

Ingredients

- 6 chicken thigh, skin on
- 2 tablespoons extra virgin olive oil
- 2 garlic cloves, crushed
- Salt and pepper to taste
- ½ teaspoon red chili flakes
- 14 and ½ ounces tomatoes, chopped
- 6 ounces black olives, pitted
- 1 tablespoon capers
- 1 tablespoon fresh basil, chopped
- ¾ cup of water

Directions

1. Set your Ninja Foodi to Saute mode and add oil, allow the oil to heat up
2. Add chicken pieces and Saute for 5 minutes until browned, transfer the browned chicken to a platter
3. Add chopped tomatoes, olives, water, capers, garlic, chopped basil, salt, pepper, red chili flakes and stir well, bring the mix to a simmer. Add the chicken pieces to your pot
4. Lock up the lid and cook on HIGH pressure for 12 minutes
5. Release the pressure naturally. Serve with a side of veggies if wanted, enjoy!

Awesome Ligurian Chicken

(Prepping time: 10 minutes\ Cooking time: 15 minutes |For 4 servings)

Ingredients

- 2 garlic cloves, chopped
- 3 sprigs fresh rosemary
- 2 sprigs fresh sage
- ½ bunch parsley
- 3 lemon, juiced
- 4 tablespoons extra virgin olive oil
- 1 teaspoon salt
- ¼ teaspoon pepper
- 1 and ½ cup of water
- 1 whole chicken, cut into parts
- 3 and ½ ounces black gourmet salt-cured olives
- 1 fresh lemon

Directions

1.Take a bowl and add chopped up garlic, parsley, sage, and rosemary
2.Pour lemon juice, olive oil to a bowl and season with salt and pepper
3.Remove the chicken skin and from the chicken pieces and carefully transfer them to a dish
4.Pour the marinade on top of the chicken pieces and allow them to chill for 2-4 hours
5.Set your Ninja Foodi to Saute mode and add olive oil, allow it to heat up. Add chicken and browned on all sides

6.Measure out the marinade and add to the pot (it should cover the chicken, add a bit of water if needed). Lock up the lid and cook on HIGH pressure for 10 minutes

7.Release the pressure naturally. The chicken out and transfer to a platter

8.Cover with a foil and allow them to coolSet your pot in Saute mode and reduce the liquid to ¼

9.Add the chicken pieces again to the pot and allow them to warm

10.Sprinkle a bit of olive, lemon slices, and rosemary. Enjoy!

Garlic And Lemon Chicken Dish

(Prepping time: 10 minutes\ Cooking time: 30 minutes |For 4 servings)

Ingredients

- 2-3 pounds chicken breast
- 1 teaspoon salt
- 1 onion, diced
- 1 tablespoon ghee
- 5 garlic cloves, minced
- ½ cup organic chicken broth
- 1 teaspoon dried parsley
- 1 large lemon, juiced
- 3-4 teaspoon arrowroot flour

Directions

1. Set your pot to Saute mode. Add diced up onion and cooking fat

2. Allow the onions to cook for 5 -10 minutes

3. Add the rest of the ingredients except arrowroot flour

4. Lock up the lid and set the pot to poultry mode. Cook until the timer runs out

5. Allow the pressure to release naturally

6. Once done, remove ¼ cup of the sauce from the pot and add arrowroot to make a slurry

7. Add the slurry to the pot to make the gravy thick. Keep stirring well. Serve!

The Hungarian Chicken Meal

(Prepping time: 10 minutes\ Cooking time: 8 hours |For 6 servings)

Ingredients

- 1 tablespoon extra-virgin olive oil
- 2 pounds boneless chicken thigh
- ½ cup chicken broth
- Juice and zest of 1 lemon
- 2 teaspoon garlic, minced
- 2 teaspoon paprika
- ½ teaspoon salt
- 1 cup cashew cream
- 1 tablespoon parsley, chopped

Directions

1. Lightly grease the inner pot of your Ninja Foodi with olive oil. Add chicken thigh to Ninja Foodi

2. Take a bowl and add broth, lemon juice, garlic, paprika, zest, and salt

3. Mix and pour the mixture over chicken. Cook on LOW for 7-8 hours

4. Remove heat and stir in cashew cream. Serve with a topping of parsley. Enjoy!

Lime And Cilantro Chicken Meal

(Prepping time: 10 minutes\ Cooking time: 2 hours 45 minutes |For 4 servings)

Ingredients

- 2 small limes
- ¼ cup cilantro, chopped
- ½ tablespoon fresh garlic, minced
- 1 teaspoon salt
- ½ teaspoon pepper
- 4 pounds chicken drumsticks

Directions

1. Juice the lime and add them to your Ninja Foodi

2. Add ¼ cup of chopped cilantro, 1 teaspoon of salt, ½ a tablespoon of freshly minced garlic
3. Add the chicken drumsticks to the Ninja Foodi and coat them well
4. Cover and cook on SLOW COOK MODE (HIGH) for 2 and a ½ hour
5. Pre-heat your oven to a temperature of 500 degrees F. Line up a cookie sheet with foil
6. Transfer the cooker drumstick from the cooker to the foil using tongs
7. Bake for 10 minutes until they are nicely browned, making sure to turn them halfway through
8. Serve with the cooking juices. Enjoy!

The Original Mexican Chicken Cacciatore
(Prepping time: 10 minutes\ Cooking time: 33 minutes |For 4 servings)

Ingredients

- Extra virgin olive oil'
- 3 shallots, chopped
- 4 garlic cloves, crushed
- 1 green bell pepper, sliced
- ½ cup organic chicken broth
- 10 ounces mushrooms, sliced
- 5-6 skinless chicken breasts
- 2 cans (14.5 ounces) organic crushed tomatoes
- 2 tablespoons organic tomato paste
- 1 can (14.5 ounces) black olives, pitted
- Fresh parsley
- Salt and pepper to taste

Directions

1. Add oil to your pot and set the Ninja Foodi to Saute mode
2. Add shallots, bell pepper and cook for 2 minutes
3. Add broth and bring to a boil for 23 minutes. Add garlic and mushrooms
4. Gently place the chicken on the top of the whole mixture
5. Cover the chicken with tomato paste and crushed tomatoes
6. Lock up the lid and cook on HIGH pressure for 8 minutes
7. Release the pressure naturally over 10 minutes and stir in parsley, olive oil, pepper, salt, and red pepper flakes. Serve!

Magnificent Chicken Curry Soup
(Prepping time: 10 minutes\ Cooking time: 30 minutes |For 4 servings)

Ingredients

- 1 and ½ cups unsweetened coconut milk
- 1 pound chicken thigh, skinless
- 3-4 garlic cloves, crushed
- ½ an onion, finely diced
- 2-inch knob ginger, minced
- 1 cup mushrooms, sliced
- 4 ounces baby spinach
- ½ teaspoon of cayenne pepper
- ½ teaspoon turmeric
- 1 teaspoon salt
- 1 teaspoon Garam Masala
- ¼ cup cilantro, chopped

Directions

1. Add the listed ingredients to Ninja Foodi
2. Lock lid and cook on HIGH pressure for 10 minutes. Naturally, release pressure over 10 minutes
3. Remove meat and shred it, return the shredded meat to the pot
4. Set your pot to Saute mode and stir for a minute
5. Serve and enjoy!. Enjoy!

Summer Time Chicken Salad
(Prepping time: 10 minutes\ Cooking time: 10 minutes |For 4 servings)

Ingredients

- 8 boneless chicken thighs
- Kosher salt
- 1 tablespoon of ghee
- 1 small onion, chopped
- 2 medium carrots, chopped
- ½ a pound of cremini mushrooms
- 3 garlic cloves, peeled and crushed
- 2 cups of 14-ounce cherry tomatoes
- ½ a cup of 2 ounces of pitted green olives
- ¼ teaspoon of freshly cracked black pepper
- ½ a cup of thinly sliced basil leaves
- ¼ a cup of coarsely chopped Italian parsley

Directions

1. Season the chicken thigh with ¾ teaspoon of kosher salt and keep it in your fridge for about 2 days
2. Set your Ninja Foodi to Saute mode and add ghee and allow it to melt
3. Once the Ghee is simmering, add carrots, onions, mushrooms and ½ a teaspoon of salt
4. Saute the veggies until they are tender (should be around 3-5 minutes)
5. Drop the tomato paste and garlic to your pot and cook for 30 seconds
6. Add seasoned chicken to the pot alongside olives and cherry tomatoes
7. Give everything a stir
8. Lock up the lid and cook for 7-10 minutes at HIGH pressure
9. Once done, allow the pressure to quick release
10. Stir in fresh herbs and enjoy!

Ham And Stuffed Turkey Rolls

(Prepping time: 10 minutes\ Cooking time: 20 minutes |For 4 servings)

Ingredients

- 4 tablespoons fresh sage leaves
- 8 ham slices
- 8 (6 ounces) turkey cutlets
- Salt and pepper to taste
- 2 tablespoons butter, melted

Directions

1. Season turkey cutlets with salt and pepper
2. Roll turkey cutlets and wrap each of them with ham slices tightly
3. Coat each roll with butter and gently place sage leaves evenly over each cutlet
4. Transfer to Ninja Foodi
5. Lock lid and select Bake/Roast mode and bake for 10 minutes at 360 degrees F
6. Open lid and flip, lock lid and bake for 10 minutes more. Enjoy!

High-Quality Belizean Chicken Stew

(Prepping time: 10 minutes\ Cooking time: 20 minutes |For 4 servings)

Ingredients

- 4 whole chicken
- 1 tablespoon coconut oil
- 2 tablespoons achiote seasoning
- 2 tablespoons white vinegar
- 3 tablespoons Worcestershire sauce
- 1 cup yellow onion, sliced
- 3 garlic cloves, sliced
- 1 teaspoon ground cumin
- 1 teaspoon dried oregano
- ½ teaspoon black pepper
- 2 cups chicken stock

Directions

1. Take a large sized bowl and add achiote paste, vinegar, Worcestershire sauce, oregano, cumin and pepper. Mix well and add chicken pieces and rub the marinade all over them
2. Allow the chicken to sit overnight. Set your pot to Saute mode and add coconut oil

3. Once the oil is hot, add the chicken pieces to the pot and brown them in batches (each batch for 2 minutes). Remove the seared chicken and transfer them to a plate
4. Add onions, garlic to the pot and Saute for 2-3 minutes . Add chicken pieces back to the pot
5. Pour chicken broth to the bowl with marinade and stir well. Add the mixture to the pot
6. Seal up the lid and cook for about 20 minutes at high pressure
7. Once done, release the pressure naturally . Season with a bit of salt and serve!

The Great Poblano Chicken Curry
(Prepping time: 10 minutes\ Cooking time: 15 minutes |For 4 servings)

Ingredients

- 1 cup onion, diced
- 3 poblano peppers, chopped
- 5 garlic cloves,1 cup cauliflower, diced
- 1 and ½ pounds large chicken breast chunks
- ¼ cup cilantro, chopped

- 1 teaspoon ground coriander
- 1 teaspoon ground cumin
- 1-2 teaspoons salt
- 2 and ½ cups of water
- 2 ounces cream cheese

Directions

1. Add everything to your Ninja Foodi except cheese and lock up the lid
2. Cook on HIGH pressure for 15 minutes. Release the pressure naturally over 10 minutes
3. Remove the chicken with tongs and place it on the side
4. Use an immersion blender to blend the soup and veggies. Set your pot to Saute mode
5. Once the broth is hot add cream cheese (Cut in chunks). Whisk well
6. Shred the chicken and transfer it back to the pot. Serve and enjoy!

Hearty Chicken Yum
(Prepping time: 30 minutes\ Cooking time: 40 minutes |For 4 servings)

Ingredients

- 2 tablespoons fresh boneless chicken thigh
- 3 tablespoons homemade ketchup
- 1 and ½ teaspoon salt
- 2 teaspoons garlic powder

- ¼ cup ghee
- ½ teaspoon ground black pepper
- 3 tablespoons organic tamari
- ¼ cup stevia

Directions

1. Add the listed ingredients to your Ninja Foodi and give it a nice stir
2. Lock up the lid and cook for about 18 minutes under HIGH pressure
3. Quick release the pressure. Open the lid and transfer the chicken to a bowl
4. Shred it u using a fork
5. Set your pot to Saute mode and allow the liquid to be reduced for 5 minutes
6. Pour the sauce over your chicken Yum and serve with vegetables. Enjoy!

The Turkey Pizza Casserole
(Prepping time: 10 minutes\ Cooking time: 10 minutes |For 4 servings)

Ingredients

- 2 cups tomatoes, crushed
- 1 pound ground turkey
- 1 pack pepperoni
- ½ cup mozzarella cheese
- ½ cup oregano cheese

- ½ teaspoon salt
- 2 garlic cloves, minced
- ½ teaspoon pepper
- ½ teaspoon onion powder

Direction

1. Take a medium sized bowl and add crushed tomatoes, seasoning
2. Pour ¼ of crushed tomatoes to your Ninja Foodi
3. Layer ¼ of ground turkey, pepperoni and cheese on top
4. Keep repeating until the ingredients are used up
5. Lock up the lid and cook on HIGH pressure for 6 minutes
6. Remove and allow it to cool for about 15 minutes. Cut it up and serve. Enjoy!

Heartfelt Chicken Curry Soup
(Prepping time: 10 minutes\ Cooking time: 10 minutes |For 4 servings)

Ingredients

- 1 teaspoon Garam Masala
- ½ teaspoon cayenne
- ½ teaspoon ground turmeric
- 1 teaspoon salt
- 4 ounces baby spinach
- 1 cup mushrooms, sliced
- 1 (2-inch piece) ginger, finely chopped
- 3-4 garlic cloves, crushed
- ½ onion, diced
- 1 and ½ cups unsweetened coconut milk
- 1 pound boneless, skinless chicken thighs
- ¼ cup chopped fresh cilantro

Directions

1. Add chicken, coconut milk, onion, garlic, ginger, mushrooms, spinach, salt, turmeric, cayenne, garam masala and cilantro to the inner pot of your Ninja Foodi
2. Lock lid and cook on HIGH pressure for 10 minutes
3. Release pressure naturally over 10 minutes. Use tongs to transfer chicken to a plate, shred it
4. Stir chicken back to the soup and stir. Enjoy!

Your's Truly Lime Chicken Chili
(Prepping time: 10 minutes\ Cooking time: 23 minutes |For 6 servings)

Ingredients

- ¼ cup cooking wine (Keto-Friendly)
- ½ cup organic chicken broth
- 1 onion, diced
- 1 teaspoon salt
- ½ teaspoon paprika
- 5 garlic cloves, minced
- 1 tablespoon lime juice
- ¼ cup butter
- 2 pounds chicken thighs
- 1 teaspoon dried parsley
- 3 green chilies, chopped

Directions

1. Set your Ninja-Foodi to Sauté mode and add onion and garlic
2. Sauté for 3 minutes, add remaining ingredients
3. Lock lid and cook on Medium-HIGH pressure for 20 minutes
4. Release pressure naturally over 10 minutes. Serve and enjoy!

Hungry Man's Indian Chicken Keema
(Prepping time: 10 minutes\ Cooking time: 10 minutes |For 6 servings)

Ingredients

- 1 tablespoon coconut oil
- 1 teaspoon cumin seeds
- ½ teaspoon turmeric
- 1 tablespoon garlic, grated
- 1 tablespoon ginger, grated
- 1 large onion, diced

- 2 tomatoes, diced
- 2 teaspoons mild red chili powder
- 1 teaspoon Garam masala
- 1 teaspoon salt
- 2 tablespoons coriander powder
- 1 pound ground chicken
- ½ cup cilantro

Directions

1. Set your Ninja Foodi to Saute mode and add cumin seeds
2. Toast for 30 seconds. Add turmeric powder and give it a nice mix
3. Add garlic, ginger and mix well again. Add onion and Saute for 2 minutes
4. Add tomatoes, Garam Masala, red chili powder, coriander, salt and mix well
5. Add ground chicken and keep Sautéing it while breaking it up with a spatula
6. Add ½ a cup of water . Lock up the lid and cook on HIGH pressure for 4 minutes
7. Release the pressure naturally over 10 minutes
8. Garnish with a bit of cilantro and serve . Enjoy!

The Borderline Crack Chicken

(Prepping time: 10 minutes\ Cooking time: 25 minutes |For 4 servings)

Ingredients

- 4 ounces cheddar cheese
- 3 tablespoons arrowroot
- 1 cup of water
- 8 ounces cream cheese
- 1 pack ranch seasoning
- 2 pounds boneless chicken breast
- 6-8 cooked bacon

Directions

1. Add chicken to your Ninja Foodi. Add cream cheese
2. Sprinkle ranch seasoning over chicken add water
3. Lock lid and cook for 25 minutes on HIGH pressure. Quick release pressure
4. Take the chicken out and shred into pieces
5. Set your pot to SAUTE mode and add a mixture of arrowroot and water
6. Add cheese and shredded chicken. Stir and bacon. Enjoy!

The Decisive Red Curry Chicken

(Prepping time: 10 minutes\ Cooking time: 10 minutes |For 6 servings)

Ingredients

- 1 tablespoon of olive oil
- 2-4 tablespoon of red curry paste
- 1 and a ½ pound of thin chicken breast
- 1-2 tablespoon of fish sauce
- 1 tablespoon of stevia
- 1 jalapeno chili
- 1 cup yellow onion, sliced
- 1 cup red pepper, sliced
- 1 cup yellow pepper, sliced
- 1 cup orange pepper, sliced
- A handful of Thai basil leaves

Directions

1. Set your Ninja Foodi to Saute mode and add oil, allow the oil to heat up
2. Add 2 tablespoon of red curry paste. Saute for 30 seconds
3. Add chicken and mix it well with the curry paste. Add coconut milk
4. Lock up the lid and cook on HIGH pressure for 2 minutes
5. Release the pressure naturally over 10 minutes. Open and stir in fish sauce and stevia
6. Add onion, red, yellow, orange peppers and stir well
7. Set your Ninja Foodi to Saute mode and bring the curry to a gentle boil. Serve and enjoy!

Spinach And Chicken Curry

(Prepping time: 10 minutes\ Cooking time: 12 minutes |For 4 servings)

Ingredients

- 10 ounce of Spinach
- 1 pound of chicken thigh cut up into 2-3 pieces
- 1 tablespoon of oil

- ½ a teaspoon of cumin seeds
- 1-inch ginger chopped up
- 6 pieces of cloves
- 2 medium onions cut up into pieces

Spices

- ¼ teaspoon of turmeric
- ½ a teaspoon of red chili powder

- 2 teaspoon of coriander
- 1 teaspoon of salt

Direction

1. Set your Ninja Foodi to Saute mode and add oil, allow the oil to heat up
2. Add cumin seeds, garlic, and ginger and cook for 30 seconds
3. Stir in garlic and the cut onions and Saute them for 1 minute more
4. Add spices and give it a nice stir. Add spinach with the chicken pieces on top of the spinach
5. Lock up the lid and allow them to cook at HIGH pressure for 8 minutes
6. Once done, do a quick release and open up the lid. Remove the chicken pieces from the pot and keep them on the side
7. Take an immersion blender and blend the whole mixture until you have a creamy texture
8. Cut up your chicken in small portions and add them back to the curry
9. Set the pot to Saute mode once more and give the whole curry a quick boil (without lid).Enjoy!

Cheese Dredged Lemon Chicken

(Prepping time: 10 minutes\ Cooking time: 8 minutes |For 4 servings)

Ingredients

- 1 tablespoon olive oil
- 3 chicken breast, boneless and skinless
- 1 cup spicy salsa
- ½ cup feta cheese, crumbled
- ½ teaspoon ground cumin
- ½ teaspoon red chili powder
- ¼ cup fresh lime juice

Directions

1. Add olive oil to Instant Pot and set your pot to Saute mode
2. Add chicken breast to the pot and brown both sides. Transfer chicken to a plate
3. Add cumin, chili powder, lime juice, salsa to pot. Stir and return chicken
4. Lock lid and cook on HIGH pressure for 8 minutes. Quick release pressure
5. Transfer chicken breast and sauté to plate. Sprinkle crumbled cheese. Serve and enjoy!

Best Chicken Wings

(Prepping time: 10 minutes\ Cooking time: 25 minutes |For 4 servings)

Ingredients

- 24 chicken wing segments
- 2 tablespoons toasted sesame oil
- 2 tablespoons Asian-Chile-Garlic sauce

- 2 tablespoons stevia
- 2 garlic cloves, minced
- 1 tablespoon toasted sesame seeds

Directions

1. Add 1 cup water to Foodie's inner pot, place reversible rack in the pot in lower portions, place chicken wings in the rack. Place lid into place and seal the valve
2. Select pressure mode to HIGH and cook for 10 minutes
3. Make the glaze by taking a large bowl and whisking in sesame oil, Chile-Garlic sauce, honey and garlic
4. Once the chicken is cooked, quick release the pressure and remove pressure lid
5. Remove rack from the pot and empty remaining water. Return inner pot to the base
6. Cover with crisping lid and select Air Crisp mode, adjust the temperature to 375 degrees F, pre-heat for 3 minutes
7. While the Foodi pre-heats, add wings to the sauce and toss well to coat it
8. Transfer wings to the basket, leaving any excess sauce in the bowl
9. Place the basket in Foodi and close with Crisping mode, select Air Crisp mode and let it cook for 8 minutes, gently toss the wings and let it cook for 8 minutes more
10. Once done, drizzle any sauce and sprinkle sesame seeds. Enjoy!

Simple And Juicy Chicken Stock
(Prepping time: 10 minutes\ Cooking time: 2hours |For 4 servings)

Ingredients

- 2 pounds meaty chicken bones
- ¼ teaspoon salt
- 3 and ½ cups of water

Directions

1. Place chicken parts in Foodi and season with salt
2. Add water, place the pressure cooker lid and seal the valve, cook on HIGH pressure for 90 minutes. Release the pressure naturally over 10 minutes
3. Line a colander with cheesecloth and place it over a large bowl, pour chicken parts and stock into the colander and strain out the chicken and bones
4. Let the stock cool and let it peel off any layer of fat that might accumulate on the surface
5. Use as needed!

Keto-Friendly Chicken Tortilla
(Prepping time: 15 minutes\ Cooking time: 15 minutes |For 4 servings)

Ingredients

- 1 tablespoon avocado oil
- 1 pound pastured organic boneless chicken breasts
- ½ cup of orange juice
- 2 teaspoons gluten-free Worcestershire sauce
- 1 teaspoon garlic powder
- 1 teaspoon salt
- ½ teaspoon chili powder
- ½ teaspoon paprika

Directions

1. Set your Ninja Foodi to Sauté mode and add oil, let the oil heat up
2. Add chicken on top, take a bowl and add remaining ingredients mix well
3. Pour the mixture over chicken. Lock lid and cook on HIGH pressure for 15 minutes
4. Release pressure naturally over 10 minutes
5. Shred the chicken and serve over salad green shells such as cabbage or lettuce. Enjoy!

Chapter 5: Heart-Warming Pork Recipes

Awesome Korean Pork Lettuce Wraps

(Prepping time: 10 minutes\ Cooking time: 60 minutes |For 8 servings)

Ingredients

- ¼ cup of miso
- ¼ cup of soy sauce (Low Sodium)/Coconut Aminos
- 3 tablespoon of Korean red paste

- 1 teaspoon of ground sesame oil
- 1 teaspoon of ground black pepper
- 1 pork shoulder trimmed of excess fat

Serving

- Lettuce leaves
- Radishes

- Cucumbers
- Green onion

Directions

1. Take a small bowl and add miso, soy sauce, ¼ cup of water Korean red paste, black pepper, and sesame oil. Mix well until smooth
2. Pour half of the sauce into your Ninja Foodi . Add pork and pour the rest of the sauce on top
3. Lock up the lid and cook on HIGH pressure for 1 hour. Release the pressure naturally
4. Shred the pork and serve in lettuce wraps with cucumbers, radish, green onion etc.

Spicy "Faux" Pork Belly

(Prepping time: 10 minutes\ Cooking time: 15 minutes |For 4 servings)

Ingredients

- 1 pound of pork belly, chopped
- 4 cups cauliflower, riced
- ½ a cup of bone broth
- ½ red onion, sliced
- ½ a cup of cilantro
- 2 green onion, sliced

- 1 tablespoon of lime juice
- 3 cloves garlic cloves, sliced
- 1 teaspoon turmeric
- 1 tablespoon oregano
- 1 tablespoon cumin
- ½ a teaspoon salt

Directions

1. Add all of the ingredients to your Instant Pot except ¼ cup of cilantro
2. Lock up the lid and cook on HIGH pressure for 15 minutes
3. Release the pressure naturally over 10 minutes
4. Open the lid and serve with sprinkled cilantro leaves
5. Enjoy!

Spiced Up Chipotle Pork Roast

(Prepping time: 5 minutes\ Cooking time:605 minutes |For 4 servings)

Ingredients

- 6 ounces bone broth
- 7 and ¼ ounces tomatoes, diced
- 2 ounces green chilies, diced

- 2 pounds pork roast
- ½ teaspoon cumin, onion powder each
- 1 teaspoon chipotle powder

Direction

1. Add listed ingredients to your Ninja Foodi. Lock lid and cook on HIGH pressure for 60 minutes
2. Release pressure naturally over 10 minutes. Serve and enjoy!

Happy Burrito Bowl Pork

(Prepping time: 10 minutes\ Cooking time: 5 minutes |For 4 servings)

Ingredients

- 1 and ½ tablespoons pork lard
- 1 onion, sliced
- 2 bell peppers, sliced
- 1 garlic clove, chopped
- Salt and pepper to taste
- 1 pound pulled pork
- ½ cup of chicken pork
- ½ cup chicken broth
- 6 cups lettuce, chopped
- 6 cups cabbage, chopped
- ¼ cup guacamole

Directions

1. Set your Ninja Foodi to Saute mode and add lard, let it melt and add onion and bell pepper
2. Cook for 2 minutes, stirring for 2 minutes. Add garlic, salt, and pepper
3. Stir well. Add pulled pork and chicken pork
4. Lock lid and cook on HIGH pressure for 1 minute. Quick release pressure
5. Arrange lettuce and green cabbage in serving bowls and add pulled pork on top
6. Top with guacamole and serve. Enjoy!

Awesome Sauerkraut Pork

(Prepping time: 10 minutes\ Cooking time: 35 minutes |For 4 servings)

Ingredients

- 3 pounds of pork shoulder
- Salt and pepper to taste
- 3 tablespoons butter
- 2 onions, chopped
- 3 cloves garlic, sliced
- 6 cups sauerkraut, divided
- 1 pound hot dog, sliced and cooked
- ½ pound kielbasa, sliced and cooked

Directions

1. Season pork roast with salt and pepper
2. Set your Ninja Foodi to Saute mode and add butter, let the butter melt
3. Add pork roast and brown. Pour 2 cups water, onion and garlic
4. Season with salt and pepper and lock lid. Cook on HIGH pressure for 35 minutes
5. Release pressure naturally over 10 minutes
6. Shred pork and stir in sauerkraut, hotdog, and kielbasa. Serve and enjoy!

Spice Lover's Jalapeno Hash

(Prepping time: 5 minutes\ Cooking time: 10 minutes |For 4 servings)

Ingredients

- 4 jalapeno peppers, chopped
- ½ cup chicken stock
- 3 ounces bacon, chopped and cooked
- 6 ounces zucchini, chopped
- 1 teaspoon ground black pepper
- 1 teaspoon butter

Directions

1. Add jalapeno peppers and zucchini into the Ninja Foodi pot
2. Put bacon, ground black pepper, butter, and chicken stock
3. Seal the lid. Set Pressure High. Cook the meat for 5 minutes
4. Then make natural pressure release for 10 minutes
5. Once cooked, let the meal chill for a few minutes. Serve with chicken stock and enjoy!

The Premium Red Pork
(Prepping time: 10 minutes\ Cooking time: 40 minutes |For 6 servings)

Ingredients

- 2 pounds of pork belly
- 2 tablespoons maple syrup
- 3 tablespoons sherry
- 1 tablespoon blackstrap molasses
- 2 tablespoons coconut amino
- 1 teaspoon salt
- 1/3 cup water
- 1 piece ginger, peeled and smashed
- Few sprigs of cilantro, garnish

Directions

1. Add the pork cubes to a pot and place it over medium heat
2. Add enough water to submerge them. Allow the water to come to a boil
3. Boil the cubes for 3 minutes and drain and rinse the cubes to remove any impurities
4. Keep them on the side. Set your Ninja Foodi to Saute mode and add maple syrup
5. Add cooked cubes and cook them for 1 minute until browned
6. After 10 minutes, add the remaining ingredients into the mix and bring the whole mixture to a boil. Lock up the lid and cook for 25 minutes at HIGH pressure
7. Allow the pressure to release naturally.
8. Open up the lid and set your Ninja Foodi to Saute mode again
9. Allow the contents to simmer for a while until the liquid has been reduced sufficiently enough to just coat the cubes. Serve with a garnish of cilantro. Enjoy!

Cool Spicy Pork Salad Bowl
(Prepping time: 10 minutes\ Cooking time: 90 minutes |For 6 servings)

Ingredients

- 4 pounds pork shoulder butter
- 2 teaspoons salt
- 2 cups chicken stock
- 1 teaspoon smoked paprika powder
- 1 teaspoon garlic powder
- 1 teaspoon black pepper
- 1 pinch dried oregano leaves
- 4 tablespoons coconut oil
- 6 garlic cloves

Directions

1. Remove rind from pork and cut meat from the bone, slice into large chunks
2. Trim fat off met
3. Set your Foodi to Saute mode and add oil, let it heat up
4. Once the oil is hot, layer chunks of meat in the bottom of the pot and Saute for around 30 minutes until browned
5. While the meat is being browned, peel garlic cloves and cut into small chunks
6. Once the meat is browned, transfer it to a large-sized bowl
7. Add a few tablespoons of chicken stock to the pot a deglaze it, scraping off browned bits
8. Transfer browned bits to the bowl with meat chunks. Repeat if any more meat is left
9. Once done, add garlic, oregano leaves, smoked paprika, Garlic powder, pepper, and salt to the meat owl and mix it up. Add all chicken stock to the pot and bring to a simmer over Saute mode
10. Once done, return seasoned meat to the pot and lock lid, cook on HIGH pressure for 45 minutes. Release pressure naturally over 10 minutes
11. Open the lid and shred the meat using a fork, transfer shredded meat to a bowl and pour cooking liquid through a mesh to separate fat into the bowl with shredded meat
12. Serve with lime and enjoy!

Dill And Butter Pork Chops
(Prepping time: 10 minutes\ Cooking time: 20 minutes |For 4 servings)

Ingredients

- 2 tablespoons unsalted butter
- 4 pieces ½ inch thick pork loin chops
- ½ teaspoon salt
- ½ teaspoon pepper
- 16 baby carrots
- ½ cup white wine vinegar
- ½ cup chicken broth

Directions

1. Set your Ninja Foodi to Saute mode. Season the chops with pepper and salt
2. Toss your chops into your pot and cook for 4 minutes
3. Transfer the chops to a plate and repeat to cook and brown the rest
4. Pour in 1 tablespoon of butter and Toss in your carrots, dill to the cooker and let it cook for about 1 minute
5. Pour in the wine and scrape off any browned bits in your cooker while the liquid comes to a boil
6. Stir in the broth. return the chops to your pot
7. Lock up the lid and let it cook for about 18 minutes at high pressure
8. Naturally, release the pressure by keeping it aside for 8 minutes
9. Unlock and serve with some sauce poured over

Cranberry Pork BBQ Dish

(Prepping time: 10 minutes\ Cooking time: 45 minutes |For 4 servings)

Ingredients

- 3-4 pounds pork shoulder, boneless, fat trimmed

For Sauce

- 3 tablespoons of liquid smoke
- 2 tablespoons tomato paste
- 2 cups fresh cranberries
- ¼ cup hot sauce (Keto-Friendly)
- 1/3 cup blackstrap molasses
- ½ cup of water
- ½ cup apple cider vinegar
- 1 teaspoon salt
- 1 tablespoon adobo sauce (Keto Friendly and Sugar-Free)
- 1 cup tomato puree (Keto-Friendly and Sugar-Free)
- 1 chipotle pepper in adobo sauce, diced

Directions

1. Cut pork against halves/thirds and keep it on the side
2. Set your Ninja Foodi to "SAUTE" mode and let it heat up. Add cranberries and water to the pot
3. Let them simmer for 4-5 minutes until cranberries start to pop, add rest of the sauce ingredients and simmer for 5 minutes more. Add pork to the pot and lock lid
4. Cook on HIGH pressure for 40 minutes. Quick release pressure
5. Use a fork to shred the pork and serve on your favorite greens

Definitive Pork Carnita

(Prepping time: 10 minutes\ Cooking time: 25 minutes |For 4 servings)

Ingredients

- 2 pounds pork butt, chopped into 2-inch pieces
- 1 teaspoon salt
- ½ teaspoon oregano
- ½ teaspoon cumin
- 1 yellow onion, cut into half
- 6 garlic cloves, peeled and crushed
- ½ cup chicken broth

Directions

1. Insert a pan into your Ninja Foodi and add pork

2. Season with salt, cumin, oregano and mix well, making sure that the pork is well seasoned
3. Take the orange and squeeze the orange juice all over
4. Add squeezed orange to into the insert pan as well
5. Add garlic cloves and onions. Pour ½ cup chicken broth into the pan
6. Lock the lid of the Ninja Foodi, making sure that the valve is sealed well
7. Set pressure to HIGH and let it cook for 20 minutes
8. Once the timer beeps, quick release the pressure
9. Open the lid and take out orange, garlic cloves, and onions
10. Set your Nina Foodi to Sauté mode and adjust the temperature to medium-high
11. Let the liquid simmer for 10-15 minutes
12. After most of the liquid has been reduced, press the stop button
13. Close the Ninja Foodi with "Air Crisp" lid. Pressure broil option and set timer to 8 minutes
14. Take the meat and put it in wraps. Garnish with cilantro and enjoy!

Technical Keto Pork Belly

(Prepping time: 10 minutes\ Cooking time: 40 minutes |For 4 servings)

Ingredients

- 1 pound pork belly
- ½-1 cup white wine vinegar
- 1 garlic clove
- 1 tablespoon olive oil
- Salt and pepper to taste

Directions

1. Set your Ninja Foodi to "SAUTE" mode and add oil, let it heat up
2. Add pork and sear for 2-3 minutes until both sides are golden and crispy
3. Add vinegar until about a quarter inch, season with salt, pepper, and garlic
4. Add garlic clove and Saute until the liquid comes to a boil
5. Lock lid and cook on HIGH pressure for 40 minutes
6. Once done, quick release pressure. Slice the meat and serve with the sauce. Enjoy!

Jamaican Pork Pot

(Prepping time: 10 minutes\ Cooking time: 45 minutes |For 4 servings)

Ingredients

- ½ cup beef stock
- 1 tablespoon olive oil
- ¼ cup Jamaican jerk spice blend
- 4 ounces of pork shoulder

Directions

1. Rub roast with olive oil and spice blend
2. Set your Ninja Foodi to Saute mode and add meat, brown all sides
3. Pour beef broth. Lock lid and cook on HIGH pressure for 45 minutes
4. Quick release pressure. Shred pork and serve!

The Mexican Pulled Pork Ala Lettuce

(Prepping time: 10 minutes\ Cooking time: 60 minutes |For 4 servings)

Ingredients

- 4 pounds pork roast
- 1 head butter lettuce, washed and dried
- 2 carrots, grated
- 2 tablespoons olive oil
- **For Spice Mix**
- 2 lime wedges
- 1 onion, chopped
- 1 tablespoon salt
- 2-3 cups water

- 1 tablespoon unsweetened cocoa powder
- 2 teaspoons oregano
- 1 teaspoon red pepper flakes
- 1 teaspoon garlic powder
- 1 teaspoon white pepper
- 1 teaspoon cumin
- 1/8 teaspoon cayenne
- 1/8 teaspoon coriander

Directions

1. Marinate pork overnight by transferring the meat to a bowl and mixing in all of the spices
2. Set your Ninja Foodi to "SAUTE" mode and add roast, let it brown
3. Add 2-3 cups water to fully submerge the roast
4. Lock lid and cook on HIGH pressure for 55 minutes
5. Release pressure naturally over 10 minutes
6. Set your pot to "SAUTE" mode again and take out the meat, shred the meat and keep it on the side. Reduce the liquid by half and strain/skim any excess fat
7. Mix pork with cooking liquid and serve with lettuce, grated carrots, squire of lime and any other topping you desire. Enjoy!

Pork With Cranberries And Pecan
(Prepping time: 10 minutes\ Cooking time: 45 minutes |For 4 servings)

Ingredients

- ¼ cup of spicy brown mustard
- ½ a teaspoon of garlic powder
- ½ a teaspoon of stevia
- ½ a teaspoon of salt
- ¼ teaspoon of pepper freshly ground
- 3 and a ½ pound of pork shoulder, boneless and trimmed of excess fat
- 2 cups onion, chopped
- 1 cup of fresh cranberries
- 3 cups of cabbage, finely shredded
- ½ a cup of toasted pecans
- ½ a cup of dried cranberries

Directions

1. Take a small bowl and add mustard, stevia, garlic powder, pepper, and salt and mix them well
2. Rub the mix all over the pork
3. Add pork to the Ninja Foodi
4. Top with cranberries and onion
5. Lock up the lid and cook on HIGH pressure for 45 minutes
6. Release the pressure naturally
7. Transfer the pork to cutting board and shred using two forks
8. Strain the liquid making sure to discard the cranberries and onion
9. Pour the strained liquid over pork
10. Serve over shredded cabbage topped with pecans and cranberries
11. Enjoy!

Cuban And Garlic Pork Meal
(Prepping time: 10 minutes\ Cooking time: 80 minutes |For 4 servings)

Ingredients

- 3 pounds boneless pork shoulder blade roast, fat trimmed and removed
- 6 garlic cloves, minced
- 2/3 cup grapefruit juice
- ½ tablespoon fresh oregano
- ½ tablespoon cumin
- 1 lime, juiced
- 1 tablespoon salt
- 1 bay leaf
- Lime wedges as needed
- Cilantro, chopped, for garnish
- Hot sauce as needed
- Salsa as needed

Directions

9. Cut the pork chops in 4 individual pieces and add them to a bowl
10. Take a small sized blender and add garlic, grapefruit juice, lime, oregano, cumin, salt, and blend well. Pour the marinade over your pork and allow it to sit for 60 minutes
11. Transfer the mix to your Ninja Foodi and add bay leaf
12. Cover and cook on HIGH pressure for 80 minutes. Release the pressure naturally
13. Remove the pork and shred it up. Return the pork back to the Foodi and add 1 cup of liquid
14. Season with some salt and allow it warm for a while (over Saute mode)
15. Enjoy!

Mean Cream Mushroom Garlic Chicken
(Prepping time: 10 minutes\ Cooking time: 15 minutes |For 4 servings)

Ingredients

- 2 pounds chicken thighs
- 7 ounces Cremini mushrooms
- 2 teaspoons garlic, minced
- ½ cup chicken broth
- ½ cup whipping cream
- 1 teaspoon cayenne pepper
- 1 tablespoon lemon juice
- 1 tablespoon parsley, chopped
- 1 tablespoon olive oil
- Salt and pepper to taste

Directions

1. Trim the stems of mushrooms. Wash and rinse chicken thighs under cold water
2. Pat dry with paper towels
3. Use kitchen scissors to trim excess skin and d fat from chicken thighs
4. Season both sides with salt and pepper, keep them on the side (covered)
5. Set your Ninja Foodi to Saute mode and add olive oil, let it heat up
6. Add chicken thighs and brown both sides. Scoop out excess fat and discard
7. Add garlic, whipping cream, mushrooms, broth, salt and pepper
8. Lock lid and cook on HIGH pressure for 10 minutes. Release pressure naturally over 10 minutes
9. Open the lid and set your pot to Saute mode. Add lemon juice and parsley. Serve and enjoy!

Pork Roast And Cauliflower Gravy
(Prepping time: 10 minutes\ Cooking time: 90 minutes |For 4 servings)

Ingredients

- 2-3 pounds pork roast
- 1 teaspoon salt
- ½ teaspoon pepper
- 4 cups cauliflower, chopped
- 1 medium onion, chopped
- 4 garlic cloves
- 2 ribs celery
- 8 ounces portabella mushrooms, sliced
- 2 tablespoons organic coconut oil
- 2 cups of filtered water

Directions

1. Pre-heat your oven to 400 degrees Fahrenheit
2. Add cauliflower, celery, garlic, onion, and water to your Ninja Foodi
3. Top them up with the roast . Season with a bit of pepper and salt
4. Lock up the lid and cook under HIGH pressure for 90 minutes
5. Release the pressure naturally. Remove the pork roast and transfer to a baking dish
6. Bake at 400 degrees Fahrenheit
7. Transfer the cooked veggies and broth to a blender and blend to obtain a smooth texture
8. Set your pot to Saute and add the mushrooms, cook them in coconut oil for about 3-5 minutes
9. Add the blended veggies and keep Sautéing until a thick mixture is obtained
10. Shred the roasted pork and serve over the gravy. Enjoy!

Premium Pork Chili Colorado

(Prepping time: 5 minutes\ Cooking time: 8 hours |For 6 servings)

Ingredients

- 3 pounds pork shoulder, cut into 1-inch cubes
- 1 teaspoon garlic powder
- 1 onion, chopped
- 1 teaspoon chipotle chili powder
- 1 tablespoon chili powder
- 1 teaspoon of sea salt

Directions

1. Add listed ingredients to Ninja Foodi
2. Lock lid and cook on SLOW COOK Mode (LOW) for 8-10 hours. Serve and enjoy!

Advanced Smothered Pork Chops

(Prepping time: 5 minutes\ Cooking time: 28 minutes |For 6 servings)

Ingredients

- 6 ounce of boneless pork loin chops
- 1 tablespoon of paprika
- 1 teaspoon of garlic powder
- 1 teaspoon of onion powder
- 1 teaspoon of black pepper
- 1 teaspoon of salt
- ¼ teaspoon of cayenne pepper
- 2 tablespoon of coconut oil
- ½ of a sliced medium onion
- 6-ounce baby Bella mushrooms, sliced
- 1 tablespoon of butter
- ½ a cup of whip cream
- ¼ teaspoon of xanthan gum
- 1 tablespoon parsley, chopped

Directions

1. Take a small bowl and add garlic powder, paprika, onion powder, black pepper, salt, and cayenne pepper. Rinse the pork chops and pat them dry
2. Sprinkle both sides with 1 teaspoon of the mixture making sure to rub the seasoning all over the meat. Reserve the remaining spice
3. Set your Ninja Foodi to Saute mode and add coconut oil, allow the oil to heat up
4. Brown the chops 3 minutes per sides. Remove and cancel the Saute mode
5. Add sliced onion to the base of your pot alongside mushrooms
6. Top with the browned pork chops. Lock up the lid and cook on HIGH pressure for 25 minutes
7. Release the pressure naturally over 10 minutes, remove the pork chops and keep them on a plate. Set your pot to Saute mode and whisk in remaining spices mix, heavy cream, and butter
8. Sprinkle ¼ teaspoon of xanthan gum and stir. Simmer for 3-5 minutes and remove the heat
9. Add a bit more xanthan gum if you require a heavier gravy
10. Top the pork chops with the gravy and sprinkle parsley. Serve!

The Big Deal Bone-y Pork Chops

(Prepping time: 10 minutes\ Cooking time: 13 minutes |For 4 servings)

Ingredients

- 4 and ¾ thick bone-in pork chops
- Salt and pepper as needed
- 1 cup baby carrots
- 1 onion, chopped
- 1 cup of mixed vegetables
- 3 tablespoons Worcestershire sauce

Directions

1. Take a bowl and add pork chops, season with pepper and salt
2. Take a skillet and place it over medium heat, add 2 teaspoons of butter and melt it
3. Toss the pork chops and brown them. Each side should take about 3-5 minutes

4. Set your Ninja Foodi to Saute mode and add 2 tablespoons of butter, add carrots and Saute them. Pour broth and Worcestershire
5. Add pork chops and lock up the lid. Cook on HIGH pressure for 13 minutes
6. Release the pressure naturally over 10 minutes. Enjoy!

Coconut And Ginger Pork Dish

(Prepping time: 5 minutes\ Cooking time: 45 minutes |For 6 servings)

Ingredients

- 1 tablespoon avocado oil
- ¾ pound pork butt
- 1 teaspoon ground coriander
- 1 teaspoon ground cumin
- 1 teaspoon salt
- 1 teaspoon pepper
- 2-inch piece ginger, peeled and chopped
- 1 onion, peeled and cut
- ½ a can coconut milk
- Lime wedges, garnish

Directions

1. Take a bowl and add coriander, salt, pepper, and cumin
2. Use your finger to rub the seasoning all over the roast
3. Coat the bottom of your Ninja Foodi with 1 tablespoon of avocado oil
4. Add the meat to the pot. Surround it with onions, ginger, garlic and a half can of coconut milk
5. Lock up the lid and cook on HIGH pressure for 45 minutes. Serve in bowls and garnish with lime
6. Enjoy!

Bacon Kale And Winning Delight

(Prepping time: 5 minutes\ Cooking time: 6 hours |For 6 servings)

Ingredients

- 2 tablespoons bacon fat
- 2 pounds kale, rinsed and chopped
- 2 bacon slices, cooked and chopped
- 2 teaspoons garlic, minced
- 2 cups vegetable broth
- Salt and pepper to taste

Directions

1. Grease inner pot of your Ninja Foodi with bacon fat
2. Add kale, garlic, bacon, and broth to insert and toss to coat
3. Cover and cook on SLOW COOK Mode (LOW for 6 hours
4. Season with salt and pepper. Serve and enjoy!

Rosemary Pork Roast

(Prepping time: 5 minutes\ Cooking time: 8 hours |For 6 servings)

Ingredients

- 3 pounds pork shoulder roast
- 1 cup bone broth
- 6 sprigs fresh rosemary
- 4 sprigs basil leaves
- 1 tablespoon chives, chopped
- ¼ teaspoon ground black pepper

Directions

1. Add listed ingredients to Ninja Foodi
2. Lock lid and cook on SLOW COOK Mode (LOW) for 8-10 hours. Serve and enjoy!

Nutrition Values (Per Serving)

- Calories: 248
- Fat: 8g

- Carbohydrates: 0.7g
- Protein: 39g

Apple And Sauerkraut Loin

(Prepping time: 5 minutes\ Cooking time: 50 minutes |For 6 servings)

Ingredients

- 2-3 pounds pork loin roast
- ½ teaspoon salt
- ½ teaspoon fresh ground pepper
- 2 large onion, chopped
- 3 garlic cloves, chopped
- 2-3 cups chicken bone broth
- 4-6 cups sauerkraut, rinsed and drained
- 3 apples, peeled and cored

Directions

1. Season the roast with pepper and salt. Set your pot to Saute mode and add ghee
2. Add roast and brown on all sides. Remove the roast and keep it on the side
3. Add garlic, onion, and broth and Scrap brown bits from the Ninja Foodi
4. Return the roast to your Ninja Foodi to lock up the lid. Cook on HIGH pressure for 45 minutes
5. Perform quick release. Add sauerkraut, apple to the cooker
6. Lock up the lid and cook on HIGH pressure for 5 minutes longer
7. Quick release the pressure. Slice the roast and serve with the sauce. Enjoy!

Bacon And Brussels Platter

(Prepping time: 10 minutes\ Cooking time: 5 minutes |For 4 servings)

Ingredients

- 5 bacon slices, chopped
- 6 cups Brussels sprouts, chopped
- ¼ teaspoon salt
- Pepper as needed
- 2 tablespoons water
- 2 tablespoons balsamic vinegar

Directions

1. Set your Ninja Foodi to Saute mode and add chopped bacon, Saute until crispy
2. Add chopped Brussels sprouts and stir well to coat it
3. Add water and sprinkle a bit of salt
4. Lock up the lid and cook on HIGH pressure for 4-6 minutes
5. Release the pressure naturally
6. Set your pot to Saute mode and Saute the Brussels for a while longer
7. Transfer to serving the dish
8. Drizzle balsamic vinegar on top and enjoy!

Healthy Oxtail Ragout

(Prepping time: 5 minutes\ Cooking time: 35 minutes |For 6 servings)

Ingredients

- 2 tablespoons butter
- 1 large onion, diced
- 2 carrots, diced
- 1 and ½ cups beef bone broth
- 1 can tomatoes
- 2 bay leaves
- 1-2 teaspoons thyme
- ½ teaspoon rosemary
- ½ teaspoon salt
- 3 peppercorns
- 3 oxtails, joins separated
- 2 teaspoons red wine vinegar

Directions

1. Set your Ninja Foodi to Saute mode and add onions, butter, celery, and carrots and Saute for 2 minutes. Add beef bone broth, thyme, bay leaves, salt, rosemary, peppercorns, and stir
2. Add oxtails. Lock up the lid and cook on HIGH pressure for 30 minutes

3. Release the pressure naturally. Skim any excess fat
4. Discard the peppercorn and bay leaves and add red wine vinegar. Serve and enjoy!

Lemon And Pork Chops Artichokes

(Prepping time: 10 minutes\ Cooking time: 24 minutes |For 4 servings)

Ingredients

- 2 tablespoons clarified butter
- 2 pieces 2-inch thick bone-in pork chops
- 3 ounces pancetta, diced
- 2 teaspoons ground black pepper
- 1 medium shallot, minced
- 4 lemon zest strips, 2-inch size
- 1 teaspoon dried rosemary
- 2 teaspoons garlic, minced
- 1 box (9 ounces) box frozen artichoke heart, quarters
- ¼ cup chicken broth

Directions

1. Set your pot to Saute mode and add pancetta, cook for 5 minutes
2. Transfer the browned pancetta to a plate and season your chops with pepper
3. Add the chops to your pot and cook for 4 minutes
4. Transfer the chops to a plate and keep repeating until they all of them are browned
5. Add shallots to the pot and cook for 1 minute
6. Add lemon zest, garlic, rosemary, and garlic, and stir until aromatic
7. After a while, stir in broth and artichokes. Return the pancetta back to the cooker
8. return the chops to your pot
9. Lock up the lid and let it cook for about 24 minutes at high pressure
10. Release pressure quickly. Unlock and transfer the chops to a carving board
11. Slice up the eye of your meat off the bone and slice the meat into strips
12. Divide in serving bowls and sauce ladled up

Simple Pressure Cooked Lamb Meat

(Prepping time: 5 minutes \ Cooking time: 55 minutes |For 4 servings)

Ingredients

- 2 tablespoons butter
- ½ teaspoon turmeric powder
- 1 pound ground lamb meat
- 1 cup onions, chopped
- 1 teaspoon salt
- 1 tablespoon garlic, minced
- ½ teaspoon ground coriander
- ½ teaspoon cayenne pepper
- 1 tablespoon ginger, minced
- ½ teaspoon cumin powder

Directions

1. Set your Ninja Foodi to Saute mode and add garlic, ginger, and onions
2. Saute for 3 minutes and add ground meat, spices
3. Lock lid and cook on HIGH pressure for 20 minutes
4. Release pressure naturally over 10 minutes.Serve and enjoy!

Sassy Evergreen Pork Chops

(Prepping time: 10 minutes\ Cooking time: 4 hours |For 4 servings)

Ingredients

- 6-8 boneless pork chops
- ¼ cup arrowroot flour
- 2 teaspoons dry mustard
- 1 teaspoon garlic powder
- 1 and ½ cups beef stock
- Cooking fat
- Salt and pepper to taste

Directions

1. Take a bowl and add flour, garlic powder, black pepper, dry mustard and salt
2. Coat the pork chop with the mixture and keep any extra flour on the side
3. Take a skillet and place it over medium-high heat. Add cooking fat and allow the fat to melt
4. Brown the chops for 1-2 minutes per side and transfer to your Ninja Foodi
5. Add beef stock to the flour mixture and mix well
6. Pour the beef stock mix to the chops and place lid
7. Cook on SLOW COOK MODE (HIGH) for 3 hours. Enjoy!

The Pork "Loin" With Pear

(Prepping time: 5 minutes\ Cooking time: 12 minutes |For 4 servings)

Ingredients

- 2 tablespoons clarified butter
- 4 pieces ½ inch thick bone-in pork loin
- ½ teaspoon salt
- ½ teaspoon pepper
- 2 medium yellow onion, peeled and cut up into 8 wedges
- 2 large Bosc pears, peeled and cored, cut into 4 wedges
- ½ cup unsweetened pear, cider
- ½ teaspoon ground allspice
- Dash of hot pepper

Directions

1. Set your Ninja Foodi to Saute mode and add 1 tablespoon of butter, allow the butter to melt
2. Add chops and Saute for 4 minutes
3. Transfer the chops to a plate and cook the remaining and brown them
4. Add onion and pears in the pot and allow them to Saute for 3 minutes more until the pears are slightly browned. Pour cider and stir in allspice, pepper sauce
5. Nestle the chops back. Lock up the lid and cook on HIGH pressure for 10 minutes
6. Perform quick release. Serve over rice!

Creative Garlic And Butter Pork

(Prepping time: 5 minutes + marinate time \ Cooking time: 40 minutes |For 4 servings)

Ingredients

- 1 tablespoon coconut butter
- 1 tablespoon coconut oil
- 2 teaspoons garlic cloves, grated
- 2 teaspoons parsley
- Salt and pepper to taste
- 4 pork chops, sliced into strips

Directions

1. Add listed ingredients to Pork Strips and mix well
2. Marinate for 1 hour. Transfer pork to Ninja Foodi
3. Lock Crisping Lid and Air Crisp for 10 minutes at 400 degrees F. Serve and enjoy!

Elegant Lamb Spare Ribs

(Prepping time: 4-5 hours\ Cooking time: 20 minutes |For 4 servings)

Ingredients

Ingredients for the Lamb

- 2.5 pounds of pastured lamb spare ribs
- 2 teaspoons of kosher salt
- 1 tablespoon of curry powder

Ingredients for the sauce

- 1 t tablespoon of coconut oil
- 1 large sized coarsely chopped onion

- ½ a pound of minced garlic
- 1 tablespoon of curry powder
- 1 tablespoon of kosher salt
- Juice from about 1 lemon
- 1 and a 1/4th cup of divided cilantro
- 4 thinly sliced scallion

Directions

1. Take a bowl and add spare ribs
2. Season with 2 teaspoons of salt, 1 teaspoon of curry powder and mix well making sure that the ribs are coated fully. Cover it up and allow them to chill for 4 hours
3. Cover it up and let them freeze for at least 4 hours
4. Set your Ninja Foodi to Saute mode and add coconut oil and allow it to heat up
5. Add spare ribs and allow them to brown. Once done, transfer them to another plate
6. Take a blender and add tomatoes and onion and blend them well to a paste
7. Add the minced garlic to your Ninja Foodi (still in Saute mode)
8. Keep stirring the garlic while carefully pouring the prepared paste
9. Add curry powder, chopped up cilantro, salt, and lemon juice
10. Allow the whole mixture to come to a boil. Add spare ribs and stir until it is coated well
11. Lock up the lid and cook for 20 minutes at HIGH pressure
12. Allow the pressure to release naturally once done.Scoop out the grease and season with some salt. Enjoy!

Cool Lamb Tajine

(Prepping time: 5 minutes\ Cooking time: 50 minutes |For 6 servings)

Ingredients

- 2 and a /13 pound of lamb shoulder
- 1 teaspoon of cinnamon powder
- 1 teaspoon of ginger powder
- 1 teaspoon of turmeric powder
- 2 cloves of crushed garlic
- 3 tablespoon of olive oil
- 10 ounce of prunes pitted and soaked
- 1 cup of vegetable stock
- 2 medium roughly sliced onion
- 1 piece of bay leaf
- 1 stick of cinnamon
- 1 teaspoon of pepper
- 1 and a ½ teaspoon of salt
- 3 and a ½ ounce of almonds
- 1 tablespoon of sesame seeds

Directions

5. Take a bowl and add ground cinnamon, ginger, turmeric, garlic and 2 spoons of olive oil
6. Make a paste. Cover the lamb with the paste
7. Take a bowl and add dried prunes with boiling water and cover, keep it on the side
8. Set your Ninja Foodi to Saute mode and add olive oil. Add onion and cook for 3 minutes
9. Transfer the onion to a bowl and keep it on the side
10. Add meat and brown all sides for about 10 minutes. Deglaze using vegetable stock
11. Add onions, cinnamon stick, bay leaf.Lock up the lid and cook on HIGH pressure for 35 minutes
12. Release the pressure naturally. Add rinsed and drained prunes and set the pot to Saute mode
13. Reduce the liquid by simmer for 5 minutes
14. Discard the bay leaf and sprinkle toasted almonds alongside sesame seeds. Enjoy

Pork And Cauliflower Dish

(Prepping time: 10 minutes\ Cooking time: 65 minutes |For 4 servings)

Ingredients

- 1 onion, chopped
- 4 cloves garlic, crushed and minced
- 4 cups cauliflower, chopped
- 2 ribs celery
- Salt and pepper to taste
- 3-pound pork roast
- 8 ounces mushrooms, sliced
- 2 tablespoons coconut oil

- 2 tablespoons ghee

Directions

1. Add onion, garlic, cauliflower, celery to Ninja Foodi
2. Put pork roast on top. Season with salt and pepper
3. Add 2 cups of water. Lock lid and cook on HIGH pressure 60 minutes
4. Quick release pressure. Transfer roast to baking pan
5. Add pan to oven and bake for 5 minutes at 400 degrees F
6. Prepare gravy by transfer the remaining contents from the pot to a blender
7. Blend until smooth. Set your pot to Saute mode and add coconut oil and ghee
8. Add mushrooms and blended mixture. Cook for 5 minutes
9. Serve pot roast with mushroom gravy and enjoy!

Nutrition Values (Per Serving)

- Calories: 697
- Fat: 56g
- Carbohydrates: 8g
- Protein: 81g

Lime And Ginger Low Carb Pork

(Prepping time: 10 minutes\ Cooking time:4-7 hours |For 4 servings)

Ingredients

- 1 tablespoon avocado oil
- 2 and ½ pounds pork loin
- Salt and pepper to taste
- 1 teaspoon stevia drops
- ¼ cup tamari
- 1 tablespoon Worcestershire sauce
- Juice of 1 lime
- 2 garlic cloves, minced
- 1 tablespoon fresh ginger
- Fresh cilantro

Directions

1. Set your Ninja Foodi to Saute mode and add oil, let the oil heat up
2. Season pork with salt and pepper and add to the pot
3. Take a bowl and whisk in remaining ingredients except for cilantro and pour it over pork
4. Lock lid and cook on SLOW COOK mode. Cook for 4-7 hours on HIGH pressure
5. Naturally, release pressure over 10 minutes. Garnish with cilantro. Serve and enjoy!

Generous Indian Lamb Shanks

(Prepping time: 5 minutes\ Cooking time: 45 minutes |For 5 servings)

Ingredients

- 3 pounds lamb shanks
- Salt as needed
- Fresh ground pepper as needed
- 2 tablespoons ghee
- 2 onion, chopped
- 2 celery, chopped
- 1 large onion, chopped
- 1 tablespoon tomato paste
- 3 garlic cloves, peeled and mashed
- 1 cup bone broth
- 1 teaspoon red boat fish sauce
- 1 tablespoon vinegar

Directions

1. Season the shanks with pepper and salt
2. Set your pot to Saute mode and add ghee, allow the ghee to melt and heat up
3. Add shanks and cook for 8-10 minutes until a nice brown texture appears
4. In the meantime, chop the vegetables
5. Once you have a nice brown texture on your lamb, remove it from the Instant Pot and keep it on the side. Add vegetables and season with salt and pepper
6. Add a tablespoon of ghee and mix
7. Add vegetables, garlic clove, tomato paste and give it a nice stir

8. Add shanks and pour broth, vinegar, fish sauce. Sprinkle a bit of pepper and lock up the lid
9. Cook on HIGH pressure for 45 minutes. Release the pressure naturally over 10 minutes
10. Serve the shanks and enjoy!

Greek Lamb Gyros
(Prepping time: 5 minutes \ Cooking time: 25 minutes |For 4 servings)

Ingredients

- 8 garlic cloves
- 1 and ½ teaspoon salt
- 2 teaspoons dried oregano
- 1 and ½ cups of water
- 2 pounds lamb meat, ground

- 2 teaspoons rosemary
- ½ teaspoon pepper
- 1 small onion, chopped
- 2 teaspoons ground marjoram

Directions

4. Add onion, garlic, marjoram, rosemary, salt and pepper to food processor and process
5. Add ground lamb meat and process again. Press meat mixture into pan
6. Transfer loaf to Ninja Foodi and "BAKE/ROAST" for 25 minutes at 375 degrees f
7. Serve and enjoy!

Pork Dish With Coconut Added In
(Prepping time: 10 minutes\ Cooking time: 4 hours |For 4 servings)

Ingredients

- 2 tablespoons coconut oil
- 4 pounds boneless pork shoulder, cut into 2-inch pieces
- Salt and pepper to taste
- 1 large onion, chopped
- 3 tablespoons garlic cloves, minced
- 3 tablespoons fresh ginger, minced

- 1 tablespoon curry powder
- 1 tablespoon ground cumin
- ½ teaspoon ground turmeric
- 1 cup unsweetened coconut milk
- Chopped cilantro, green onions for garnish

Directions

1. Take a large sized skillet and add coconut oil
2. Allow it to heat up and add pork in batches, brown them and season with a bit of salt and pepper. Transfer to a Ninja Foodi
3. Making sure that there are 2 tablespoons of the worth of fat in the skillet, add onion, garlic, ginger, cumin, curry, turmeric and cook over low heat for 5 minutes
4. Add the mix to your Ninja Foodi and place the lid
5. Cook on SLOW COOK MODE (LOW) for 4 hours
6. Serve with a garnish of cilantro and scallions. Enjoy!

Tastiest Pork Cheek Stew
(Prepping time: 10 minutes\ Cooking time: 45 minutes |For 4 servings)

Ingredients

- 4 pounds of pork cheeks
- 2 tablespoons avocado oil
- 1 and ½ cups of chicken broth
- 8 ounces cremini mushrooms
- 1 large leek, cut into ½ inch chunks

- 1 small onion, diced
- 6 garlic cloves, peeled
- 1 teaspoon salt
- Juice of ½ lemon

Directions

1. Set your Ninja Foodi to Saute mode and add oil
2. Cut up the cheeks into 2 x 3 inch even pieces and add them to the Pot
3. Sear them until nicely browned
4. Pour broth over the browned cheeks alongside mushroom, onion, leek, garlic, sea salt
5. Lock up the lid and cook on HIGH pressure for 45 minutes
6. Release the pressure naturally and shred the meat. Stir the meat well with the sauce and serve!

Veal And Rosemary Stew
(Prepping time: 10 minutes\ Cooking time: 20 minutes |For 4 servings)

Ingredients

- 2 sprigs rosemary
- 1 tablespoon olive oil
- 1 tablespoon butter
- 8 ounces shallots
- 2 carrots, chopped

- 2 stalks celery, chopped
- 2 tablespoons almond flour
- 3 pounds veal
- Water as needed
- 2 teaspoon salt

Directions

1. Set the Ninja Foodi to Saute mode and add olive oil, allow the oil to heat up
2. Add butter and chopped rosemary and stir. Add celery, shallots, carrots and Saute for a while
3. Shove the veggies on the side and add the meat cubes, brown them slightly and pour just enough stock to gently cover them
4. Lock up the lid and cook on 20 minutes on HIGH pressure
5. Release the pressure naturally over 10 minutes
6. Open and set the pot to Saute mode, allow it to simmer. Enjoy!

Keto – Suitable Steamed Pork
(Prepping time: 5 minutes\ Cooking time: 45 minutes |For 4 servings)

Ingredients

- 2 boneless pork chops
- 2 tablespoons fresh orange juice
- 2 cups of water
- ¼ teaspoon ground cloves

- ¼ teaspoon ground coriander
- ¼ teaspoon cinnamon, ground
- 1 pinch cayenne pepper

Directions

1. Add listed ingredients to Ziploc bag and let them marinate for 2 hours
2. Place a reversible rack inside the pot and attach Crisping Lid
3. Pour water into a pot and place marinated meat on the rack
4. Lock lid and STEAM for 45 minutes
5. Serve and enjoy!

Refined Carrot And Bacon Soup
(Prepping time: 10 minutes\ Cooking time: 4 minutes |For 4 servings)

Ingredients

- 2 pounds carrots, peeled
- 4 cups broth
- ½ cup yellow onion, chopped

- ½ pack bacon cut into ¼ inch pieces
- ½ cup apple cider vinegar
- ½ cup white vinegar

Directions

1. Set your Ninja Foodi to Saute mode and add butter, allow the butter to melt and add bacon and onion, Saute for a while. Slice 1 -2 heirloom carrots thinly and add them to a small bowl

2. Add vinegar to cover them, allow them to pickle
3. Chop the remaining carrots into inch long pieces
4. Add chopped carrots and broth to your Instant Pot
5. Lock up the lid and cook on HIGH pressure for 4 minutes. Perform a natural release
6. Use an immersion blender break down the carrots until you have a smooth mix
7. Stir in onions and bacon, salt and apple cider vinegar. Serve and enjoy!

Lovely Pulled Pork Ragu
(Prepping time: 10 minutes\ Cooking time: 45 minutes |For 4 servings)

Ingredients

- 18 ounce of pork tenderloin
- 1 teaspoon of kosher salt
- Black pepper as needed
- 1 teaspoon of olive oil
- 5 cloves of garlic

- 1 can of 28-ounce tomatoes, crushed
- 1 small sized jar of roasted red peppers
- 2 sprigs of thyme
- 2 pieces of bay leaves
- 1 tablespoon fresh parsley, chopped

Directions

1. Set your Ninja Foodi to Saute mode. Season the pork with pepper and salt
2. Add oil to your pot and allow the oil to heat up. Add garlic and Saute for 1 and a ½ minute
3. Remove with a slotted spoon. Add pork and brown for 2 minutes on both sides
4. Add the remaining ingredients and garlic (make sure to reserve half of the kale for later use)
5. Lock up the lid and cook on HIGH pressure for 45 minutes
6. Naturally, release the pressure over 10 minutes and discard the bay leaves
7. Shred the pork using a fork and garnish with parsley. Enjoy!

The Calabacita Squash meal
(Prepping time: 10 minutes\ Cooking time: 90 minutes |For 4 servings)

Ingredients

- 1 pork tenderloin
- 1 tablespoon of chili powder
- 1 tablespoon of ground cumin
- 1 tablespoon of garlic powder
For the chipotle cream sauce

- 1/3 cup of canola-oil free mayo
- 3 tablespoon of fresh lime juice

- 1 and a ½ teaspoon of salt
- 1 tablespoon of butter/ghee
- 14 ounce of tomatoes, diced
- 6 Calabacita squash, deseeded

- 1 and a ½ a teaspoon of chipotle/ chili powder

Directions

1. Prepare the tenderloin by dusting it with half of the chili powder, garlic, cumin and salt
2. Set your Ninja Foodi to Saute mode and add butter, allow the butter to melt
3. Add seasoned pork and sear all sides for 3-4 minutes until browned
4. Add 4-6 cups of water and lock up the lid
5. Cook on MEAT mode at default settings and release the pressure naturally over 10 minutes
6. Transfer the pork to a large mixing bowl and shred it into small pieces
7. Add canned tomatoes and remaining spice to the bowl. Stir well
8. Spread the deseeded squash into a large rimmed baking sheet with the cut side facing up
9. Stuff the squash with the pork mixture and bake for 45 minutes at 350 degrees Fahrenheit
10. Prepare the sauce by mixing the sauce ingredients
11. Pour the sauce on top of the pork and garnish with cilantro. Serve and enjoy!

Chapter 6: Healthy Vegan/Vegetarian Ninja Foodi Recipes

Comfortable Mushroom Soup

(Prepping time: 10 minutes\ Cooking time: 10 minutes |For 6 servings)

Ingredients

- 1 small onion, diced
- 8 ounces white button mushrooms, chopped
- 8 ounces portabella mushrooms
- 2 garlic cloves, minced

Cashew Cream

- 1/3 cup of raw cashew

- ¼ cup dry white wine vinegar
- 2 and ½ cup mushroom stock
- 2 teaspoons salt
- 1 teaspoon fresh thyme
- ¼ teaspoon black pepper

- ½ a cup of mushroom stock

Directions

1. Add onion, mushroom to the pot and set your Ninja Foodi to Saute mode
2. Cook for 8 minutes and stir from time to time
3. Add garlic and Saute for 2 minutes more. Add wine and Saute until evaporated
4. Add thyme, pepper, salt, Mushroom stock, and stir
5. Lock up the lid and cook on HIGH pressure for 5 minutes
6. Perform quick release. Transfer cashew and water to the blender and blend well
7. Remove lid and transfer mix to the blender. Blend until smooth. Server and enjoy!

Chives And Radishes Platter

(Prepping time: 10 minutes\ Cooking time: 7 minutes |For 4 servings)

Ingredients

- 2 cups radishes, quartered
- ½ cup chicken stock
- Salt and pepper to taste

- 2 tablespoons melted ghee
- 1 tablespoon chives, chopped
- 1 tablespoon lemon zest, grated

Direction

1. Add radishes, stock, salt, pepper, zest to your Ninja Foodi and stir
2. Lock lid and cook on HIGH pressure for 7 minutes
3. Quick release pressure. Add melted ghee, toss well. Sprinkle chives and enjoy!

Garlic And Swiss Chard Garlic

(Prepping time: 10 minutes \ Cooking time: 4 minutes |For 4 servings)

Ingredients

- 2 tablespoons ghee
- 3 tablespoons lemon juice
- ½ cup chicken stock
- 4 bacon slices, chopped

- 1 bunch Swiss chard, chopped
- ½ teaspoon garlic paste
- Salt and pepper to taste

Directions

1. Set your Ninja Foodi to Saute mode and add bacon, stir well and cook for a few minutes
2. Add ghee, lemon juice, garlic paste, and stir. Add Swiss chard, salt, pepper, and stock
3. Lock lid and cook on HIGH pressure for 3 minutes. Quick release pressure and serve. Enjoy!

Healthy Rosemary And Celery Dish
(Prepping time: 10 minutes\ Cooking time: 5 minutes |For 4 servings)

Ingredients

- 1 pound celery, cubed
- 1 cup of water
- 2 garlic cloves, minced
- Salt and pepper
- ¼ teaspoon dry rosemary
- 1 tablespoon olive oil

Direction

1. Add water to your Ninja Foodi and place steamer basket
2. Add celery cubs to basket and lock lid, cook on HIGH pressure for 4 minutes
3. Quick release pressure. Take a bowl and add mix in oil, garlic, and rosemary. Whisk well
4. Add steamed celery to the bowl and toss well, spread on a lined baking sheet
5. Broil for 3 minutes using the Air Crisping lid at 250 degrees F. Serve and enjoy!

Awesome Veggie Hash
(Prepping time: 10 minutes \ Cooking time: 15 minutes |For 4 servings)

Ingredients

- 1 cups cauliflower, chopped
- 1 teaspoon mustard
- ½ cup dark leaf kale, chopped
- 1 tablespoon lemon juice
- ½ cup spinach, chopped
- ½ teaspoon salt
- 2 garlic cloves
- ½ teaspoon pepper
- 6 whole eggs
- 3 teaspoons coconut oil

Directions

1. Set your Ninja Foodi to Saute mode and add coconut oil, add garlic, cook until fragrant
2. Add chopped cauliflower and cook for 5 minutes
3. Stir in all ingredients except eggs, cook for 2 minutes
4. Stir in eggs, lock lid and cook for 2 minutes on HIGH pressure. Quick release pressure.Enjoy!

Thyme And Carrot Dish With Dill
(Prepping time: 5 minutes\ Cooking time: 5 minutes |For 4 servings)

Ingredients

- ½ cup of water
- 1 pound baby carrots
- 3 tablespoons stevia
- 1 tablespoon thyme, chopped
- 1 tablespoon dill, chopped
- Salt and pepper to taste
- 2 tablespoons ghee

Direction

1. Add trivet to your Ninja Foodi, add carrots and add water
2. Lock lid and cook on HIGH pressure for 3 minutes. Quick release pressure
3. Drain and transfer to a bowl. Set your Ninja Foodi to Saute mode and add ghee, let it melt
4. Add stevia, thyme dill, and carrots. Stir well for a few minutes. Serve and enjoy!

Creative Coconut Cabbage
(Prepping time: 10 minutes \ Cooking time: 7 minutes |For 4 servings)

Ingredients

- 2 tablespoons lemon juice
- 1/3 medium carrot, sliced

- ½ ounces, yellow onion, sliced
- 1/2 cup cabbage, shredded
- 1 teaspoon turmeric powder
- 1 ounce dry coconut
- ½ tablespoon mustard powder
- ½ teaspoon mild curry powder
- 1 large garlic cloves, diced
- 1 and ½ teaspoons salt
- 1/3 cup water
- 3 tablespoons olive oil
- 3 large whole eggs
- 3 large egg yolks

Directions

1. Set your Ninja Foodi to Saute mode and add oil, stir in onions, salt and cook for 4 minutes
2. Stir in spices, garlic and Saute for 30 seconds
3. Stir in rest of the ingredients, lock lid and cook on HIGH pressure for 3 minutes
4. Naturally, release pressure over 10 minutes. Serve and enjoy!

Complete Cauliflower Zoodles

(Prepping time: 10 minutes\ Cooking time: 8 minutes |For 6 servings)

Ingredients

- 2 tablespoons butter
- 2 cloves garlic
- 7-8 cauliflower florets
- 1 cup vegetable broth

Garnish

- Chopped sun-dried tomatoes
- Balsamic vinegar

- 2 teaspoons salt
- 2 cups spinach, coarsely chopped
- 2 green onions, chopped
- 1 pound of zoodles (Spiralized Zucchini)

- Gorgonzola cheese

Directions

1. Set your Ninja Foodi to Saute mode and add butter, allow the butter to melt
2. Add garlic cloves and Saute for 2 minutes
3. Add cauliflower, broth, salt and lock up the lid and cook on HIGH pressure for 6 minutes
4. Prepare the zoodles. Perform a naturally release over 10 minutes
5. Use an immersion blender to blend the mixture in the pot to a puree
6. Pour the sauce over the zoodles
7. Serve with a garnish of cheese, sun-dried tomatoes and a drizzle of balsamic vinegar. Enjoy!

Simple Mushroom Hats And Eggs

(Prepping time: 10 minutes\ Cooking time: 9 minutes |For 1 serving)

Ingredients

- 4 ounces mushroom hats
- 1 teaspoon butter, melted
- 4 quail eggs

- ½ teaspoon ground black pepper
- ¼ teaspoon salt

Directions

1. Spread the mushroom hats with the butter inside. Then beat the eggs into mushroom hats
2. Sprinkle with salt and ground black pepper. Transfer the mushroom hats on the rack
3. Lower the air fryer lid. Cook the meat for 7 minutes at 365 F
4. Check the mushroom, if it is not cooked fully then cook them for 2 minutes more
5. Serve and enjoy!

Ginger And Butternut Bisque Yum

(Prepping time: 10 minutes\ Cooking time: 8 minutes |For 6 servings)

Ingredients

- 1 cup of diced yellow onion
- 4 minced cloves of garlic
- 2 teaspoon of peeled and chopped ginger
- 1 cup of chopped carrot
- 1 green apple chopped
- 1 peeled and chopped butternut squash
- 1 teaspoon salt
- 2 cups of water
- ¼ cup of finely chopped parsley
- Black pepper

Directions

1. Prepare the ingredients accordingly and keep them on the side
2. Set your Ninja Foodie to Saute mode and add onions, cook for minutes
3. Add just a splash of water . Add garlic, carrot, ginger, apple, squash, and salt
4. Give it a nice stir. Add water and lock up the lid
5. Cook on HIGH pressure for 5 minutes. Naturally, release the pressure
6. Allow it to cool for 15 minutes
7. Blend the soup in batches, or you may use an immersion blender as well to blend in the pot until it is creamy. Add parsley and season with some black pepper. Serve and enjoy!

Hearty Cheesy Cauliflower

(Prepping time: 10 minutes\ Cooking time: 35 minutes |For 6 servings)

Ingredients

- 1 tablespoon Keto-Friendly mustard
- 1 head cauliflower
- 1 teaspoon avocado mayonnaise
- ½ cup parmesan cheese, grated
- ¼ cup butter, cut into small pieces

Directions

1. Set your Ninja Foodi to Saute mode and add butter, let it melt
2. Add cauliflower and Saute for 3 minutes
3. Add rest of the ingredients and lock lid, cook on HIGH pressure for 30 minutes
4. Release pressure naturally over 10 minutes. Serve and enjoy!

Mesmerizing Spinach Quiche

(Prepping time: 10 minutes\ Cooking time: 33 minutes |For 4 servings)

Ingredients

- 1 tablespoon butter, melted
- 1 pack (10 ounces) frozen spinach, thawed
- 5 organic eggs, beaten
- Salt and pepper to taste
- 3 cups Monterey Jack Cheese, shredded

Directions

1. Set your Ninja Foodi to Saute mode and let it heat up, add butter and let the butter melt
2. Add spinach and Saute for 3 minutes, transfer the Sautéed spinach to a bowl
3. Add eggs, cheese, salt, and pepper to a bowl and mix it well
4. Transfer the mixture to greased quiche molds and transfer the mold to your Foodi
5. Close the lid and choose the "Bake/Roast" mode and let it cook for 30 minutes at 360 degrees F. Once done, open lid and transfer the dish out
6. Cut into wedges and serve. Enjoy!

Running Away Broccoli Casserole

(Prepping time: 10 minutes\ Cooking time: 7 minutes |For 4 servings)

Ingredients

- 1 tablespoon extra-virgin olive oil
- 1 pound broccoli, cut into florets
- 1 pound cauliflower, cut into florets
- ¼ cup almond flour

- 2 cups of coconut milk
- ½ teaspoon ground nutmeg
- Pinch of pepper
- 1 and ½ cup shredded Gouda cheese, divided

Directions

1. Pre-heat your Ninja Foodi by setting it to Saute mode
2. Add olive oil and let it heat up, add broccoli and cauliflower
3. Take a medium bowl stir in almond flour, coconut milk, nutmeg, pepper, 1 cup cheese and add the mixture to your Ninja Foodi. Top with ½ cup cheese and lock lid, cook on HIGH pressure for 5 minutes. Release pressure naturally over 10 minutes . Serve and enjoy!

Spaghetti Squash Fancy Noodles
(Prepping time: 10 minutes\ Cooking time: 7 minutes |For 6 servings)

Ingredients

- 2 pound of spaghetti squash

- 1 cup of water

Directions

1. Take a paring knife and cut the spaghetti squash in half
2. Take a largely sized spoon and scoop out the center seeds and discard the gunk
3. Place the Ninja Foodi steamer insert inside the inner pot of your Ninja Foodi. Add 1 cup of water
4. Add the half-cut squashes to the steamer insert, making sure that the cut part if facing up
5. Lock up the lid and cook on HIGH pressure for 7 minutes
6. Once done, perform a quick release. Take the squash out and fork out the strings
7. Serve with sauce or your favorite topping!

Dill And Garlic Fiesta Platter
(Prepping time: 10 minutes\ Cooking time: 10-15 minutes |For 6 servings)

Ingredients

- 3 cups carrots, chopped
- 1 tablespoon melted butter
- ½ teaspoon garlic salt

- 1 tablespoon fresh dill, minced
- 1 cup of water

Directions

1. Add listed ingredients to Ninja Foodi. Stir and lock lid, cook on HIGH pressure for 10 minutes
2. Release pressure naturally over 10 minutes. Quick release pressure
3. Serve with topping of dill, enjoy

Quick Red Cabbage
(Prepping time: 10 minutes\ Cooking time: 10 minutes |For 6 servings)

Ingredients

- 6 cups red cabbage, chopped
- 1 tablespoon apple cider vinegar
- ½ cup Keto-Friendly applesauce
- 1 cup of water

- 3 garlic cloves, minced
- 1 small onion, chopped
- 1 tablespoon olive oil
- Salt and pepper to taste

Directions

1. Add olive oil to Ninja Foodi
2. Set it to Saute mode and let it heat up, add onion and garlic and Saute for 2 minutes
3. Add remaining ingredients and stir. Lock lid and cook on HIGH pressure for 10 minutes
4. Quick release pressure. Stir well and serve. Enjoy!

Simple Rice Cauliflower
(Prepping time: 10 minutes\ Cooking time: 15 minutes |For 4 servings)

Ingredients

- 1 large cauliflower head
- 2 tablespoons olive oil
- ¼ teaspoon salt
- ½ teaspoon dried parsley
- ½ teaspoon cumin
- ¼ teaspoon turmeric
- ¼ teaspoon paprika
- Fresh cilantro
- Lime wedges

Directions

1. Wash the cauliflower well and trim the leaves
2. Place a steamer rack on top of the pot and transfer the florets to the rack
3. Add 1 cup of water into the Ninja Foodi.Lock up the lid and cook on HIGH pressure for 1 minute
4. Once done, do a quick release.Transfer the flower to a serving platter
5. Set your pot to Saute mode and add oil, allow the oil to heat up
6. Add flowers back to the pot and cook, making sure to break them using a potato masher
7. Add spices and season with a bit of salt. Give a nice stir and squeeze a bit of lime
8. Serve and enjoy!

Very Spicy Cauliflower Steak
(Prepping time: 10 minutes\ Cooking time: 4 minutes |For 6 servings)

Ingredients

- 1 large head cauliflower
- 2 tablespoon extra-virgin olive oil
- 2 teaspoon paprika
- 2 teaspoon ground cumin
- ¾ teaspoon kosher salt
- 1 cup fresh cilantro, chopped
- 1 lemon, quartered

Directions

1. Place the steamer rack into your Ninja Foodi. Add 1 and a ½ cups of water
2. Remove the leaves from the cauliflower and trim the core to ensure that it is able to sit flat
3. Carefully place it on the steam rack. Take a small bowl and add olive oil, cumin, paprika, salt
4. Drizzle the mixture over the cauliflower
5. Lock up the lid and cook on HIGH pressure for 4 minutes
6. Quick release the pressure. Lift the cauliflower to a cutting board and slice into 1-inch steaks
7. Divide the mixture among serving plates and sprinkle with cilantro. Serve and enjoy!

Authentic Indian Palak Paneer
(Prepping time: 10 minutes\ Cooking time: 5 minutes |For 4 servings)

Ingredients

- 2 teaspoons olive oil
- 5 garlic cloves, chopped
- 1 tablespoon fresh ginger, chopped
- 1 large yellow onion, chopped
- ½ jalapeno chile, chopped
- 1 pound fresh spinach
- 2 tomatoes, chopped
- 2 teaspoons ground cumin
- ½ teaspoon cayenne
- 2 teaspoons Garam masala

- 1 teaspoon ground turmeric
- 1 teaspoon salt
- ½ cup of water
- 1 and ½ cup paneer cubes
- ½ cup heavy whip cream

Directions

1. Pre-heat your Ninja Foodi using Saute mode on HIGH heat, once the pot is hot, add oil and let it shimmer. Add garlic, ginger and chile, Saute for 2-3 minutes
2. Add onion, spinach, tomatoes, cumin, cayenne, garam masala, turmeric, salt, and water
3. Lock lid and cook on HIGH pressure for 2 minutes. Release pressure naturally over 10 minutes
4. Use an immersion blender to puree the mixture to your desired consistency
5. Gently stir in paneer and top with a drizzle of cream. Enjoy!

All-Time Mixed Vegetable Curry

(Prepping time: 10 minutes\ Cooking time: 3 minutes |For 6 servings)

Ingredients

- 3 cups leeks, sliced
- 6 cups rainbow chard, stems and leaves, chopped
- 1 cup celery, chopped
- 2 tablespoons garlic, minced
- 1 teaspoon dried oregano
- 1 teaspoon salt
- 2 teaspoons fresh ground black pepper
- 3 cups chicken broth
- 2 cups yellow summer squash, sliced into 1/ inch slices
- ¼ cup fresh parsley, chopped
- ¾ cup heavy whip cream
- 4-6 tablespoons parmesan cheese, grated

Directions

1. Add leeks, chard, celery, 1 tablespoon garlic, oregano, salt, pepper and broth to your Ninja Foodi
2. Lock lid and cook on HIGH pressure for 3 minutes. Quick release pressure
3. Open the lid and add more broth, set your pot to Saute mode and adjust heat to HIGH
4. Add yellow squash, parsley and remaining 1 tablespoon garlic
5. Let it cook for 2-3 minutes until the squash is soft. Stir in cream and sprinkle parmesan
6. Serve and enjoy!

Worthy Caramelized ONion

(Prepping time: 10 minutes\ Cooking time: 30-35 minutes |For 6 servings)

Ingredients

- 2 tablespoons unsalted butter
- 3 large onions sliced
- 2 tablespoons water
- 1 teaspoon salt

Directions

1. Set your Ninja Foodi to Sauté mode and add set temperature to medium heat, pre-heat the inner pot for 5 minutes. Add butter and let it melt, add onions, water, and stir
2. Lock lid and cook on HIGH pressure for 30 minutes. Quick release the pressure
3. Remove lid and set the pot to sauté mode, let it sear in Medium-HIGH mode for 15 minutes until all liquid is gone. Serve and enjoy!

A Very Greeny Green Beans Platter

(Prepping time: 10 minutes\ Cooking time: 5 minutes |For 6 servings)

Ingredients

- 2-3 pounds fresh green beans
- 2 tablespoons butter

- 1 garlic clove, minced
- Salt and pepper to taste
- 1 and ½ cups of water

Directions

1. Add listed ingredients to Ninja Foodi. Lock lid and cook on HIGH pressure for 5 minutes
2. Quick release pressure

A Mishmash Cauliflower Mash
(Prepping time: 10 minutes\ Cooking time: 5 minutes |For 3 servings)

Ingredients

- 1 tablespoon butter, soft
- ½ cup feta cheese
- Salt and pepper to taste
- 1 large head cauliflower, chopped into large pieces
- 1 garlic cloves, minced
- 2 teaspoons fresh chives, minced

Directions

1. Add water to your Ninja Foodi and place steamer basket
2. Add cauliflower pieces and lock lid, cook on HIGH pressure for 5 minutes
3. Quick release pressure. Open the lid and use an immersion blender to mash the cauliflower
4. Blend until you have a nice consistency. Enjoy!

Zucchini And Artichoke Platter
(Prepping time: 10 minutes\ Cooking time: 10 minutes |For 4 servings)

Ingredients

- 2 tablespoon coconut oil
- 1 bulb garlic, minced
- 1 large artichoke heart, cleaned sliced
- 2 medium zucchinis, sliced
- ½ cup vegetable broth
- Salt and pepper as needed

Directions

1. Set your Ninja Foodi to Saute mode and add oil, allow the oil the heat up
2. Add garlic and Saute until nicely fragrant. Add rest of the ingredients and stir
3. Lock lid and cook on HIGH pressure for 10 minutes. Quick release, serve and enjoy!

Winning Broccoli Casserole
(Prepping time: 10 minutes\ Cooking time: 6 hours |For 4 servings)

Ingredients

- 1 tablespoon extra-virgin olive oil
- 1 pound broccoli, cut into florets
- 1 pound cauliflower, cut into florets
- ¼ cup almond flour
- 2 cups of coconut milk
- ½ teaspoon ground nutmeg
- Pinch of fresh ground black pepper
- 1 and ½ cups cashew cream

Directions

1. Grease the Ninja Foodi inner pot with olive oil. Place broccoli and cauliflower to your Ninja Foodi
2. Take a small bowl and stir in almond flour, coconut milk, pepper, 1 cup of cashew cream
3. Pour coconut milk mixture over vegetables and top casserole with remaining cashew cream
4. Cover and cook on SLOW COOK Mode (LOW) for 6 hours. Server and enjoy!

Spaghetti Squash Drizzled With Sage Butter Sauce
(Prepping time: 10 minutes\ Cooking time: 10 minutes |For 4 servings)

Ingredients

- 1 medium-sized spaghetti squash
- 1 and a ½ cup of water
- 1 bunch of fresh sage
- 3-4 garlic cloves, sliced
- 2 tablespoon of olive oil
- 1 teaspoon of salt
- 1/8 teaspoon of nutmeg

Directions

1. Halve the squash and scoop out the seeds
2. Add water to your Ninja Foodi and lower down the squash with the squash halves facing up
3. Stack them on top of one another. Lock up the lid and cook on HIGH pressure for 3 minutes
4. Release the pressure over 10 minutes
5. Take a cold Saute pan and add sage, garlic and olive oil and cook on LOW heat, making sure to stir and fry the sage leaves. Keep it on the side
6. Release the pressure naturally and tease the squash fibers out from the shell and plop them into the Saute Pan. Stir well and sprinkle salt and nutmeg . Serve with a bit of cheese and enjoy!

Uber-Keto Caper And Beet Salad

(Prepping time: 10 minutes\ Cooking time: 25 minutes |For 4 servings)

Ingredients

- 4 medium beets

For Dressing

- Small bunch parsley, stems removed
- 1 large garlic clove
- ½ teaspoon salt
- 2 tablespoons of rice wine vinegar

- Pinch of black pepper
- 1 tablespoon extra-virgin olive oil
- 2 tablespoons capers

Directions

1. Pour 1 cup of water into your steamer basket and place it on the side
2. Snip up the tops of your bits and wash them well. Put the beets in your steamer basket
3. Place the steamer basket in your instant pot and lock up the lid
4. Let it cook for about 25 minutes at high pressure. Once done, release the pressure naturally
5. While it is being cooked, take a small jar and add chopped up parsley and garlic alongside olive oil, salt, pepper and capers. Shake it vigorously to prepared your dressing
6. Open up the lid once the pressure is released and check the beets for doneness using a fork
7. Take out the steamer basket to your sink and run it under cold water
8. Use your finger to brush off the skin of the beets
9. Use a plastic cutting board and slice up the beets
10. Arrange them on a platter and sprinkle some vinegar on top

The Greeny And Beany Horseradish Mix

(Prepping time: 5 minutes\ Cooking time: 10-15 minutes |For 4 servings)

Ingredients

- 2 large beets with greens, scrubbed and root ends trimmed
- 1 cup water, for steaming
- 2 tablespoons sour cream
- 1 tablespoon whole milk
- 1 teaspoon prepared horseradish
- ¼ teaspoon lemon zest
- 1/8 teaspoon salt
- 2 teaspoon unsalted butter
- 1 tablespoon minced fresh chives

Directions

1. Trim off beet greens and keep them on the side
2. Add water to the Ninja Foodi and place steamer basket, place beets in a steamer basket

3. Lock lid and cook on HIGH pressure for 10 minutes, release pressure naturally over 10 minutes
4. While the beets are being cooked, wash greens and slice them into ½ inch thick ribbons
5. Take a bowl and whisk in sour cream, horseradish, lemon zest, 1/16 teaspoon of salt
6. Once the cooking is done, remove the lid and remove beets, let them cool
7. Use a paring knife to peel them and slice them into large bite-sized pieces
8. Remove steamer from the Ninja Foodi and pour out water
9. Set your Foodi to "Saute" mode and add butter, let it melt
10. Once the butter stops foaming, add beet greens sprinkle remaining 1/6 teaspoon salt and cook for 3-4 minutes. Return beets to the Foodi and heat for 1-2 minutes, stirring
11. Transfer beets and greens to a platter and drizzle sour cream mixture
12. Sprinkle chives and serve. Enjoy!

Fully Stuffed Whole Chicken
(Prepping time: 5 minutes\ Cooking time: 8 hours |For 4 servings)

Ingredients

- 1 cup mozzarella cheese
- 4 garlic clove, peeled
- 1 whole chicken, 2 pounds, cleaned and dried

- Salt and pepper to taste
- 2 tablespoons lemon juice

Directions

1. Stuff chicken cavity with garlic cloves, cheese. Season with salt and pepper
2. Transfer to Ninja Foodi and drizzle lemon juice. Lock lid and SLOW COOK on LOW for 8 hours
3. Transfer to a plate, serve and enjoy!

Rosemary Dredged Green Beans
(Prepping time: 5 minutes\ Cooking time: 3 hours |For 4 servings)

Ingredients

- 1 pound green beans
- 1 tablespoon rosemary, minced
- 1 teaspoon fresh thyme, minced

- 2 tablespoons lemon juice
- 2 tablespoons water

Directions

1. Add listed ingredients to Ninja Foodi
2. Lock lid and cook on SLOW COOK MODE(LOW) for 3 hours . Unlock lid and stir. Enjoy!

Italian Turkey Breast
(Prepping time: 5 minutes\ Cooking time: 2 hours |For 4 servings)

Ingredients

- 1 and ½ cups Italian dressing
- 2 garlic cloves, minced
- 1 (2 pounds) turkey breast, with bone

- 2 tablespoons butter
- Salt and pepper to taste

Directions

1. Mix in garlic cloves, salt, black pepper and rub turkey breast with mix
2. Grease Ninja Foodi pot and arrange turkey breast. Top with Italian dressing
3. Lock lid and BAKE/ROAST for 2 hours at 230 degrees F. Serve and enjoy!

Crazy Fresh Onion Soup

(Prepping time: 5 minutes\ Cooking time: 10-15 minutes |For 4 servings)

Ingredients

- 2 tablespoons avocado oil
- 8 cups yellow onion
- 1 tablespoon balsamic vinegar
- 6 cups of pork stock
- 1 teaspoon salt
- 2 bay leaves
- 2 large sprigs, fresh thyme

Directions

1. Cut up the onion in half through the root
2. Peel them and slice into thin half moons
3. Set the pot to Saute mode and add oil, one the oil is hot and add onions
4. Cook for about 15 minutes
5. Add balsamic vinegar and scrape any fond from the bottom
6. Add stock, bay leaves, salt, and thyme
7. Lock up the lid and cook on HIGH pressure for 10 minutes
8. Release the pressure naturally
9. Discard the bay leaf and thyme stems
10. Blend the soup using an immersion blender and serve!

Elegant Zero Crust Kale And Mushroom Quiche

(Prepping time: 5 minutes\ Cooking time: 9 hours |For 6 servings)

Ingredients

- 6 large eggs
- 2 tablespoons unsweetened almond milk
- 2 ounces low –fat feta cheese, crumbled
- ¼ cup parmesan cheese, grated
- 1 and ½ teaspoons Italian seasoning
- 4 ounces mushrooms, sliced
- 2 cups kale, chopped

Directions

1. Grease the inner pot of your Ninja Foodi
2. Take a large bowl and whisk in eggs, cheese, almond milk, seasoning and mix it well
3. Stir in kale and mushrooms. Pour the mix into Ninja Foodi. Gently stir
4. Place lid and cook on SLOW COOK Mode(LOW) for 8-9 hours. Serve and enjoy!

Delicious Beet Borscht

(Prepping time: 5 minutes\ Cooking time: 45 minutes |For 6 servings)

Ingredients

- 8 cups beets
- ½ cup celery, diced
- ½ cup carrots, diced
- 2 garlic cloves, diced
- 1 medium onion, diced
- 3 cups cabbage, shredded
- 6 cups beef stock
- 1 bay leaf
- 1 tablespoon salt
- ½ tablespoon thyme
- ¼ cup fresh dill, chopped
- ½ cup of coconut yogurt

Directions

1. Add the washed beets to a steamer in the Ninja Foodi
2. Add 1 cup of water. Steam for 7 minutes
3. Perform a quick release and drop into an ice bath
4. Carefully peel off the skin and dice the beets

5. Transfer the diced beets, celery, carrots, onion, garlic, cabbage, stock, bay leaf, thyme and salt to your Instant Pot. Lock up the lid and set the pot to SOUP mode, cook for 45 minutes
6. Release the pressure naturally. Transfer to bowls and top with a dollop of dairy-free yogurt
7. Enjoy with a garnish of fresh dill!

Pepper Jack Cauliflower Meal
(Prepping time: 5 minutes\ Cooking time: 3 hours 35 minutes |For 6 servings)

Ingredients

- 1 head cauliflower
- ¼ cup whipping cream
- 4 ounces cream cheese
- ½ teaspoon pepper
- 1 teaspoon salt
- 2 tablespoons butter
- 4 ounces pepper jack cheese
- 6 bacon slices, crumbled

Directions

1. Grease Ninja Foodi and add listed ingredients (except cheese and bacon)
2. Stir and Lock lid, cook SLOW COOK MODE (LOW) for 3 hours
3. Remove lid and add cheese, stir. Lock lid again and cook for 1 hour more
4. Garnish with bacon crumbles and enjoy!

Slow-Cooked Brussels
(Prepping time: 5 minutes\ Cooking time: 4 hours |For 4 servings)

Ingredients

- 1 pound Brussels sprouts, bottom trimmed and cut
- 1 tablespoon olive oil
- 1 -1/2 tablespoon Dijon mustard
- ¼ cup of water
- Salt and pepper as needed
- ½ teaspoon dried tarragon

Directions

1. Add Brussels, salt, water, pepper, mustard to Ninja Foodi
2. Add dried tarragon and stir
3. Lock lid and cook on SLOW COOK MODE (LOW) for 5 hours until the Brussels are tender
4. Stir well and add Dijon over Brussels. Stir and enjoy!

Slowly Cooked Lemon Artichokes
(Prepping time: 10 minutes\ Cooking time: 5 hours |For 4 servings)

Ingredients

- 5 large artichokes
- 1 teaspoon of sea salt
- 2 stalks celery, sliced
- 2 large carrots, cut into matchsticks
- Juice from ½ a lemon
- ¼ teaspoon black pepper
- 1 teaspoon dried thyme
- 1 tablespoon dried rosemary
- Lemon wedges for garnish

Directions

1. Remove the stalk from your artichokes and remove the tough outer shell
2. Transfer the chokes to your Ninja Foodi and add 2 cups of boiling water
3. Add celery, lemon juice, salt, carrots, black pepper, thyme, rosemary
4. Cook on Slow Cook mode (HIGH) for 4-5 hours
5. Serve the artichokes with lemon wedges. Serve and enjoy!

Well Dressed Brussels

(Prepping time: 10 minutes\ Cooking time: 4-5 hours |For 4 servings)

Ingredients

- 2 pounds Brussels, halved
- 2 red onions, sliced
- 2 tablespoons apple cider vinegar
- 1 tablespoon extra-virgin olive oil
- 1 teaspoon ground cinnamon
- ½ cup pecans, chopped

Directions

1. Add Brussels and onions to Ninja Foodi. Take a small bowl and add cinnamon, vinegar, olive oil
2. Pour mixture over sprouts and toss
3. Place lid and cook on SLOW COOK MODE (LOW) for 4-5 hours. Enjoy!

Cheddar Cauliflower Bowl

(Prepping time: 10 minutes\ Cooking time: 5 minutes |For 8 servings)

Ingredients

- ¼ cup butter
- ½ sweet onion, chopped
- 1 head cauliflower, chopped
- 4 cups herbed vegetable stock
- ½ teaspoon ground nutmeg
- 1 cup heavy whip cream
- Salt and pepper as needed
- 1 cup cheddar cheese, shredded

Directions

1. Set your Ninja Foodi to sauté mode and add butter, let it heat up and melt
2. Add onion and Cauliflower, Saute for 10 minutes until tender and lightly browned
3. Add vegetable stock and nutmeg, bring to a boil
4. Lock lid and cook on HIGH pressure for 5 minutes, quick release pressure once done
5. Remove pot and from Foodi and stir in heavy cream, puree using an immersion blender
6. Season with more salt and pepper and serve with a topping of cheddar. Enjoy!

A Prosciutto And Thyme Eggs

(Prepping time: 10 minutes\ Cooking time: 5 minutes |For 4 servings)

Ingredients

- 4 kale leaves
- 4 prosciutto slices
- 3 tablespoons heavy cream
- 4 hardboiled eggs
- ¼ teaspoon pepper
- ¼ teaspoon salt
- 1 and ½ cups of water

Directions

1. Peel eggs and wrap in kale. Wrap in prosciutto and sprinkle salt and pepper
2. Add water to your Ninja Foodi and lower trivet. Place eggs inside and lock lid
3. Cook on HIGH pressure for 5 minutes. Quick release pressure. Serve and enjoy!

The Authentic Zucchini Pesto Meal

(Prepping time: 10 minutes\ Cooking time: 10 minutes |For 4 servings)

Ingredients

- 1 tablespoon olive oil
- 1 onion, chopped
- 2 and ½ pound roughly chopped zucchini
- ½ cup of water

- 1 and ½ teaspoon salt
- 1 bunch basil leaves
- 2 garlic cloves, minced
- 1 tablespoon extra-virgin olive oil
- Zucchini for making zoodles

Direction

5. Set the Ninja Foodi to Saute mode and add olive oil
6. Once the oil is hot, add onion and Saute for 4 minutes
7. Add zucchini, water, and salt. Lock up the lid and cook on HIGH pressure for 3 minutes
8. Release the pressure naturally. Add basil, garlic, and leaves
9. Use an immersion blender to blend everything well until you have a sauce-like consistency
10. Take the extra zucchini and pass them through a Spiralizer to get noodle like shapes
11. Toss the Zoodles with sauce and enjoy!

Supreme Cauliflower Soup

(Prepping time: 10 minutes\ Cooking time: 5 minutes |For 4 servings)

Ingredients

- ½ a small onion, chopped
- 2 tablespoons butter
- 1 large head of cauliflower, leaves and stems removed, coarsely chopped
- 2 cups chicken stock
- 1 teaspoon garlic powder
- 1 teaspoon salt
- 4 ounces cream cheese, cut into cubes
- 1 cup sharp cheddar cheese, cut
- ½ cup cream
- Extra cheddar, sour cream bacon strips, green onion for topping

Directions

1. Peel the onion and chop up into small pieces
2. Cut the leaves of the cauliflower and steam, making sure to keep the core intact
3. Coarsely chop the cauliflower into pieces
4. Set your Ninja Foodi to Saute mode and add onion, cook for 2-3 minutes
5. Add chopped cauliflower, stock, salt, and garlic powder
6. Lock up the lid and cook on HIGH pressure for 5 minutes. Perform a quick release
7. Prepare the toppings. Use an immersion blender to puree your soup in the Ninja Foodi
8. Serve your soup with a topping of sliced green onions, cheddar, crumbled bacon. Enjoy!

Very Rich And Creamy Asparagus Soup

(Prepping time: 10 minutes\ Cooking time: 5-10 minutes |For 4 servings)

Ingredients

- 1 tablespoon olive oil
- 3 green onions, sliced crosswise into ¼ inch pieces
- 1 pound asparagus, tough ends removed, cut into 1 inch pieces
- 4 cups vegetable stock
- 1 tablespoon unsalted butter
- 1 tablespoon almond flour
- 2 teaspoon salt
- 1 teaspoon white pepper
- ½ cup heavy cream

Directions

8. Set your Ninja Foodi to "Saute" mode and add oil, let it heat up
9. Add green onions and Saute for a few minutes, add asparagus and stock
10. Lock lid and cook on HIGH pressure for 5 minutes
11. Take a small saucepan and place it over low heat, add butter, flour and stir until the mixture foams and turns into a golden beige, this is your blond roux
12. Remove from heat. Release pressure naturally over 10 minutes
13. Open the lid and add roux, salt, and pepper to the soup
14. Use an immersion blender to puree the soup

15. Taste and season accordingly, swirl in cream and enjoy!

Summertime Vegetable Platter
(Prepping time: 5 minutes\ Cooking time: 3 hours 5 minutes |For 6 servings)

Ingredients

- 1 cup grape tomatoes
- 2 cups okra
- 1 cup mushrooms
- 2 cups yellow bell peppers
- 1 and ½ cup red onions

- 2 and ½ cups zucchini
- ½ cup olive oil
- ½ cup balsamic vinegar
- 1 tablespoon fresh thyme, chopped
- 2 tablespoons fresh basil, chopped

Directions

1.Slice and chop okra, onions, tomatoes, zucchini, mushrooms
2.Add veggies to a large container and mix
3.Take another dish and add oil and vinegar, mix in thyme and basil
5.Toss the veggies into Ninja Foodi and pour marinade. Stir well
6.Close lid and cook on 3 hours on SLOW COOK MOD (HIGH), making sure to stir after every hour

The Creative Mushroom Stroganoff
(Prepping time: 5 minutes\ Cooking time: 10 minutes |For 6 servings)

Ingredients

- ¼ cup unsalted butter, cubed
- 1 pound cremini mushrooms, halved
- 1 large onion, halved
- 4 garlic cloves, minced
- 2 cups vegetable broth

- ½ teaspoon salt
- ¼ teaspoon fresh black pepper
- 1 and ½ cups sour cream
- ¼ cup fresh flat-leaf parsley, chopped
- 1 cup grated parmesan cheese

Directions

1. Add butter, mushrooms, onion, garlic, vegetable broth, salt, pepper, and paprika
2. Gently stir and lock lid. Cook on HIGH pressure for 5 minutes
3. Release pressure naturally over 10 minutes
4. Serve by stirring in sour cream and with a garnish of parsley and parmesan cheese. Enjoy!

Garlic And Ginger Red Cabbage Platter
(Prepping time: 10 minutes\ Cooking time: 8 minutes |For 6 servings)

Ingredients

- 2 tablespoon coconut oil
- 1 tablespoon butter
- 3 garlic cloves, crushed
- 2 teaspoon fresh ginger, grated

- 8 cups red cabbage, shredded
- 1 teaspoon salt
- ½ a teaspoon pepper
- 1/3 cup water

Directions

1. Set your Ninja Foodi to Saute mode and add coconut oil and butter, allow to heat up
2. Add garlic and ginger and mix. Add cabbage, pepper, salt, and water
3. Mix well and lock up the lid, cook on HIGH pressure for 5 minutes
4. Perform a quick release and mix. Serve and enjoy!

The Veggie Lover's Onion And Tofu Platter

(Prepping time: 8 minutes\ Cooking time: 12 minutes |For 4 servings)

Ingredients

- 4 tablespoons butter
- 2 tofu blocks, pressed and cubed into 1-inch pieces
- Salt and pepper to taste
- 1 cup cheddar cheese, grated
- 2 medium onions, sliced

Directions

1. Take a bowl and add tofu, season with salt and pepper
2. Set your Foodi to Saute mode and add butter, let it melt
3. Add onions and Saute for 3 minutes. Add seasoned tofu and cook for 2 minutes more
4. Add cheddar and gently stir
5. Lock the lid and bring down the Air Crisp mode, let the dish cook on "Air Crisp" mode for 3 minutes at 340 degrees F. Once done, take the dish out, serve and enjoy!

Feisty Maple Dredged Carrots

(Prepping time: 10 minutes\ Cooking time: 4 minutes |For 6 servings)

Ingredients

- 2-pound carrot
- ¼ cup raisins
- Pepper as needed
- 1 cup of water
- 1 tablespoon butter
- 1 tablespoon sugar-free Keto friendly maple syrup

Directions

1. Wash, peel the skin and slice the carrots diagonally
2. Add the carrots, raisins, water to your Ninja Foodi
3. Lock up the lid and cook on HIGH pressure for 4 minutes. Perform a quick release
4. Strain the carrots . Add butter and maple syrup to the warm Ninja Foodi and mix well
5. Transfer the strained carrots back to the pot and stir to coat with maple sauce and butter
6. Serve with a bit of pepper. Enjoy!

The Original Sicilian Cauliflower Roast

(Prepping time: 10 minutes\ Cooking time: 10 minutes |For 4 servings)

Ingredients

- 1 medium cauliflower head, leaves removed
- ¼ cup olive oil
- 1 teaspoon red pepper, crushed
- ½ cup of water
- 2 tablespoons capers, rinsed and minced
- ½ cup parmesan cheese, grated
- 1 tablespoon fresh parsley, chopped

Directions

1. Take the Ninja Foodi and start by adding water and place the cook and crisp basket inside the pot. Cut an "X" on the head of cauliflower by using a knife and slice it about halfway down
2. Take a basket and transfer the cauliflower in it
3. Then put on the pressure lid and seal it and set it on low pressure for 3 minutes
4. Add olive oil, capers, garlic, and crushed red pepper into it and mix them well
5. Once the cauliflower is cooked, do a quick release and remove the lid
6. Pour in the oil and spice mixture on the cauliflower
7. Spread equally on the surface then sprinkle some Parmesan cheese from the top
8. Close the pot with crisping lid. Set it on Air Crisp mode to 390 degrees F for 10 minutes

9. Once done, remove the cauliflower flower the Ninja Foodi transfer it into a serving plate
10. Cut it up into pieces and transfer them to serving plates. Sprinkle fresh parsley from the top
11. Serve and enjoy!

Chapter 7: Holiday And Weekend Ninja Recipes

Simple Weeknight Vanilla Yogurt

(Prepping time: 10 minutes + 9 hours\ Cooking time: 3 hours |For 4 servings)

Ingredients

- ½ cup full-fat milk
- ¼ cup yogurt started
- 1 cup heavy cream
- ½ tablespoon vanilla extract
- 2 teaspoons stevia

Directions

1. Add milk to your Ninja Foodi and stir in heavy cream, vanilla extract, stevia
2. Stir well, let the yogurt sit for a while. Lock lid and cook on SLOW COOKER mode for 3 hours
3. Take a small bowl and add 1 cup milk with the yogurt starter, bring this mixture to the pot
4. Lock lid and wrap Foodi in two small towels. Let it sit for 9 hours (to allow it to culture)
5. Refrigerate and serve. Enjoy!

The Great Family Lemon Mousse

(Prepping time: 10 minutes \ Cooking time: 12 minutes |For 4 servings)

Ingredients

- 1-2 ounces cream cheese, soft
- ½ cup heavy cream
- 1/8 cup fresh lemon juice
- ½ teaspoon lemon liquid stevia
- 2 pinch salt

Directions

1. Take a bowl and mix in cream cheese, heavy cream, lemon juice, salt, and stevia
2. Pour mixture into a ramekin and transfer to Ninja Foodi
3. Lock lid and choose the Bake/Roast mode and bake for 12 minutes at 350 degrees F
4. Check using a toothpick if it comes out clean. Serve and enjoy!

Tangy Berry Slices

(Prepping time: 20 minutes\ Cooking time: 15 minutes |For 4 servings)

Ingredients

- 1 cup cottage cheese
- ½ teaspoon stevia
- ¼ cup ground pecans
- ½ cup strawberries
- ¼ cup whipped cream
- ¼ cup butter

Directions

1. Set your Ninja Food to Saute mode and add butter, add pecans and toss until coated
2. Divide mixture into 3 ramekins and press them down
3. Blend cheese and stevia, puree until smooth. Place cheese mixture on top of the pecan crust
4. Cover with fresh strawberry slices, top with whipped cream. Chill and enjoy!

Over The Weekend Apple And Sprouts

(Prepping time: 10 minutes\ Cooking time: 10 minutes |For 4 servings)

Ingredients

- 1 green apple, julienned
- 1 and ½ teaspoon olive oil
- 4 cups alfalfa sprouts
- Salt and pepper to taste
- ¼ cup of coconut milk

Direction

1. Set your Ninja Foodi to Saute mode and add oil, let it heat up
2. Add apple, sprouts, and stir. Lock lid and cook on HIGH pressure for 5 minutes
3. Add salt, pepper, coconut milk and stir well. Serve3 and enjoy!

Generous Gluten Free Pancakes
(Prepping time: 10 minutes\ Cooking time: 16 minutes |For 4 servings)

Ingredients

- 1/3 cup almond flour
- ½ cup of water
- ½ teaspoon chili powder
- 1 Serrano pepper, minced
- 4 tablespoons coconut oil
- 3 tablespoons coconut cream
- ¼ teaspoon turmeric powder
- 1 handful cilantro, chopped
- 6 large eggs
- 1 teaspoon salt
- ¼ teaspoon pepper
- ½ inch ginger, grated
- ½ red onion, chopped

Directions

1. Take a bowl and add coconut milk, almond flour, spices, and blend well
2. Stir in ginger, Serrano, cilantro, red onion and mix
3. Grease interior of Ninja Foodi with coconut oil, pour batter in pot and Lock lid, cook on LOW pressure for 30 minutes. Release pressure naturally over 10 minutes
4. Remove pancake to a platter and serve. Enjoy!

Fancy Holiday Lemon Custard
(Prepping time: 10 minutes \ Cooking time: 20 minutes |For 4 servings)

Ingredients

- 5 egg yolks
- ¼ cup fresh squeezed lemon juice
- 1 tablespoon lemon zest
- 1 teaspoon pure vanilla extract
- 1/3 teaspoon liquid stevia
- 2 cups heavy cream
- 1 cup whipped coconut cream

Directions

1. Take a medium sized bowl and whisk in yolks, lemon juice, zest, vanilla, and liquid stevia
2. Whisk in heavy cream, divide the mixture between 4 ramekins
3. Place the included rack in your Ninja Foodi and place ramekins in the rack
4. Add just enough water to reach halfway to the sides of the ramekins
5. Lock lid and cook on HIGH pressure for 20 minutes. Release pressure naturally over 10 minutes
6. Remove ramekins and let them cool down
7. Chill in fridge, top with whipped coconut cream and enjoy!

Gentle Peanut Butter Cheesecake
(Prepping time: 10 minutes \ Cooking time: 20 minutes |For 4 servings)

Ingredients
- 1/8 cup smooth peanut butter
- 2 whole eggs
- ½ teaspoon stevia
- ½ teaspoon vanilla extract
- ½ cup sour cream

- 2 tablespoons smooth peanut butter (additional)
- Pinch of stevia
- 2 cups cream cheese

Directions

1. Use a blender and mix in cheese, peanut butter, eggs, stevia and vanilla extract
2. Pour mixture in springform pan, cover with aluminum foil
3. Add 2 cups water to your Ninja Foodi, place pan on a trivet
4. Lock lid and cook on HIGH pressure for 20 minutes. Release pressure naturally over 10 minutes
5. Let it cool down. Add your desired toppings and spread on top. Enjoy!

Decisive Crème Brulee
(Prepping time: 10 minutes \ Cooking time: 20 minutes |For 4 servings)

Ingredients

- 1 cup heavy cream
- ½ tablespoon vanilla extract
- 3 egg yolks
- 1 pinch salt
- ¼ cup stevia

Directions

1. Take a bowl and mix in egg yolks, vanilla extract, salt, and heavy cream
2. Mix well and beat the mixture until combined well
3. Divide mixture between 4 greased ramekins and evenly transfer the ramekins to your Ninja Foodi. Lock lid and select the "Bake/Roast" mode, bake for 35 minutes at 365 degrees F
4. Remove ramekin from Ninja Foodi and wrap with plastic wrap. Refrigerate to chill for 3 hours
5. Serve and enjoy!

The Cool Pot-De-Crème
(Prepping time: 10 minutes \ Cooking time: 20 minutes |For 4 servings)

Ingredients

- 6 egg yolks
- 2 cups heavy whip cream
- 1/3 cup cocoa powder
- 1 tablespoon pure vanilla extract
- ½ teaspoon liquid stevia
- Whipped coconut cream for garnish
- Shaved dark chocolate for garnish

Directions

1. Take a medium sized bowl and whisk in yolks, heavy cream, cocoa powder, vanilla and stevia
2. Pour mixture in 1 and ½ quart baking dish, transfer to Nina Foodi insert
3. Add water to reach about half of the ramekin
4. Lock lid and cook on HIGH pressure for 12 minutes, quick release pressure
5. Remove baking dish from the insert and let it cool
6. Chill in fridge and serve with a garnish of coconut cream, shaved chocolate shavings. Enjoy!

Humming Key Lime Curd
(Prepping time: 10 minutes \ Cooking time: 10 minutes |For 4 servings)

Ingredients

- 3 ounces unsalted butter
- 1 cup liquid stevia
- 2 large eggs
- 2 large egg yolks
- 2/3 cup fresh key lime juice
- 1-2 teaspoons key lime zest

Directions

1. Take food How Toor and add butter and stevia for 2 minutes

2. Slowly add the eggs and yolks to the processor and process To for 1 minute
3. Add Key Lime Juice to the blender and mix well. The mix should look curdled
4. Pour the mix into 3 one cup sized Mason Jars and lock up the lid
5. Place 1 and a ½ cups of water to your Ninja Foodi. Add the steamer basket/trivet
6. Place jars on the basket. Lock up the lid and cook for 10 minutes at HIGH pressure
7. Once done, allow the pressure to release naturally. Remove the jars and open the lids
8. Add Key Lime Zest to the curd and stir well. Place the lid and slightly tighten it
9. Cool for 20 minutes or chill in your fridge overnight. Enjoy!

Runny Eggs In A Cup

(Prepping time: 5 minutes\ Cooking time: 5 minutes |For 4 servings)

Ingredients

- 4 whole eggs
- 1 cup mixed veggies, diced
- ½ cup cheddar cheese, shredded
- ¼ cup half and half
- Salt and pepper to taste
- ½ cup shredded cheese

Directions

1. Take a bowl and add eggs, cheese, veggies, half and a half, pepper, salt and chop up cilantro
2. Mix well and divide the mix amongst four ½ a pint wide mouth mason jars (or similar containers). Slightly put the lid on top
3. Add 2 cups of water to your pot and place a steamer rack on top
4. Place the egg jars on your steamer. Lock up the lid and cook for 5 minutes at HIGH pressure
5. Quick release the pressure. Remove the jars and top them up with ½ a cup of cheese
6. Serve immediately or broil a bit to allow the cheese to melt

Simple Party Week Poached Pears

(Prepping time: 10 minutes \ Cooking time: 10 minutes |For 6 servings)

Ingredients

- 6 firm pears, peeled
- 1 bottle of dry red wine
- 1 bay leaf
- 4 garlic cloves, minced
- 1 stick cinnamon
- 1 fresh ginger, minced
- 1 and 1/3 cup stevia
- Mixed Italian herbs as needed

Directions

1. Peel the pears leaving the stems attached. Pour wine into your Ninja Foodi
2. Add bay leaf, cinnamon, cloves, ginger, stevia, and stir
3. Add pears to the pot and lock up the lid and cook on HIGH pressure for 9 minutes
4. Perform a quick release. Take the pears out using tong and keep them on the side
5. Set the pot to Saute mode and allow the mixture to reduce to half
6. Drizzle the mixture over the pears and enjoy!

A Wedding Worthy Coconut Cake

(Prepping time: 10 minutes \ Cooking time: 10 minutes |For 4 servings)

Ingredients

Dry Ingredients

- 1 cup almond flour
- ½ cup unsweetened shredded coconut
- 1/3 cup Truvia
- 1 teaspoon of apple pie spice
- 1 teaspoon of baking powder

Wet Ingredients

- ¼ cup melted butter
- 2 lightly whisked eggs
- ½ cup heavy whipping cream

Directions

1. Add all dry ingredients in a bowl and add the wet ingredients one at a time, making sure to gently stir after each addition. Empty batter into a pan and cover with foil
2. Add water 1-2 cups of water to Ninja Foodi, place steamer rack
3. Place pan in a steamer rack and lock lid. Cook on HIGH pressure for 40 minutes
4. Naturally, release pressure over 10 minutes. Quick release pressure
5. Remove pan and let it cool for 15-20 minutes. Flip it over onto a platter and garnish as needed. Serve and enjoy!

Uniform Dark Chocolate Cake
(Prepping time: 10 minutes\ Cooking time: 3 hours 10 minutes |For 4 servings)

Ingredients
- 1 cup + 2 tablespoons almond flour
- 1 and ½ teaspoons baking powder
- ½ cup of cocoa powder
- ½ cup granular swerve
- 3 tablespoons unflavored whey powder/egg white protein powder
- ¼ teaspoon salt
- 2/3 cup almond milk, unsweetened
- 3 large whole eggs
- ¾ teaspoon vanilla extract
- 6 tablespoons melted butter
- 1/3 cup chocolate chips, sugar-free

Directions

1. Prepare a six quart Ninja Foodi and grease with oil
2. Add whey protein powder, almond flour, sweetener, baking powder, salt, cocoa powder
3. Fold in butter, eggs, vanilla extract, milk and mix well. Stir in chips and pour batter into the pot
4. Lock lid and SLOW COOK (HIGH) for 3 hours until a toothpick comes out clean from the center
5. Remove heat and let it cool for 20 minutes, slice and serve. Enjoy!

Party Night Lamb Gyros
(Prepping time: 10 minutes\ Cooking time: 25 minutes |For 8 servings)

Ingredients

- 8 garlic cloves
- 1 and ½ teaspoon salt
- 2 teaspoons dried oregano
- 1 and ½ cups of water
- 2 pounds lamb meat, ground
- 2 teaspoons rosemary
- ½ teaspoon pepper
- 1 small onion, chopped
- 2 teaspoons ground marjoram

Directions

1. Add onions, garlic, marjoram, rosemary, salt and pepper to a food processor
2. Process until combined well, add ground lamb meat and process again
3. Press meat mixture gently into a loaf pan. Transfer the pan to your Ninja Foodi pot
4. Lock lid and select "Bake/Roast" mode. Bake for 25 minutes at 375 degrees F
5. Transfer to serving the dish and enjoy!

Extreme Choco Fudge Eatery For The Party
(Prepping time: 20 minutes\ Cooking time: 10 minutes

\ Freeze Time: 3-5 hours |For 24 servings)

Ingredients

- ½ teaspoon organic vanilla extract
- 1 cup heavy whipping cream
- 2 ounces butter, soft
- 2 ounces 70% dark chocolate, finely chopped

Directions

1. Set your Ninja-Foodi to Saute mode with "Medium-HIGH" temperature, add vanilla and heavy cream. Saute for 5 minutes and select "LOW" temperature
2. Saute for 10 minutes more, add butter and chocolate. Saute for 2 minutes more
3. Transfer the mix to a serving dish and refrigerate for a few hours. Serve chilled and enjoy!

The Delightful Cauliflower And Cheese "Cake"
(Prepping time: 10 minutes \ Cooking time: 15 minutes |For 4 servings)

Ingredients

- 2 cups cauliflower, riced
- 2 tablespoons cream cheese
- ½ cup half and half
- ½ cup cheddar cheese, shredded
- Salt and pepper to taste

Directions

1. Take a heatproof dish and add all of the listed ingredients
2. Cover the dish with an aluminum foil. Add 1 and a ½ cup of water to your Ninja Foodi
3. Place a trivet or steamer basket on top. Transfer the covered trivet on top of your basket
4. Lock up the lid and cook for 5 minutes at HIGH pressure. Allow the pressure to release naturally over 10 minutes
5. Heat up your oven broiler and broil the cauliflowers a bit and broil them well until the cheese Is brown. Enjoy!

Fan-Favorite Aunt's Coconut Custard
(Prepping time: 10 minutes \ Cooking time: 5 hours |For 8 servings)

Ingredients

- 1 tablespoon coconut oil
- 8 large eggs, lightly beaten
- 4 cups of coconut milk
- 1 cup Erythritol
- 2 teaspoons stevia powder
- 1 teaspoon coconut extract

Directions

1. Coat the inside of your Ninja Foodi with coconut oil
2. Stir in eggs, coconut milk, stevia, Erythritol, coconut extract to your Ninja Foodi
3. Stir and lock the lid. Cook on SLOW COOKER MODE (LOW) for 5 hours
4. Let it cool for 1-2 hours. Serve and enjoy!

The Christmas Strawberry Shortcake
(Prepping time: 10 minutes \ Cooking time: 15 minutes |For 4 servings)

Ingredients

- 1 whole egg
- ½ cup almond flour
- ½ teaspoon vanilla extract
- 1 tablespoon agave nectar
- 1 tablespoon ghee
- 3 tablespoons strawberries, chopped
- 1 cup of water
- 3 tablespoons coconut whip cream

Directions

1. Add all ingredients except whip cream to a heat resistant mug, add a cup of water to the Ninja Foodi pot. Place a steaming rack in your pot and place the mug in the rack

2. Lock lid and cook on HIGH pressure for 12 minutes. Quick release pressure
3. Remove lid and remove the mug. Top with coconut whipped cream and more strawberries.Enjoy!

Kid-Friendly Peanut Butter Cheesecake
(Prepping time: 10 minutes \ Cooking time: 10 minutes |For 4 servings)

Ingredients

- 2 whole eggs
- 16 ounces cheese
- 2 tablespoons powdered peanut butter
- 1 teaspoon vanilla extract
- 1 tablespoons cocoa
- ½ cup stevia

Directions

1. Take a blender and add eggs, cream cheese and blend until smooth
2. Add rest of the ingredients and blend well. Add the mixture into 4 ounces mason jars
3. Cover with aluminum foil. Add a cup of water to Ninja Foodi
4. Place mason jars and lock lid, cook on HIGH pressure for 15 minutes
5. Naturally, release pressure naturally over 10 minutes. Serve and enjoy!

Quick Lava Molten Cake For Keto Lovers
(Prepping time: 10 minutes\ Cooking time: 10 minutes |For 4 servings)

Ingredients

- 1 whole egg
- 2 tablespoons extra virgin olive oil
- 3 tablespoons stevia
- 4 tablespoons coconut milk
- 4 tablespoons all-purpose almond flour
- 1 tablespoon cacao powder
- Pinch of salt
- Butter for grease

Direction

1. Take a ramekin and grease it up with clarified butter
2. Add 1 cup of water to your Ninja Foodi. Place a steamer rack or trivet on top of your pot
3. Take an e medium sized bowl and add all of the listed ingredients, mix them well until you have a nice batter. Transfer the batter to your ramekins
4. Transfer the ramekins to the steamer rack and lock up the lid
5. Cook on HIGH pressure for 6 minutes
6. Allow the pressure to release naturally over 10 minutes and take the cake out. Serve and enjoy!

Grandmother's Pumpkin Carrot Cake
(Prepping time: 10 minutes\ Cooking time: 15 minutes |For 4 servings)

Ingredients

- 1 tablespoon extra-virgin olive oil
- 2 cups carrots, shredded
- 2 cups pureed pumpkin
- ½ sweet onion, finely chopped
- 1 cup heavy whip cream
- ½ cup cream cheese, soft
- 2 whole eggs
- 1 tablespoon granulated Erythritol
- 1 teaspoon ground nutmeg
- ½ teaspoon salt
- ¼ cup pumpkin seeds, garnish
- ¼ cup of water

Directions

1.Add oil to your Ninja Foodi pot and whisk In carrots, pumpkin, onion, heavy cream, cream cheese, eggs, Erythritol, nutmeg, salt, and water. Stir and lock lid
2.Cook on HIGH pressure for 10 minutes Release pressure naturally over 10 minutes
3.Serve with a topping of pumpkin seeds. Enjoy!

Spiced Up Jack Cheese Muffin

(Prepping time: 10 minutes\ Cooking time: 10 minutes |For 4 servings)

Ingredients

- ¼ cup pepper jack cheese, shredded
- 4 bacon slices
- 4 whole eggs
- 1 Green onion, chopped
- Pinch of garlic powder
- Pinch of pepper
- ¼ teaspoon salt
- 1 and ½ cups of water

Directions

1. Set your Ninja Foodi to Saute mode and add bacon, cook for a few minutes until crispy
2. Wipe bacon grease, pour water and lower rack
3. Take a bowl and beat eggs, pepper, garlic powder, salt. Crumbled bacon and add to the mixture
4. Stir in onion and cheese. Pour mix into 4 silicone muffin cups
5. Arrange on rack and lock lid. Cook on HIGH for 8 minutes
6. Quick release pressure. Serve and enjoy!

Early Morning Vegetable Stock

(Prepping time: 10 minutes\ Cooking time: 15 minutes |For 4 servings)

Ingredients

- 2 small onion, chopped
- 2 stocks celery, diced
- 2 bay leaves
- 2 carrots, diced
- 1 dried shiitake mushroom
- 6 cremini mushrooms, sliced
- 4 crushed garlic cloves
- 1 teaspoon whole peppercorn
- 2 tablespoons coconut aminos
- 8 cups cold water
- Dried herbs as needed

Directions

1. Prepare the ingredients as mentioned above. Add all of the ingredients to the Ninja Foodi
2. Lock up the lid and cook on HIGH pressure for 15 minutes
3. Release the pressure naturally over 10 minutes. Strain the stock through a metal mesh strainer
4. Allow it to cool and chill, serve!

Grandmother's Carrot Halwa

(Prepping time: 10 minutes\ Cooking time: 15 minutes |For 4 servings)

Ingredients

- 2 tablespoons ghee
- 10 cups carrots, peeled and chopped
- 1 cup almond milk
- 1 tablespoon stevia
- 2 teaspoons cardamom powder
- 2 tablespoons raisins
- ½ teaspoons saffron
- 2 tablespoons almond

Directions

1.Set the Ninja Foodi to Saute mode and add ghee, allow the ghee to heat up
2.Add grated carrots and cook for 2-3 minutes. Add almond milk and lock up the lid
3.Cook on HIGH pressure for 5 minutes. Quick release the pressure
4.Add stevia, almond meal, raisins, saffron, and cardamom powder
5.Set the pot to Saute mode and add cook for 5-7 minutes more
6.Garnish with sliced almonds and enjoy chilled!

Lemon And Ricotta Party-Friendly Cheesecake
(Prepping time: 10 minutes \ Cooking time: 10 minutes |For 4 servings)

Ingredients

- 8 ounces cream cheese
- ¼ cup Truvia
- 1 lemon – zested and juiced

- 1/3 cup ricotta cheese
- ½ teaspoon lemon extract
- 2 whole eggs

For topping

- Natural sweetener as needed

- 1 tablespoon sour cream

Directions

1. Take your blender and add all the ingredients except eggs, blend well
2. Add eggs and blend on low speed, making sure to not over beat the eggs
3. Add batter to pan and cover with foil. Add trivet to Ninja Foodi and 2 cups water
4. Place baking pan in trivet and lock lid, cook on HIGH pressure for 30 minutes
5. Release pressure naturally over 10 minutes
6. Blend in sweetener and sour cream in a bowl and decorate the cake with frosting. Enjoy!

Highly Sough-After Egg Devils
(Prepping time: 5 minutes \ Cooking time: 10 minutes |For 6 servings)

Ingredients

- 8 large eggs
- 1 cup of water
- Guacamole as needed

- Sliced radishes as needed
- Furikake
- Keto-Friendly Mayo

Directions

1. Add 1 cup of water to your Ninja Foodi. Place the steamer insert in your Ninja Foodi
2. Arrange the eggs on top of the insert
3. Lock up the lid and cook for about 6 minutes at HIGH pressure
4. Allow the pressure to release naturally. Transfer the eggs to an ice bath and peel the skin
5. Cut the eggs in half and garnish them with dressings of Guacamole, sliced up radishes, Mayonnaise, Furikake, Sliced up Parmesan etc.!

Hearty Mushroom Stock
(Prepping time: 10 minutes\ Cooking time: 30 minutes |For 4 servings)

Ingredients

- 1 ounce dried porcini mushrooms
- 1 ounce dried shiitake mushrooms
- 16 ounces white mushrooms, diced
- 1 large onion, diced
- 1 carrot, diced
- 1 cup dry white wine

- 2 tablespoons coconut aminos
- 1 bay leaf
- 3 sprigs fresh thyme
- 2 sprigs fresh parsley
- 1 teaspoon black peppercorn
- 12 cups water

Directions

1. Soak the porcini and shitake mushroom in 4 cups of hot water
2. Prepare your other ingredients
3. Add mushroom and onion to the Ninja Foodi and Set the pot to sauté mode
4. Saute for a while. Add leeks, garlic, carrots, red wine and stir until the wine has evaporated
5. Add the rest of the remaining ingredients

6. Lock up the lid and cook on HIGH pressure for 30 minutes. Naturally, release the pressure
7. Strain the stock through a metal strainer. Use as needed or store in the fridge

A Christmas-y Pot De Crème
(Prepping time: 10 minutes \ Cooking time: 3 hours |For 8 servings)

Ingredients

- 6 egg yolks
- 2 cups heavy whipping cream
- ½ cup of cocoa powder
- 1 tablespoon pure vanilla extract
- ½ teaspoon stevia
- Whipped coconut cream for garnish
- Shaved dark chocolate for garnish

Directions

1. Take a medium sized bowl and whisk in yolks, heavy cream, cocoa powder, vanilla, stevia
2. Pour mix into 1 and ½ quart baking dish and place dish in the insert of your Ninja Foodi
3. Add just enough water until it reaches halfway up the sides of the baking dish
4. Lock lid and cook on SLOW COOK MODE (LOW) for 3 hours
5. Remove baking dish and let it cool
6. Chill the dessert completely and garnish with whipped coconut cream and shaved dark chocolate.
Enjoy!

Creative Almond And Carrot Cake
(Prepping time: 10 minutes \ Cooking time: 50 minutes |For 4 servings)

Ingredients

- 3 whole eggs
- 1 cup almond flour
- 2/3 cup Swerve
- 1 teaspoon baking powder
- 1 and ½ teaspoons apple pie spice
- ¼ cup of coconut oil
- ½ cup heavy whip cream (Keto friendly)
- 1 cup carrots, shredded
- ½ cup walnuts, chopped

Directions

6. Take a 6-inch pan and grease it up well
7. Take a bowl and add all of the listed ingredients, mix them well until you have a nice and fluffy
mix. Use a hand mixer if needed. Pour the batter into your pan and cover with a foil
8. Place a steamer rack/trivet on top of your Ninja Foodi
9. Add 2 cups of water and transfer the pan to the rack
10. Lock up the lid and cook for 40 minutes on BAKE mode at 350 degrees F
11. Once done, release the pressure naturally over 10 minutes
12. Enjoy the cake as it is or if you want, then add some Keto friendly frosting/toppings

Heavenly Zucchini Bread
(Prepping time: 10 minutes\ Cooking time: 3 hours 15 minutes |For 12 servings)

Ingredients

- 1 cup almond flour
- 2 teaspoons cinnamon
- 1/3 cup coconut flour
- ½ teaspoon salt
- ½ teaspoon baking soda
- 1 and ½ teaspoon baking powder
- 1/3 cup soft coconut oil
- 3 whole eggs
- 2 teaspoons vanilla bean extract
- 1 cup sweetener
- 2 cups shredded zucchini
- ½ cup pecans, chopped

Directions

1. Take a bowl Add coconut and almond flour, salt, baking soda and powder, cinnamon and xanthan gum. Keep it on the side. Take another bowl and mix oil, vanilla, eggs, and sugar, mix well
2. Blend in shredded zucchini and nuts. Pour the baking soda into the bowl with zucchini and stir well. Pour the mixture into your prepared pan
3. Place your trivet/rack in your Ninja Foodi and place pan on top of the trivet
4. Cook on SLOW COOK MODE (HIGH) for 3 hours. Let it cool and wrap in foil, place in the fridge. Serve and enjoy!

Heart Melting Choco-Mousse

(Prepping time: 10 minutes + 6 hours chill times \ Cooking time: 10 minutes |For 4 servings)

Ingredients

- 4 egg yolks
- ¼ cup of water
- ¼ cup cacao
- ½ cup Swerve

- ½ cup whipping cream
- ½ teaspoon vanilla
- ½ cup almond milk
- ¼ teaspoon of sea salt

Directions

1. Take a bowl and whisk in eggs. Add water, swerve, cacao in a saucepan and mix well
2. Stir in milk and cream, let the mixture warm over medium heat until it reaches a boil, remove heat. Measure 1 tablespoon of chocolate mix into the dish with eggs
3. Whisk and slowly empty the remaining chocolate into the mixture
4. Empty the mousse mix into 5 ramekins. Add 1 and ½ cups water to Instant Pot. Place a trivet
5. Place the trivets into the trivet and lock lid, cook on HIGH pressure for 6 minutes
6. Quick release pressure. Chill in the fridge for 6 hours, enjoy!

Chapter 8: 5 Ingredients Or Less Ninja Foodi Recipes

The Coolest New York Strip Steak
(Prepping time: 10 minutes\ Cooking time: 9 minutes |For 4 servings)

Ingredients

- 24 ounces NY strip steak
- ½ teaspoon ground black pepper
- 1 teaspoon salt

Directions

1. Add steaks on a metal trivet and place trivet on your Ninja Foodi
2. Season with salt and pepper
3. Add 1 cup water to the pot (below steaks). Lock lid and cook on HIGH pressure for 1 minute
4. Quick release pressure.
5. Place Air Crisp lid and Air Crisp for 8 minutes for a medium-steak. Remove from pot and enjoy!

French Onion Pork Chops
(Prepping time: 5 minutes\ Cooking time: 20 minutes |For 4 servings)

Ingredients

- 4 pork chops
- 10 ounces French Onion Soup
- ½ cup sour cream
- 10 ounces chicken broth

Directions

1. Add pork chops to your Ninja Foodi. Add broth. Lock lid and cook on HIGH pressure for 12 minutes. Release pressure naturally over 10 minutes.
2. Whisk sour cream and French Onion Soup and pour mixture over pork.
3. Set your Ninja Foodi to Saute mode and cook for 6-8 minutes more. Serve and enjoy!

Hearty Apple Infused Water
(Prepping time: 10 minutes \ Cooking time: 4 minutes |For 4 servings)

Ingredients

- 1 whole apple, chopped
- 5 sticks of cinnamon

Directions

1. Place the above-mentioned ingredients to a mesh steamer basket
2. Place the basket in your pot. Add water to barely cover the content.
3. Lock up the lid and cook on HIGH pressure for 5 minutes
4. Once the cooking is done, quick release the pressure
5. Remove the steamer basket and discard the cooked produce
6. Allow the flavored water to cool and chill. Serve!

Simple And Easy Chicken Breast
(Prepping time: 5 minutes\ Cooking time: 10 minutes |For 4 servings)

Ingredients

- 4 chicken breasts, skinless
- 1 and ¼ cup of water

Direction

1. Add water to Ninja Foodi . Add frozen chicken and lock lid. Cook on HIGH pressure for 10 minutes. Quick release pressure. Open the lid and use just as you want it.

Italian Dark Kale Crisps

(Prepping time: 5 minutes\ Cooking time: 10 minutes |For 4 servings)

Ingredients

- 2 cups kale, Italian dark-leaf
- 1 teaspoon yeast
- 2 tablespoons coconut oil
- ½ teaspoon chili flakes
- ¼ teaspoon salt

Directions

1. Take a bowl and tear the kale roughly and place it into the bowl
2. Sprinkle the kale with coconut oil, yeast, chili flakes and salt
3. Mix up the kale well till it becomes consistent
4. Insert the air fryer basket and in the Ninja Foodi and then transfer the kale
5. Air fryer the meal for 10 minutes. Serve and enjoy!

Quick Ginger And Sesame Chicken

(Prepping time: 5 minutes\ Cooking time: 10 minutes |For 4 servings)

Ingredients

- 1 and ½ pounds chicken thighs, no skin
- 2 tablespoons coconut aminos
- 1 tablespoon agave
- 1 tablespoon ginger, minced
- 1 tablespoon garlic-sesame oil
- 1 tablespoon rice vinegar
- Red onion, sliced for salad
- Carrots julienned for salad
- Cucumbers julienned for salad

Direction

1. Slice thigh into large chunks and add rest of the ingredients to a heat-safe dish
2. Place foil over the bowl. Add 2 cups water to Ninja Foodi
3. Place steamer rack in Ninja Foodi and place the bowl over the rack
4. Lock lid and cook on HIGH pressure for 10 minutes. Naturally, release pressure over 10 minutes
5. Shred meat and serve with a tossing of the salad. Enjoy!

Butter Melted Broccoli Florets

(Prepping time: 10 minutes\ Cooking time: 8 minutes |For 4 servings)

Ingredients

- 4 tablespoons butter
- Salt and pepper to taste
- 2 pounds broccoli florets
- 1 cup whip cream

Directions

1. Arrange basket in the bottom of your Ninja Foodi and add water
2. Place florets on top of the basket. Lock lid and cook on HIGH pressure for 5 minutes
3. Quick release pressure and transfer florets to the pot itself
4. Season with salt, pepper and add butter
5. Lock crisping lid and Air Crisp on 360 degrees F 3 minutes
6. Transfer to a serving plate. Serve and enjoy!

The Epic Fried Eggs

(Prepping time: 5 minutes\ Cooking time: 10 minutes |For 2 servings)

Ingredients

- 4 eggs
- ¼ teaspoon ground black pepper
- 1 teaspoon butter, melted
- ¾ teaspoon salt

Directions

1. Take a small egg pan and brush it with butter. Beat the eggs in the pan
2. Sprinkle with the ground black pepper and salt. Transfer the egg pan in the pot
3. Lower the air fryer lid. Cook the meat for 10 minutes at 350 F. Serve immediately and enjoy!

Gentle Keto Butter Fish

(Prepping time: 10 minutes\ Cooking time: 30 minutes |For 6 servings)

Ingredients

- 1 pound salmon fillets
- 2 tablespoons ginger/garlic paste
- 3 green chilies, chopped
- Salt and pepper to taste
- ¾ cup butter

Directions

5. Season salmon fillets with ginger, garlic paste, salt, pepper
6. Place salmon fillets to Ninja Foodi and top with green chilies and butter
7. Lock lid and BAKE/ROAST for 30 minutes at 360 degrees F
8. Bake for 30 minutes and enjoy!

Sensational Carrot Puree

(Prepping time: 10 minutes \ Cooking time: 4 minutes |For 4 servings)

Ingredients

- 1 and a ½ pound carrots, chopped
- 1 tablespoon of butter at room temperature
- 1 tablespoon of agave nectar
- ¼ teaspoon of sea salt
- 1 cup of water

Directions

1. Clean and peel your carrots properly. Roughly chop up them into small pieces
2. Add 1 cup of water to your Pot
3. Place the carrots in a steamer basket and place the basket in the Ninja Foodi
4. Lock up the lid and cook on HIGH pressure for 4 minutes. Perform a quick release
5. Transfer the carrots to a deep bowl and use an immersion blender to blend the carrots
6. Add butter, nectar, salt, and puree. Taste the puree and season more if needed. Enjoy!

Simple Broccoli Florets

(Prepping time: 10 minutes\ Cooking time: 6 minutes |For 4 servings)

Ingredients

- 4 tablespoons butter, melted
- Salt and pepper to taste
- 2 pounds broccoli florets
- 1 cup whipping cream

Directions

1. Place a steamer basket in your Ninja Foodi (bottom part) and add water
2. Place florets on top of the basket and lock lid
3. Cook on HIGH pressure for 5 minutes. Quick release pressure
4. Transfer florets from the steamer basket to the pot. Add salt, pepper, butter, and stir
5. Lock crisping lid and cook on Air Crisp mode for 360 degrees F. Serve and enjoy!

Awesome Magical 5 Ingredient Shrimp

(Prepping time: 10 minutes\ Cooking time: 15 minutes |For 4 servings)

Ingredients

- 2 tablespoons butter
- ½ teaspoon smoked paprika
- 1 pound shrimps, peeled and deveined
- Lemongrass stalks
- 1 red chili pepper, seeded and chopped

Directions

1. Take a bowl and mix all of the ingredients well, except lemongrass and marinate for 1 hour
2. Transfer to Ninja Foodi and lock lid, BAKE/ROAST for 15 minutes at 345 degrees F
3. Once done, serve and enjoy!

Romantic Mustard Pork

(Prepping time: 10 minutes\ Cooking time: 30 minutes |For 4 servings)

Ingredients

- 2 tablespoons butter
- 2 tablespoons Dijon mustard (Keto-Friendly)
- 4 pork chops
- Salt and pepper to taste
- 1 tablespoon fresh rosemary, coarsely chopped

Directions

1. Take a bowl and add pork chops, cover with Dijon mustard and carefully sprinkle rosemary, salt, and pepper. Let it marinate for 2 hours
2. Add butter and marinated pork chops to your Ninja Foodi pot
3. Lock lid and cook on Low-Medium Pressure for 30 minutes
4. Release pressure naturally over 10 minutes. Take the dish out, serve and enjoy!

Creative And Easy Lamb Roast

(Prepping time: 10 minutes\ Cooking time: 60 minutes |For 6 servings)

Ingredients

- 2 pounds lamb roast
- 1 cup onion soup
- 1 cup beef broth
- Salt and pepper to taste

Directions

1. Transfer lamb roast to your Ninja Foodi pot. Add onion soup, beef broth, salt, and pepper
2. Lock lid and cook on Medium-HIGH pressure for 55 minutes
3. Release pressure naturally over 10 minutes. Transfer to serving bowl, serve and enjoy!

Crispy Tofu And Mushrooms

(Prepping time: 10 minutes\ Cooking time: 10 minutes |For 2 servings)

Ingredients

- 8 tablespoons parmesan cheese, shredded
- 2 cups fresh mushrooms, chopped
- 2 blocks tofu, pressed and cubed
- Salt and pepper to taste
- 8 tablespoons butter

Directions

1. Take a bowl and mix in tofu, salt, and pepper

2. Set your Ninja Foodi to Saute mode and add seasoned tofu, Saute for 5 minutes
3. Add mushroom, cheese and Saute for 3 minutes. Lock crisping lid and Air Crisp for 3 minutes at 350 degrees F. Transfer to serving plate and enjoy!

A Hearty Sausage Meal

(Prepping time: 10 minutes\ Cooking time: 20 minutes |For 6 servings)

Ingredients

- 4 whole eggs
- 4 sausages, cooked and sliced
- 2 tablespoons butter
- ½ cup mozzarella cheese, grated
- ½ cup cream

Directions

1. Take a bowl and mix everything
2. Add egg mix to your Ninja Foodi, top with cheese and sausage slices
3. Lock pressure lid and select "BAKE/ROAST" mode and cook for 20 minutes at 345 degrees F
4. Take it out once done, serve and enjoy!

Deserving Mushroom Saute

(Prepping time: 10 minutes\ Cooking time: 15 minutes |For 8 servings)

Ingredients

- 1 pound white mushrooms, stems trimmed
- 2 tablespoons unsalted butter
- ½ teaspoon salt
- ¼ cup of water

Directions

1. Quarter medium mushrooms and cut any large mushrooms into eight
2. Put mushrooms, butter, and salt in your Foodi's inner pot
3. Add water and lock pressure lid, making sure to seal the valve
4. Cook on HIGH pressure for 5 minutes, quick release pressure once did
5. Once done, set your pot to Saute mode on HIGH mode and bring the mix to a boil over 5 minutes until all the water evaporates
6. Once the butter/water has evaporated, stir for 1 minute until slightly browned. Enjoy!

Slightly Zesty Lamb Chops

(Prepping time: 5 minutes \ Cooking time: 40 minutes |For 4 servings)

Ingredients

- 4 tablespoons butter
- 3 tablespoons lemon juice
- 4 lamb chops, with bone
- 2 tablespoons almond flour
- 1 cup picante sauce

Directions

1. Coat chops with almond flour, keep them on the side
2. Set your Ninja Foodi to Saute mode and add butter, chops
3. Saute for 2 minutes, add picante sauce and lemon juice
4. Lock lid and cook on HIGH pressure for 40 minutes. Release naturally and serve, enjoy!

Bacon And Scrambled Egg

(Prepping time: 10 minutes\ Cooking time: 5-10 minutes |For 2 servings)

Ingredients

- 4 strips bacon
- 2 whole eggs
- 1 tablespoon milk
- Salt and pepper to taste

Directions

1. Add bacon inside your Ninja Foodi. Lock Crisping Lid and set it to Air Crisp mode
2. Cook for 3 minutes at 390 degrees F. Flip and cook for 2 minutes more
3. Remove bacon and keep it on the side. Take a bowl and whisk in eggs and milk
4. Season with salt and pepper. Set your Ninja Foodi to Saute mode
5. Add eggs, cook until firm. Serve and enjoy!

Delicious Creamy Crepes
(Prepping time: 5 minutes \ Cooking time: 30 minutes |For 4 servings)

Ingredients

- 1 and ½ teaspoon Splenda
- 3 organic eggs
- 3 tablespoons coconut flour
- ½ cup heavy cream
- 3 tablespoons coconut oil, melted and divided

Directions

1. Take a bowl and mix in 1 and ½ tablespoons coconut oil, Splenda, eggs, salt and mix well
2. Beat well until mixed. Add coconut flour and keep beating. Stir in heavy cream, beat well
3. Set your Ninja Foodi to Saute mode and add ¼ of the mixture
4. Saute for 2 minutes on each side. Repeat until all ingredients are used up. Enjoy!

Egg Stuffed Avocado Dish
(Prepping time: 10 minutes\ Cooking time: 5 minutes |For 6 servings)

Ingredients

- ½ tablespoon fresh lemon juice
- 1 medium ripe avocado, peeled, pitted and chopped
- 6 organic eggs, boiled, peeled and cut in half lengthwise
- Salt to taste
- ½ cup fresh watercress, trimmed

Directions

1. Place steamer basket at the bottom of your Ninja Foodie. Add water
2. Add watercress on the basket and lock lid
3. Cook on HIGH pressure for 3 minutes, quick release the pressure and drain the watercress
4. Remove egg yolks and transfer them to a bowl
5. Add watercress, avocado, lemon juice, salt into the bowl and mash with a fork
6. Place egg whites in a serving bowl and fill them with the watercress and avocado dish
7. Serve and enjoy!

Lovely Asparagus Bites
(Prepping time: 5 minutes \ Cooking time: 10 minutes |For 4 servings)

Ingredients

- 1 cup asparagus
- ½ cup coconut, desiccated
- ½ cup feta cheese

Directions

1. Add coconut in a shallow dish, coat asparagus with coconut
2. Transfer to Ninja Foodi and top with feta cheese
3. Lock Crisping lid and Air Crisp for 10 minutes at 360 degrees F. Serve and enjoy!

Easy to Make Mustard Pork Chops

(Prepping time: 5 minutes \ Cooking time: 30 minutes |For 4 servings)

Ingredients

- 2 tablespoons butter
- 2 tablespoons Dijon mustard
- 4 pork chops
- Salt and pepper to taste
- 1 tablespoon fresh rosemary

Directions

1. Marinate pork chops with Dijon mustard, rosemary, salt, and pepper for 2 hours
2. Put butter and marinated pork chops in Ninja Foodi. Lock lid and cook on LOW pressure for 30 minutes. Release naturally and enjoy!

Generous Lemon Mousse

(Prepping time: 5 minutes + chill time \ Cooking time: 12 minutes |For 4 servings)

Ingredients

- 1-ounce cream cheese, soft
- ½ cup heavy cream
- 1/8 cup fresh lemon juice
- ½ teaspoon lemon liquid stevia
- 2 pinch salt

Directions

1. Mix in cream cheese, heavy cream, lemon juice, salt and stevia in a bowl
2. Pour mix into ramekins and transfer ramekins to Ninja Foodi
3. Lock lid and cook on BAKE/ROAST mode for 12 minutes at 350 degrees F
4. Pour mixture into serving glass and chill for 3 hours, serve and enjoy!

Terrific Baked Spinach Quiche

(Prepping time: 10 minutes\ Cooking time: 5-10 minutes |For 2 servings)

Ingredients

- 1 tablespoons butter, melted
- 1 pack frozen spinach, thawed
- 5 organic eggs, beaten
- Salt and pepper to taste
- 3 cups monetary jack cheese, shredded

Directions

1. Set your pot to Saute mode and add butter, spinach
2. Saute for 3 minutes, transfer dish out of the bowl
3. Add eggs, Monterey Jack cheese, salt, pepper to a bowl and transfer to the greased mold
4. Place molds inside Ninja Foodi and lock lid, cook on BAKE/ROAST mode for 30 minutes at 360 degrees F. Remove from Ninja Foodi and cut into wedges. Serve and enjoy!

Juicy Keto Lamb Roast

(Prepping time: 5 minutes \ Cooking time: 55 minutes |For 4 servings)

Ingredients

- 2 pounds lamb roast
- 1 cup onion soup
- 1 cup beef broth
- Salt and pepper

Directions

1. Add lamb roast to Ninja Foodi, add onion soup, beef broth, salt, and pepper
2. Lock lid and cook on HIGH pressure for 55 minutes
3. Release pressure naturally over 10 minutes. Serve and enjoy!

Warm Avocado Chips
(Prepping time: 10 minutes\ Cooking time: 10 minutes |For 4 servings)

Ingredients

- 4 tablespoons butter
- 4 raw avocados, peeled and sliced in chips
- Salt and pepper to taste

Directions

1. Season avocado slices with salt and pepper
2. Grease pot of Ninja Foodi with butter and add the avocado slices
3. Air Crisp for 10 minutes at 350 degrees F. Remove from Foodi and transfer to a plate
4. Serve and enjoy!

Nutty Assorted Collection
(Prepping time: 5 minutes\ Cooking time: 15 minutes |For 4 servings)

Ingredients

- 1 tablespoon butter, melted
- ½ cup raw cashew nuts
- 1 cup of raw almonds
- Salt to taste

Directions

1. Add nuts to your Ninja Foodi pot
2. Lock lid and cook on "Air Crisp" mode for 10 minutes at 350 degrees F
3. Remove nuts into a bowl and add melted butter and salt. Toss well to coat
4. Return the mix to your Ninja Foodi, lock lid and bake for 5 minutes on BAKE/ROAST mode
5. Serve and enjoy!

Exquisite Mediterranean Cheese Spinach
(Prepping time: 5 minutes\ Cooking time: 15 minutes |For 4 servings)

Ingredients

- 4 tablespoons butter
- 2 pounds spinach, chopped and boiled
- Salt and pepper to taste
- 1 and ½ cups feta cheese, grated
- 4 teaspoons fresh lemon zest, grated

Directions

1. Take a bowl and mix spinach, butter, salt, pepper and transfer the mixture to your Crisping Basket of the Ninja Foodi. Transfer basket to your Foodi and lock Crisping lid
2. Cook for 15 minutes on Air Crisp mode on 340 degrees F
3. Serve by stirring in olives, lemon zest, and feta. Enjoy!

English Green Peas And Asparagus
(Prepping time: 5 minutes\ Cooking time: 3 minutes |For 4 servings)

Ingredients

- 1-2 garlic cloves, minced
- 2 cups English Green Peas
- 2 cups asparagus
- ½ cup vegetable broth
- 1 lemon, zested
- 2-3 tablespoons pine nuts

Directions

1. Set the pot to Saute mode and add oil, allow the oil to heat up. Add garlic, cumin
2. Add the cut up bell pepper, potatoes, spices and give it a nice mix
3. Sprinkle water. Lock up the lid and cook on HIGH pressure for 2 minutes
4. Release the pressure naturally. Stir in mango powder, lemon juice
5. Mix and garnish with a bit of cilantro. Enjoy!

The Pecan Delight

(Prepping time: 10 minutes\ Cooking time: 2 hours |For 4 servings)

Ingredients

- 3 cups of raw pecans
- ¼ cup of date paste
- 2 teaspoon of vanilla beans extract
- 1 teaspoon of sea salt
- 1 tablespoon of coconut oil

Directions

1. Add all of the listed ingredients to your Ninja Foodi
2. Cook on LOW for about 3 hours, making sure to stir it from time to time
3. Once done, allow it to cool and serve!

Favorite Peanut Butter Cups

(Prepping time: 5 minutes \ Cooking time: 30 minutes |For 4 servings)

Ingredients

- 1 cup butter
- ¼ cup heavy cream
- 2 ounces unsweetened chocolate
- ¼ cup peanut butter, separated
- 4 packs stevia

Directions

1. Melt peanut butter, butter in a bowl and mix, stir in chocolate, stevia, heavy cream
2. Mix well and pour in baking mold
3. Put mold in Ninja Foodi and lock lid, BAKE/ROAST for 30 minutes at 360 degrees F
4. Transfer to transfer plate and serve. Enjoy!

Crispy Mixed Up Nuts

(Prepping time: 5 minutes \ Cooking time: 15 minutes |For 4 servings)

Ingredients

- 1 tablespoons butter, melted
- ½ cup raw cashew nuts
- 1 cup of raw almonds
- 1 cup Walnuts

Directions

1. Add nuts in Ninja Foodi, lock Air Crisping lid. Air Crisp for 10 minutes at 350 degrees F
2. Remove nuts into a bowl and add melted butter and salt
3. Toss well and return to Foodi. Lock lid and BAKE/ROAST for 5 minutes. Serve and enjoy!

Quick And Simple Pork Carnitas

(Prepping time: 5 minutes\ Cooking time: 23 minutes |For 4 servings)

Ingredients

- 2 tablespoons butter
- 2 orange, juiced

- 2 pounds pork shoulder, with bone
- Salt and pepper to taste
- 1 teaspoon garlic powder

Directions

1. Season pork with salt and pepper
2. Set your Ninja Foodi to Saute mode and add butter, garlic powder
3. Saute for 1 minute, add seasoned pork. Saute for 3 minutes, pour orange juice
4. Lock lid and cook on HIGH pressure for 15 minutes. Release pressure naturally
5. Add crisping lid and lock, broil for 8 minutes at 375 degrees F. Serve and enjoy!

Simple Teriyaki Chicken
(Prepping time: 10 minutes\ Cooking time: 8 hours |For 4 servings)

Ingredients

- 2 and ½ pounds skinless chicken breasts
- 1 cup low sodium chicken broth
- 2 ounces pepperoncini, with liquid
- 2 tablespoons Italian seasoning

Directions

1. Add listed ingredients to your Ninja Foodi
2. Stir and close the lid, cook on SLOW COOK mode (LOW) for 4 hours. Slice chicken and enjoy!

Lovely Yet "Stinky" Garlic
(Prepping time: 5 minutes \ Cooking time: 15 minutes |For 6 servings)

Ingredients

- 3 large garlic bulb
- A drizzle of olive oil
- 1 cup of water

Directions

1. Place your steamer rack on top of the Ninja Foodi. Add 1 cup of water
2. Prepare the garlic by slicing the top portion
3. Place the bulbs in your steamer basket and lock up the lid
4. Cook on HIGH pressure for about 6 minutes
5. Allow the pressure to release naturally over 10 minutes. Take the garlic out using tongs (very hot!) and drizzle olive oil on top. Broil for about 5 minutes and serve!

Simple Veggie And Bacon Platter
(Prepping time: 10 minutes\ Cooking time: 25 minutes |For 2 servings)

Ingredients

- 1 green bell pepper, seeded and chopped
- 4 bacon slices
- ½ cup parmesan cheese
- 1 tablespoon avocado mayonnaise
- 2 scallions, chopped

Directions

1. Arrange bacon slices in Ninja Foodi, top with avocado mayo, pepper, scallions, cheese
2. Lock lid and Cook on "BAKE/ROAST" mode for 25 minutes at 365 degrees F
3. Remove from Foodi and serve, enjoy!

Cream Cheese And Zucchini Fries
(Prepping time: 5 minutes \ Cooking time: 10 minutes |For 4 servings)

Ingredients

- 1 pound zucchini, sliced into 2 and ½ inch
- Salt as needed
- 1 cup cream cheese
- 2 tablespoons olive oil

Directions

1. Add zucchini in a colander and add cream cheese. Add oil, zucchini to Ninja Foodi
2. Lock lid and Air Crisp for 10 minutes at 365 degrees F. Remove from Foodi, serve and enjoy! -

Creamy Beef And Garlic Steak
(Prepping time: 5 minutes + marinate time \ Cooking time: 40 minutes |For 4 servings)

Ingredients
- ½ cup butter
- 4 garlic cloves, minced
- 2 pounds beef top sirloin steak
- Salt and pepper to taste
- 1 and ½ cup cream

Directions

1. Rub beef sirloin steaks with garlic, salt, and pepper. Marinate beef with butter, cream and keep it on the side. Place grill in Ninja Foodi and transfer the steaks to the Foodi
2. Lock lid and BROIL for 30 minutes at 365 degrees F, making sure to flip about after halfway through. Serve and enjoy!

Delicious Bacon Swiss Pork Chops
(Prepping time: 5 minutes + marinate time \ Cooking time: 15 minutes |For 4 servings)

Ingredients

- ½ cup Swiss cheese, shredded
- 4 pork chops, with bone
- 6 bacon strips, cut in half
- Salt and pepper to taste
- 1 tablespoon butter

Directions

1. Season pork chops with salt and pepper
2. Set your Ninja Foodi to Saute mode and add chops and butter, Saute for 3 minutes each side. Add Swiss Cheese. Lock lid and cook on MEDIUM-LOW pressure for 15 minutes
3. Quick release pressure. Transfer steaks to a platter and enjoy!

Hearty Baked Brisket
(Prepping time: 10 minutes\ Cooking time: 4 minutes |For 4 servings)

Ingredients

- 20 garlic cloves, minced
- 2 bunch cilantro, chopped
- 1 and ¼ cups red wine vinegar
- 3 onions, sliced thinly
- 3 pounds beef brisket

Directions

8. Place reversible rack in your pot and attach crisping lid. Take a blender and add garlic, cilantro, red wine, onion, and pulse. Transfer mix to Ziploc bag and add beef brisket
9. Season with salt and pepper. Let them marinate for 2 hours
10. Transfer marinated beef to the rack and lock crisping lid, press "BAKE/ROAST" button and cook for 60 minutes
11. Take a pan and place it over medium heat, bring the marinade to simmer until reduced

12. Use sauce brush to brush the brisket halfway through. Serve and enjoy!

Nice Beef Fajitas
(Prepping time: 5 minutes\ Cooking time: 7 hours 8 minutes |For 4 servings)

Ingredients

- 2 tablespoons butter
- 2 bell pepper, sliced
- 2 pounds beef, sliced
- 2 tablespoons fajita seasoning
- 2 onions, sliced

Directions

1. Set your Ninja Foodi to Saute mode and add butter, onion, fajita seasoning, pepper, and beef. Saute for 3 minutes, Lock lid and set SLOW COOK mode, cook for 7 hours. Serve and enjoy!

Divine Keto Nut Porridge
(Prepping time: 5 minutes \ Cooking time: 15 minutes |For 4 servings)

Ingredients

- 4 teaspoons coconut oil, melted
- 1 cup pecans, halved
- 2 cups of water
- 2 tablespoons stevia
- 1 cup cashew nuts, raw and unsalted

Directions

1. Add cashews and pecans to a food processor, pulse until chunky
2. Add nuts mix to Ninja Foodi, stir in water, coconut oil, and stevia
3. Set your pot to Saute mode and cook for 15 minutes. Serve and enjoy!

Delicious Prosciutto Cane Wraps
(Prepping time: 10 minutes\ Cooking time: 5 minutes |For 4 servings)

Ingredients

- 1 pound thick asparagus
- 80 ounces prosciutto, thinly sliced

Directions

1. Take a steamer rack/trivet and place it on top of your Ninja Foodi
2. Wrap up the asparagus sticks with prosciutto and prepare your spears
3. Place them in layers on your rack
4. Lock up the lid and cook for 2-3 minutes at HIGH pressure
5. Allow the pressure to release naturally over 10 minutes
6. Open up your lid and take out the steamer basket
7. Transfer the asparagus to your serving plate. Season with some salt if you prefer and enjoy!

Green Bean Mix
(Prepping time: 5 minutes\ Cooking time: 2 hours |For 4 servings)

Ingredients

- 4 cups green beans, trimmed
- 2 tablespoons butter, melted
- 1 tablespoon date paste
- Salt and pepper as needed
- ¼ teaspoon coconut aminos

Directions

1. Add green beans, date paste, pepper, salt, coconut aminos, and stir
2. Toss and place lid. Cook SLOW COOK MODE (LOW)) for 2 hours. Serve and enjoy!

5 Ingredients Keto Choco Cheese Cake
(Prepping time: 5 minutes + chill time\ Cooking time: 15 minutes |For 4 servings)

Ingredients

- 2cups cream cheese, soft
- 2 whole eggs
- 2 tablespoons cocoa powder
- 1 teaspoon pure vanilla extract
- ½ cup Swerve

Directions

3. Add eggs, cocoa powder, vanilla extract, cheese in an immersion blender and blend until smooth. Transfer mixture to a mason jar
4. Put the insert in Ninja Foodi and place mason jars on the insert. Lock lid and "BAKE/ROAST" for 15 minutes at 360 degrees F. Let them chill for 2 hours, serve and enjoy!

Helpful Raspberry And Peach Aid
(Prepping time: 5 minutes\ Cooking time: 5 minutes |For 4 servings)

Ingredients

- 1 cup peaches, chopped
- ½ cup raspberries
- 1 lemon, zest and juiced

Directions

1. Place the above-mentioned ingredients to a mesh steamer basket
2. Place the basket in your Ninja Foodi. Add water to barely cover the content
3. Lock up the lid and cook on HIGH pressure for 5 minutes
4. Once the cooking is done, quick release the pressure
5. Remove the steamer basket and discard the cooked produce
6. Allow the flavored water to cool and chill. Serve!

The Eldar Shrub
(Prepping time: 5 minutes\ Cooking time: 20 minutes |For 4 servings)

Ingredients

- 1 cup dried elderberries
- 2 cups apple cider vinegar
- 2 cups of water
- 2 tablespoons agave nectar
- ½ cup oregano, chopped

Directions

1. Add the listed ingredients to your Ninja Foodi
2. Lock up the lid and cook on HIGH pressure for 20 minutes
3. Release the pressure naturally over 10 minutes and strain the mixture into canning jars
4. Allow it to sit and chill and enjoy!

Cool "Cooked" Ice Tea
(Prepping time: 5 minutes\ Cooking time: 4 minutes |For 4 servings)

Ingredients

- 4 teabags
- 6 cups of water

- 2 tablespoons agave nectar

Directions

5. Add the listed ingredients to your Ninja Foodi and lock up the lid
6. Cook on HIGH pressure for 4 minutes. Release the pressure naturally
7. Allow it to cool and serve over ice. Enjoy!

Chapter 9: 20 Minutes Ninja Foodi Recipes

Quick And Easy Buttery Pancake
(Prepping time: 5 minutes\ Cooking time: 10 minutes |For 4 servings)

Ingredients

- 2 cups cream cheese
- 2 cups almond flour
- 6 large whole eggs
- 1/4 teaspoon salt
- 2 tablespoons butter
- ¼ teaspoon ground ginger
- ½ teaspoon cinnamon powder

Directions

1. Take a large bowl and add cream cheese, eggs, 1 tablespoon butter. Blend on high until creamy. Slow add flour and keep beating. Add salt, ginger, cinnamon. Keep beating until fully mixed. Set your Ninja Foodi to Saute mode and grease stainless steel insert. Add butter and heat it up. Add ½ cup batter and cook for 2-3 minutes, flip and cook the other side
2. Repeat with the remaining batter, Enjoy!

Decisive Asian Brussels
(Prepping time: 5 minutes\ Cooking time: 4 minutes |For 4 servings)

Ingredients
- 1 pound Brussels, halved
- 3 tablespoons chicken stock
- Salt and pepper to taste
- 1 teaspoon toasted sesame seeds
- 1 tablespoon green onions, chopped
- 1 and ½ tablespoons stevia
- 1 tablespoon coconut aminos
- 2 tablespoons olive oil
- 1 tablespoon Keto sriracha sauce

Directions

1. Take a bowl and mix in oil, coconut aminos, Sriracha, stevia, salt, pepper and whisk well
2. Put Brussels to Ninja Foodi and add sriracha mix, stock, green onions, sesame, stir
3. Lock lid and cook on HIGH pressure for 4 minutes. Serve and enjoy!

Busy Man's Bacon Jalapeno
(Prepping time: 6 minutes\ Cooking time: 3 minutes |For 3 servings)

Ingredients

- 6 jalapeno peppers
- 6 bacon strips, chopped and cooked
- ¼ teaspoon ground cumin
- 1 teaspoon garlic, minced
- 1-ounces ground beef, cooked
- 6 tablespoons cream cheese
- ½ teaspoon salt

Directions

1. Trim the ends of the peppers and remove the seeds
2. Add cream cheese, ground cumin and salt then mix them
3. Then add ground beef and stir well. Add bacon
4. Put the mixture into the peppers. Transfer on the rack. Lower the air fryer lid
5. Cook the jalapenos for 3 minutes at 365 F. Serve immediately and enjoy!

Lovely Bok Choy Soup
(Prepping time: 5 minutes\ Cooking time: 13 minutes |For 4 servings)

Ingredients

- 4 chicken thighs
- 4 cups beef bone broth
- 1 pound Bok choy
- Salt and pepper to taste
- ¼ teaspoon dried dill weed
- 1 teaspoon bay leaf

Directions

1. Add chicken thigh to Ninja Foodi, add 1 cup broth. Lock lid and cook on HIGH pressure for 8 minutes. Release pressure naturally over 10 minutes. Add remaining ingredients and lock lid again. Cook on HIGH pressure for 5 minutes more
2. Quick release pressure. Serve and enjoy!

Mushroom Hats Stuffed With Cheese

(Prepping time: 10 minutes\ Cooking time: 6 minutes |For 3 servings)

Ingredients

- 10 ounces mushroom hats
- 2 ounces parmesan, grated
- ½ teaspoon oregano, dried
- 1-ounce fresh parsley, chopped
- 1-ounce cheddar cheese, grated
- 2 tablespoons cream cheese
- ½ teaspoon chili flakes

Directions

1. Mix together the chopped pars0ley, cream cheese, chili flakes, grated cheese, and dried oregano. Fill up the mushroom hats with the cheese mixture
2. Place the mushroom hats in the rack. Lower the air fryer lid
3. Cook the meat for 6 minutes at 400 F. Then check the mushroom cooked or not if you want you can cook for 2-3 minutes more. Serve hot and enjoy!

A King's Favorite Egg Salad

(Prepping time: 5 minutes\ Cooking time: 15 minutes |For 2 servings)

Ingredients

- 3 eggs
- 1 teaspoon olive oil
- ½ white onion, sliced
- 1 avocado, chopped
- 3 tablespoons heavy cream
- ½ teaspoon paprika
- ½ teaspoon salt

Directions

1. Take a trivet and place the eggs into it. Lower the air fryer lid
2. Cook the eggs for 15 minutes at 270 F
3. In between, combine heavy cream, salt, chopped avocado, onion and paprika
4. Once cooked, let the chill in the icy water and then peel them
5. Cut the eggs into the quarters and add in the avocado mixture
6. Then stir the salad. Serve and enjoy!

Come-Back Cauliflower And Parm

(Prepping time: 5 minutes\ Cooking time: 4 minutes |For 4 servings)

Ingredients

- 1 cauliflower head
- ½ cup vegetable stock
- 2 garlic cloves, minced
- Salt and pepper to taste
- 1/3 cup grated parmesan
- 1 tablespoons parsley, chopped

- 3 tablespoons olive oil

Directions

1. Take a bowl and add oil, garlic, salt, pepper cauliflower, and toss. Transfer to Ninja Foodi
2. Add stock and lock lid, cook on HIGH pressure for 4 minutes
3. Add parsley, parmesan and toss. Serve and enjoy!

The Chorizo Flavored Casserole
(Prepping time: 5 minutes\ Cooking time: 10 minutes |For 3 servings)

Ingredients

- 3 eggs, whisked
- 2 ounces chorizo, chopped
- 3 ounces cauliflower hash brown, cooked
- 1-ounces mozzarella, sliced
- ¾ cup almond milk
- ½ teaspoon butter
- 1/3 teaspoon chili flakes

Directions

1. Start with melting butter then whisk it with chorizo, chili flakes, eggs, and almond milk
2. Add hash brown and stir well. Take a cake pan and put the egg mixture into it
3. Then place in the Ninja Foodi. Close the Air Crisping lid and crisp on Air Crisp mode for 2 minutes at 365 F. Serve and enjoy!

Sensible Chinese Salad
(Prepping time: 5 minutes\ Cooking time: 5 minutes |For 4 servings)

Ingredients

- 2 tablespoons sesame oil
- 1 yellow onion, chopped
- 1 teaspoon garlic, minced
- 1 pound cabbage, shredded
- ¼ cup rice wine vinegar
- ¼ teaspoon Szechuan pepper
- ½ teaspoon salt
- 1 tablespoon coconut aminos

Directions

1. Set your Ninja Foodi to Saute mode and add oil, let it heat up
2. Add onion and cook until tender. Add rest of ingredients and stir
3. Lock lid and cook on HIGH pressure for 3 minutes. Quick release pressure
4. Transfer cabbage mix to the salad bowl and serve. Enjoy!

Mushroom And Bok Choy Health Bite
(Prepping time: 7 minutes\ Cooking time: 7 minutes |For 3 servings)

Ingredients

- 10 ounces bok choy, chopped
- 1 tablespoon coconut oil
- 5 ounces white mushrooms, chopped
- 1 teaspoon salt

Directions

1. Mix together the mushrooms and bok choy. Add all the ingredients and mix them well
2. Sprinkle with coconut oil and salt. Make a shake to the ingredients and place them into Ninja Foodi. Lower the air fryer lid. Cook the side dish for 7 minutes at 400 F
3. Stir generously. Serve hot and enjoy!

Cool Cabbage Soup
(Prepping time: 5 minutes\ Cooking time: 5 minutes |For 4 servings)

Ingredients

- ½ pound Capoccolo, chopped
- Salt and pepper to taste
- ½ teaspoon cayenne pepper
- 1 onion, chopped
- 1 celery stalk, chopped
- 1 parsnip, chopped
- 1 pound cabbage, cut into wedges
- 2 cups broth
- 1 cup tomatoes, pureed
- 1 cup of water
- 1 bay leaf

Directions

1. Add listed ingredients to Ninja Foodi. Lock lid and cook on HIGH pressure for 3 minutes
2. Quick release pressure once did. Ladle soup to serving bowls and serve, enjoy!

Sensible Steamed Keto Salad
(Prepping time: 5 minutes\ Cooking time: 5 minutes |For 4 servings)

Ingredients

- 1 cup of water
- 8 tomatoes, sliced
- 2 tablespoons extra virgin olive oil
- ½ cup Halloumi cheese, crumbled
- 2 garlic cloves, smashed
- 2 tablespoons fresh basil, snipped

Directions

1. Add 1 cup water to Ninja Foodi. Place steamer rack to the Foodi
2. Place tomatoes on rack and lock lid, cook on HIGH pressure for 3 minutes
3. Quick release pressure. Remove lid toss tomato with remaining ingredients. Serve and enjoy!

Okra And Bacon Delight
(Prepping time: 5 minutes\ Cooking time: 4 minutes |For 4 servings)

Ingredients

- 2 tablespoons olive oil
- 1 red onion, chopped
- ½ pound okra
- 1 teaspoon ginger-garlic paste
- 4 slices pancetta, chopped
- 1 t teaspoon celery seeds
- ½ teaspoon caraway seeds
- ½ teaspoon cayenne pepper
- ½ teaspoon turmeric powder
- 1 cup of water
- 1 cup tomato puree

Directions

1. Set your Ninja Foodi to Saute mode, add olive oil and let it heat up
2. Add onion and Saute until tender. Add okra, ginger garlic paste, Saute for 1 minute
3. Stir in remaining ingredients. Lock lid and cook on HIGH pressure for 3 minutes
4. Quick release pressure and serve. Enjoy!

Awesome Luncheon Green Beans
(Prepping time: 10 minutes\ Cooking time: 5 minutes |For 4 servings)

Ingredients

- 1 pound fresh green beans
- 2 tablespoons butter
- 1 garlic clove, minced
- Salt and pepper to taste
- 1 and ½ cups of water

Directions

1. Add listed ingredients to Ninja Foodi. Lock lid and cook on High Pressure for 5 minutes
2. Quick release pressure. Serve and enjoy!

Powerful Keto Tuscan Soup
(Prepping time: 5 minutes\ Cooking time: 5 minutes |For 4 servings)

Ingredients

- 2 tablespoons butter, melted
- ½ cup leeks, sliced
- 2 garlic cloves, minced
- 4 cups broccoli rabe, broken into pieces
- 2 cups of water
- 2 cups broth, homemade
- 1 zucchini, shredded
- 1 carrot, trimmed and grated
- Salt to taste
- ¼ teaspoon ground pepper

Directions

1. Set your Ninja Foodi to Saute mode and let it heat up
2. Add butter and let it melt, add leeks and cook for 2 minutes
3. Add minced garlic, cook for 40 seconds. Add remaining ingredients
4. Lock lid and cook on LOW pressure for 3 minutes. Quick release. Serve and enjoy!

Turnip Greens And Sausage
(Prepping time: 10 minutes \ Cooking time: 5 minutes |For 4 servings)

Ingredients

- 2 teaspoons sesame oil
- 2 pork sausage, casing removed, sliced
- 2 garlic cloves, minced
- 1 medium leek, chopped
- 1 cup of turkey bone stock
- 1 pound turnip greens
- Salt and pepper to taste
- 1 bay leaf
- 1 tablespoon black sesame seeds

Directions

1. Set your Ninja Foodi to Saute mode and add sesame oil, let it heat up
2. Add sausage and cook until browned
3. Add garlic, leeks and cook for 2 minutes. Add greens, stock, salt, pepper and bay leaf
4. Lock lid and cook for 3 minutes on LOW pressure. Quick release pressure
5. Serve with a garnish of black sesame seeds. Enjoy!

Easy And Cheesy Asparagus
(Prepping time: 10 minutes \ Cooking time: 3 minutes |For 4 servings)

Ingredients

- 1 and ½ pounds fresh asparagus
- 2 tablespoons olive oil
- 4 garlic cloves, minced
- Salt and pepper to taste
- ½ cup Colby cheese, shredded

Directions

1. Add 1 cup water to Ninja Foodi. Add steamer basket to Ninja Foodi
2. Place asparagus and drizzle asparagus with olive oil
3. Scatter garlic over asparagus. Season with salt and pepper
4. Lock lid and cook on HIGH pressure for 1 minute. Quick release pressure
5. Serve with cheese scattered on top. Enjoy!

Crisped Up Sweet Fish

(Prepping time: 10 minutes\ Cooking time: 6 minutes |For 4 servings)

Ingredients

- 2 drops liquid stevia
- ¼ cup butter
- 1 pound fish chunks
- 1 tablespoon vinegar
- Salt and pepper to taste

Directions

1. Set your Ninja Foodi to Saute mode, add butter and fish chunks
2. Saute for 3 minutes and add stevia, salt, and pepper
3. Lock crisping lid and Air Crisp for 3 minutes at 360 degrees F
4. Transfer to serving bowl and serve. Enjoy!

Flimsy Buffalo Fish

(Prepping time: 5 minutes\ Cooking time: 11 minutes |For 4 servings)

Ingredients

- 6 tablespoons butter
- ¾ cup Franks red hot sauce
- 6 fish fillets
- Salt and pepper to taste
- 2 teaspoons garlic powder

Directions

1. Set your Ninja Foodi to Saute mode and add butter, fish fillets
2. Saute for 3 minutes and add salt, pepper and garlic powder
3. BAKE/ROAST for 8 minutes at 340 degrees F. Transfer to serving plate and enjoy!

Tomato And Zucchini Rosemary

(Prepping time: 10 minutes \ Cooking time: 3 minutes |For 4 servings)

Ingredients

- 2 tablespoons olive oil
- 2 garlic cloves, chopped
- 1 pound zucchini, sliced
- ½ cup tomato puree
- ½ cup of water
- 1 teaspoon dried thyme
- ½ teaspoon dried oregano
- ½ teaspoon dried rosemary

Directions

1. Set your Ninja Foodi to Saute mode and add olive oil, let it heat up
2. Add garlic and cook until aromatic. Add rest of the ingredients and stir
3. Lock lid and cook on LOW pressure for 3 minutes. Quick release pressure and serve. Enjoy!

Herbed Up 13 Minutes Cod

(Prepping time: 5 minutes\ Cooking time: 8 minutes |For 4 servings)

Ingredients

- 4 garlic cloves, minced
- 2 teaspoons coconut aminos
- ¼ cup butter
- 6 whole eggs
- 2 small onions, chopped
- 3 cod fish fillets, skinless and cut into rectangular pieces
- 2 green chilies, chopped
- Salt and pepper to taste

Directions

1. Add listed ingredients to a shallow dish except for cod and beat well
2. Dip each fillet in the mix and keep it on the side. Transfer fillets to basket and lock lid
3. Air Crisp for 8 minutes at 330 degrees F. Serve and enjoy!

New Broccoli Pops

(Prepping time: 6 minutes\ Cooking time: 12 minutes |For 4 servings)

Ingredients

- 1/3 cup parmesan cheese, grated
- 2 cups cheddar cheese, grated
- Salt and pepper to taste
- 3 eggs, beaten
- 3 cups broccoli florets
- 1 tablespoon olive oil

Directions

1. Add broccoli into a food processor and pulse until finely crumbled
2. Transfer broccoli to a large-sized bowl and add remaining ingredients to the bowl, mix well
3. Make small balls using the mixture and let them chill for 30 minutes
4. Place balls in your Ninja Foodi pot and Air Crisping lid. Let it cook for 12 minutes at 365 degrees F on the "Air Crisp" mode. Once done, remove and enjoy!

Great Salmon Stew

(Prepping time: 5 minutes\ Cooking time: 8 minutes |For 4 servings)

Ingredients

- 1 cup homemade fish broth
- Salt and pepper to taste
- 1 medium onion, chopped
- 1 pound salmon fillet, cubed
- 1 tablespoon butter

Directions

1. Season salmon fillets with salt and pepper
2. Set your Ninja Foodi to Saute mode and add butter and onions
3. Saute for 3 minutes, add salmon and fish broth
4. Lock lid and cook on HIGH pressure for 8 minutes
5. Release pressure naturally over 10 minutes. Transfer to serving plate, serve and enjoy!

Creative Srilankan Coconut Dish

(Prepping time: 10 minutes\ Cooking time: 10 minutes |For 4 servings)

Ingredients

- 1 tablespoon coconut oil
- 1 medium brown onion, halved and sliced
- 1 and ½ teaspoon salt
- 2 large garlic cloves, diced
- ½ a long red chili, sliced
- 1 tablespoon yellow mustard seeds
- 1 tablespoon turmeric powder
- 1 medium cabbage, quartered, shredded and sliced
- 1 medium carrot, peeled and sliced
- 2 tablespoons lime juice
- ½ cup desiccated unsweetened coconut
- 1 tablespoon olive oil
- 1/3 cup water

Directions

1. Set your Ninja Foodi to Saute mode and add coconut oil, once the oil is hot and add onion and half of the salt. Saute for 3-4 minutes
2. Add garlic, chili, and spices and Saute for 30 seconds
3. Add cabbage, lime juice, carrots, coconut, and olive oil and stir well. Add water and stir

4. Lock up the lid and cook on HIGH pressure for 5 minutes
5. Release the pressure naturally over 5 minutes followed by a quick release
6. Serve as a side with chicken/fish. Enjoy!

Baked Paprika Delight
(Prepping time: 5 minutes\ Cooking time: 15 minutes |For 4 servings)

Ingredients

- 1 teaspoon smoked paprika
- 3 tablespoons butter
- 1 pound tiger shrimps
- Salt, to taste

Directions

1. Add listed ingredients in large bowl and marinate shrimps
2. Grease Ninja Foodi pot with butter and add seasoned shrimps
3. Lock lid and BAKE/ROAST for 15 minutes at 355 degrees F. Serve and enjoy!

The Good Eggs De Provence
(Prepping time: 2 minutes\ Cooking time: 18 minutes |For 4 servings)

Ingredients

- 6 whole eggs
- 1 cup cooked ham
- 1 small onion, chopped
- 1 cup cheddar cheese
- ½ cup heavy cream
- Salt to taste
- Ground black pepper to taste
- 1 cup of water

Directions

1. Add water to your Ninja Foodi. Place a trivet
2. Take a medium bowl and whisk in eggs, heavy cream
3. Add remaining ingredients and mix thoroughly. Transfer mix to a heatproof dish
4. Cover and place in your Ninja Foodi. Lock lid and cook on HIGH pressure for 18 minutes
5. Release pressure naturally over 10 minutes. Serve and enjoy!

Spiced Up Brussels
(Prepping time: 10 minutes\ Cooking time: 5 minutes |For 4 servings)

Ingredients

- 2 pounds Brussels sprouts, halved
- ¼ cup coconut aminos
- 2 tablespoons sriracha sauce
- 1 tablespoon vinegar
- 2 tablespoons sesame oil
- 1 tablespoon almonds, chopped
- 1 teaspoon red pepper flakes
- 2 teaspoons garlic powder
- 1 teaspoon onion powder
- 1 tablespoon smoked paprika
- ½ tablespoons cayenne pepper
- Salt and pepper to taste

Directions

1. Set your Ninja Foodi to Saute mode and add almonds. Toast them for a while
2. Take a bowl and add the remaining ingredients (except the Brussels) and give it a nice mix
3. Add the Brussels to the pot alongside the prepped mixture
4. Stir well and lock up the lid. Cook on HIGH pressure for 3 minutes
5. Release the pressure naturally and serve!

The Epic French Egg
(Prepping time: 10 minutes\ Cooking time: 8 minutes |For 4 servings)

Ingredients

- 4 whole eggs
- 4 slices of your desired meat/vegetable
- 4 slices cheese
- Fresh herbs, for garnish
- Olive oil
- 1 cup of water

Directions

1. Place trivet to your Ninja Foodi
2. Prepare ramekins by drizzling drop of olive oil and greasing them
3. Add meat/veggies to the ramekin. Break an egg and drop it into the ramekins
4. Top with cheese. Place into a steamer basket and lock lid
5. Cook on LOW pressure for 4 minutes. Release pressure naturally over 10 minutes
6. Remove ramekins and serve. Enjoy!

Quick Avocado And Coconut Pudding

(Prepping time: 10 minutes\ Cooking time: 5 minutes |For 4 servings)

Ingredients

- 2 avocados, pitted, peeled and chopped
- 2 teaspoons vanilla extract
- 2 tablespoons coconut sugar
- 1 tablespoon lime juice
- 14 ounces of coconut milk
- 1 and ½ cup of water

Directions

1. Take a bowl and add coconut milk, avocado, vanilla extract, sugar, lime juice, and blend well. Pour the mix into a ramekin. Add water to your pot
2. Add a steamer basket and place the ramekin in the pot
3. Close lid and cook on HIGH pressure for 5 minutes
4. Release pressure naturally over 10 minutes. Serve cold and enjoy!

Juicy Glazed Carrots

(Prepping time: 5 minutes\ Cooking time: 4 minutes |For 4 servings)

Ingredients

- 2 pounds carrots
- ¼ cup raisins
- Pepper as needed
- 1 cup of water
- 1 tablespoon butter
- 1 tablespoon sugar-free Keto-Friendly Maple Syrup

Directions

1. Wash, peel the skin and slice the carrots diagonally
2. Add the carrots, raisins, water to your Instant Pot
3. Lock up the lid and cook on HIGH pressure for 4 minutes
4. Perform a quick release. Strain the carrots
5. Add butter and maple syrup to the warm Instant Pot and mix well
6. Transfer the strained carrots back to the pot and stir to coat with maple sauce and butter
7. Serve with a bit of pepper. Enjoy!

All-Round Pumpkin Puree

(Prepping time: 5 minutes\ Cooking time: 13-15 minutes |For 2 servings)

Ingredients

- 2 pounds small sized pumpkin, halved and seeded
- ½ cup of water
- Salt and pepper to taste

Directions

1. Add water to your Ninja Foodi, place a steamer rack in the pot
2. Add pumpkin halves to the rack and lock lid, cook on HIGH pressure for 13-15 minutes
3. Once done, quick release pressure and let the pumpkin cool
4. Once done, scoop out flesh into a bowl
5. Blend using an immersion blender and season with salt and pepper. Serve and enjoy!

Broccoli And Scrambled Egg Ala Gusto

(Prepping time: 10 minutes\ Cooking time: 5 minutes |For 4 servings)

Ingredients

- 1 pack, 12 ounces frozen broccoli florets
- 2 tablespoons butter
- salt and pepper as needed
- 8 whole eggs
- 2 tablespoons milk
- ¾ cup white cheddar cheese, shredded
- Crushed red pepper, as needed

Directions

1. Add butter and broccoli to your Ninja Foodi
2. Season with salt and pepper according to your taste
3. Set the Ninja to Medium Pressure mode and let it cook for about 10 minutes, covered, making sure to keep stirring the broccoli from time to time
4. Take a medium sized bowl and add crack in the eggs, beat the eggs gently
5. Pour milk into the eggs and give it a nice stir
6. Add the egg mixture into the Ninja (over broccoli) and gently stir, cook for 2 minutes (uncovered)
7. Once the egg has settled in, add cheese and sprinkle red pepper, black pepper, and salt
8. Enjoy with bacon strips if you prefer!

Onion And Tofu Scramble

(Prepping time: 10 minutes\ Cooking time: 5 minutes |For 4 servings)

Ingredients

- 4 tablespoons butter
- 2 blocks tofu, pressed and cubed into inch pieces
- Salt and pepper to taste
- 1 cup cheddar, grated
- 2 medium onions, sliced

Directions

1. Take a bowl and mix in tofu, salt, pepper. Set your Foodi to Saute mode
2. Add butter and onions, Saute for 3 minutes and add seasoned tofu
3. Cook for 2 minutes, add Cheddar cheese. Lock lid and cook for 3 minutes on Air Crisp mode at 350 degrees F. Transfer to a plate, serve and enjoy!

Quick Gouda Sauce

(Prepping time: 10 minutes\ Cooking time: 10 minutes |For 4 servings)

Ingredients

- 1 zucchini, chopped
- ½ cup daikon, chopped
- 1 small cauliflower, cut into chunks
- 2 garlic cloves
- 1 and ½ cups of water
- ½ cup raw cashews, soaked
- ¼ cup nutritional yeast
- 1 tablespoon smoked paprika
- 2 tablespoons plum vinegar
- 2 courgettes cut into batons
- 2 carrots cut into batons
- 2 celery stalks cut into batons

Directions

1. Add the listed ingredients to the Ninja Foodi and lock up the lid
2. Cook on HIGH pressure for 3 minutes. Naturally, release the pressure
3. Remove the lid and allow it to cool for 10-15 minutes more
4. Transfer to a blender and blend for 2 minutes until creamy. Enjoy with veggie dippers!

Quick And Easy Garlic Turkey Breasts

(Prepping time: 5 minutes\ Cooking time: 15 minutes |For 4 servings)

Ingredients

- ½ teaspoon garlic powder
- 4 tablespoons butter
- ¼ teaspoon dried oregano
- 1 pound turkey breasts, boneless
- 1 teaspoon black pepper
- ½ teaspoon salt
- ¼ teaspoon dried salt

Directions

1. Season both turkey on both sides with garlic powder, dried oregano, dried basil, salt, and pepper. Set your pot to Saute mode and add breasts and butter. Saute for 2 minutes
2. Lock lid and BAKE/ROAST for 15 minutes at 355 degrees F. Serve and enjoy!

Creamy 5 Ingredients Chicken Breasts

(Prepping time: 5 minutes\ Cooking time: 15 minutes |For 4 servings)

Ingredients

- 1 small onion
- 2 tablespoons butter
- 1 pound chicken breasts
- ½ cup sour cream
- Salt as needed

Directions

1. Season breasts with salt and keeps it on the side
2. Heat butter in skillet on medium-low heat, add onions. Saute for 3 minutes, add chicken breast. Lock lid and cook HIGH pressure for 10 minutes. Quick release pressure
3. Stir in sour cream and cook on SAUTE mode for 4 minutes more
4. Stir gently and serve. Enjoy!

Tasty Pepperoni Omelette

(Prepping time: 10 minutes\ Cooking time: 5 minutes |For 4 servings)

Ingredients

- 4 tablespoons heavy cream
- 15 pepperoni slices
- 2 tablespoons butter
- Salt and pepper to taste
- 6 whole eggs

Directions

1. Take a bowl and whisk in eggs, cream, pepperoni slices, salt, and pepper
2. Set your Foodi to Saute mode and add butter and egg mix. Saute for 3 minutes, flip
3. Lock lid and Air Crisp for 2 minutes at 350 degrees F. Transfer to serving plate and enjoy!

The Cool Scrambled Eggs

(Prepping time: 10 minutes\ Cooking time: 5 minutes |For 4 servings)

Ingredients

- ½ cup milk
- 4 ounces bacon, chopped
- 7 whole eggs
- ½ teaspoon dried thyme
- ½ teaspoon dried basil
- ¼ cup fresh parsley, chopped
- 1 tablespoons cilantro, chopped
- 1 teaspoon paprika
- ¼ teaspoon salt

Directions

1. Beat eggs with milk, herbs, and spices. Set your Ninja Foodi to Saute mode
2. Add bacon and cook until crispy. Pour egg mixture over and cook for 5 minutes
3. Stir in chopped herbs and stir cook for 5 minutes more. Serve and enjoy!

Decisive Eggplant And Olive Keto Spread

(Prepping time: 10 minutes\ Cooking time: 10 minutes |For 4 servings)

Ingredients

- 4 tablespoons olive oil
- 2 pounds eggplant
- 3-4 garlic cloves, skin on
- 1 teaspoon salt
- ½ cup of water
- ¼ cup lemon juice
- 1 tablespoon tahini
- ¼ cup black olives pitted
- Sprigs of fresh thyme
- Extra virgin olive oil

Directions

1. Peel the skin off your eggplant alternatively, meaning that you are skin parts of the eggplant and leave some parts with skin on
2. Slice the eggplant into large chunks and chop up the any remaining eggplant
3. Chop up the remaining eggplant
4. Set your Ninja Foodi to Saute mode and add the large chunks with the face facing down and caramelize for 5 minutes. Add garlic cloves (skin on) and cook for a few minutes
5. Flip the eggplant slices and add chopped eggplant pieces
6. Add water and season with some salt
7. Lock up the lid and cook on HIGH pressure for 3 minutes
8. Release the pressure naturally over 10 minutes
9. Take the inner pot out and discard the brown liquid, pour lemon juice to the pot
10. Add black olives and garlic cloves
11. Use an immersion blender to blend the whole mixture and puree
12. Serve with a sprinkle of thyme and a dash of olive oil

A Ballet Of Roasted Ham And Spinach

(Prepping time: 10 minutes\ Cooking time: 8 minutes |For 4 servings)

Ingredients

- 3 pounds fresh baby spinach
- ½ cup cream
- 28 ounces ham, sliced
- 4 tablespoons butter, melted
- Salt and pepper to taste

Directions

1. Set your Ninja Foodi to Saute mode and add butter, spinach
2. Saute for 3 minutes and top with cream, ham slices, salt, and pepper
3. Lock lid and bake on BAKE/ROASTED mode for 8 minutes at 360 degrees F
4. Remove from Foodi and serve. Enjoy!

Secret Indian Fish Curry

(Prepping time: 5 minutes\ Cooking time: 4 minutes |For 4 servings)

Ingredients

- 2 tablespoons coconut oil
- 1 and ½ tablespoons fresh ginger, grated
- 2 teaspoons garlic, minced
- 1 tablespoon curry powder
- ½ teaspoon ground cumin
- 2 cups of coconut milk
- 16 ounces firm white fish, cut into 1-inch chunks
- 1 cup kale, shredded
- 2 tablespoons cilantro, chopped

Directions

1. Pre-heat your Ninja Foodi to by selecting the Saute mode and setting the temperature to HIGH heat. Add coconut oil and let it heat up, add ginger and garlic and Saute for 2 minutes until lightly brown. Stir in curry powder, cumin, Saute for 2 minutes until fragrant
2. Stir in coconut milk, reduce heat to low and simmer for 5 minutes
3. Lock lid and cook on LOW pressure for 4 minutes. Release pressure naturally over 10 minutes
4. Stir in kale and cilantro, simmer in Saute mode for 2 minutes. Serve and enjoy!

Magnificent Cauliflower Alfredo Zoodles

(Prepping time: 10 minutes\ Cooking time: 8 minutes |For 4 servings)

Ingredients

- 2 tablespoons butter
- 2 garlic cloves
- 7-8 cauliflower florets
- 1 cup broth
- 2 teaspoons salt
- 2 cups spinach, coarsely chopped
- 2 green onions, chopped
- 1 pound zoodles
- Chopped sundried tomatoes, balsamic vinegar, and cheese for garnish

Directions

1. Set your Ninja Foodi to Saute mode and add butter, allow the butter to melt
2. Add garlic cloves and Saute for 2 minutes
3. Add cauliflower, broth, salt and lock up the lid and cook on HIGH pressure for 6 minutes
4. Prepare the zoodles. Perform a naturally release over 10 minutes
5. Use an immersion blender to blend the mixture in the pot to a puree
6. Pour the sauce over the zoodles
7. Serve with a garnish of cheese, sun-dried tomatoes and a drizzle of balsamic vinegar. Enjoy!

Chicken Coriander Soup

(Prepping time: 10 minutes\ Cooking time: 10 minutes |For 4 servings)

Ingredients

- 2 tablespoon of coconut oil
- 1 tablespoon of minced garlic
- 3-6 green chilies
- 2 tablespoon of grated ginger
- 1 cup of roughly chopped cilantro stems
- 1 pound of chicken breast
- 12 black peppercorns
- 1 teaspoon of salt
- 2 cup of chicken broth
- 1 cup of thinly sliced cabbage
- 1 cup of julienned carrots
- 3-6 tablespoon of arrowroot powder mixed in 1 cup of water
- ¼ teaspoon of fresh ground pepper
- ½ a cup of chopped cilantro
- 2 tablespoon of lemon juice

Directions

1. Set your Ninja Foodi to Saute mode and add 1 tablespoon of oil
2. Add garlic, green chilies, 1 tablespoon of ginger and cilantro stems. Mix well

3. Add chicken breast, salt, peppercorn, 2 cups of water, 2 cups of broth and give it a nice stir
4. Lock up the lid and cook on HIGH pressure for 10 minutes
5. Release the pressure naturally
6. Take a large sized bowl and take the breast out, shred the chicken and keep them on the side. Strain the broth into the bowl through a metal strainer and discard the stems
7. Reserve the broth. Rinse and dry your Ninja Foodie insert
8. Put it back and set your pot to Saute mode again
9. Add remaining oil, cabbage, ginger and carrots. Stir well
10. Add shredded chicken, broth and arrowroot mix. Mix well and bring the soup to a slight boil
11. Turn the Instant Pot off and add fresh ground pepper, chopped cilantro, and lemon juice
12. Enjoy!

Garlic And Mushroom Chicken Stew

(Prepping time: 5 minutes\ Cooking time: 10 minutes |For 4 servings)

Ingredients

- 1 onion, sliced and halved
- 2 tablespoons olive oil
- 1 teaspoon salt
- 1 and ¾ pounds chicken breast, diced
- 7 ounces Swiss brown and white button mushrooms
- 4 large garlic cloves, diced
- 1-2 bay leaves

- ¼ teaspoons nutmeg powder
- ½ teaspoon pepper
- ½ cup chicken stock
- 1 teaspoon Dijon mustard
- 1/3 cup sour cream
- 1 teaspoon arrowroot
- 2-3 tablespoons parsley, chopped

Directions

1. Set your Ninja Foodi to Saute mode and add olive oil, allow the oil to heat up
2. Add onion and salt and cook for 3-4 minutes
3. Add chicken, mushroom, bay leaves, garlic, nutmeg, stock cube, pepper, water, and mustard and stir well. Lock up the lid and cook on HIGH pressure for 10 minutes
4. Release the pressure naturally over 10 minutes
5. Open the lid and scoop up a few tablespoons of liquid and mix with arrowroot, dissolve the liquid back and stir to thicken the gravy. Add sour cream and stir. Enjoy with a garnish of parsley

Spaghetti Squash In Sage And Butter Sauce

(Prepping time: 5 minutes\ Cooking time: 10 minutes |For 4 servings)

Ingredients

1 medium spaghetti squash

1 and ½ cups of water
1 bunch fresh sage

2 tablespoons olive oil
1 teaspoon salt
1/8 teaspoon nutmeg

Directions

1. Halve the squash and scoop out the seeds
2. Add water to your Ninja Foodi and lower down the squash with the squash halves facing up
3. Stack them on top of one another. Lock up the lid and cook on HIGH pressure for 3 minutes
4. Release the pressure over 10 minutes
5. Take a cold Saute pan and add sage, garlic and olive oil and cook on LOW heat, making sure to stir and fry the sage leaves . Keep it on the side
6. Release the pressure naturally and tease the squash fibers out from the shell and plop them into the Saute Pan. Stir well and sprinkle salt and nutmeg. Serve with a bit of cheese and enjoy!

Ham And Hollandaise Delight

(Prepping time: 10 minutes\ Cooking time: 5 minutes |For 4 servings)

Ingredients

- 2 whole eggs
- 2 tablespoons Hollandaise sauce
- 2 ham slices, chopped
- 1 and ½ cups + 2 tablespoons water

Directions

1. Add 1 and ½ cups water to Ninja Foodi. Lower trivet inside
2. Crack eggs into 2 ramekins. Add a tablespoon of water on top
3. Place ramekins in Ninja Foodi trivet and lock lid, cook on STEAM mode for 2-3 minutes
4. Quick release pressure and top with ham and hollandaise sauce. Serve and enjoy!

Delicious Ghee Carrots

(Prepping time: 10 minutes\ Cooking time: 5 minutes |For 4 servings)

Ingredients

- 1 pound of baby carrots
- 1 cup of water
- 1 tablespoon of clarified ghee
- 1 tablespoon of chopped up fresh mint leaves
- Sea flavored vinegar as needed

Directions

1. Place a steamer rack on top of your Ninja Foodi and add the carrots. Add water
2. Lock up the lid and cook at HIGH pressure for 2 minutes. Do a quick release
3. Pass the carrots through a strainer and drain them. Wipe the insert clean
4. Return the insert to the Ninja Foodi and set the pot to Saute mode
5. Add clarified butter and allow it to melt. Add mint and Saute for 30 seconds
6. Add carrots to the insert and Saute well
7. Remove them and sprinkle with a bit of flavored vinegar on top. Enjoy!

Simple Cheese Casserole

(Prepping time: 2 minutes\ Cooking time: 18 minutes |For 4 servings)

Ingredients

- 16 ounces marinara sauce
- 10 ounces parmesan sauce, shredded
- 2 tablespoons olive oil
- 16 ounces mozzarella cheese, shredded
- 2 pounds sausage, scrambled

Directions

1. Grease your Ninja Foodi with olive oil, arrange half of the scrambled sausage
2. Layer with half or marinara, half mozzarella, and parmesan
3. Top with remaining half of sausage, marinara, and cheese
4. Lock lid and cook using "BAKE/ROAST" mode for 20 minutes at 360 degrees F
5. Remove from Foodi and serve. Enjoy!

Chapter 10: Awesome Snacks And Appetizers

Inspiring Cauliflower Hash Browns

(Prepping time: 10 minutes\ Cooking time: 30 minutes |For 6 servings)

Ingredients

- 6 whole eggs
- 4 cups cauliflower rice
- ¼ cup milk
- 1 onion, chopped
- 3 tablespoons butter
- 1 and ½ cups cooked ham, chopped
- ½ cup shredded cheese

Directions

1. Set your Ninja Foodi to sauté mode and add butter, let the butter heat up
2. Add onions and cook for 5 minutes until tender. Add iced cauliflower to pot and stir
3. Lock the Air Crisping lid and Air Crisp for 15 minutes, making sure to give them a turn about halfway through
4. Take a small bowl and mix in eggs and milk, pour mixture over browned cauliflower
5. Sprinkle ham over top. Press Air Crispy again and crisp for 10 minutes more
6. Sprinkle cheddar cheese on top and lock lid, let the crisp for 1 minute more until the cheese melts. Serve and enjoy!

Everybody's Favorite Cauliflower Patties

(Prepping time: 5 minutes \ Cooking time: 20 minutes |For 4 servings)

Ingredients

- 3 whole eggs
- 1 chili pepper, chopped
- ½ teaspoon garlic powder
- Salt and pepper to taste
- 2 cups cauliflower, chopped
- ¾ cups olive oil
- ¼ cup cheddar cheese
- ¼ cup whole mozzarella cheese

Directions

1. Cut cauliflower into small florets, remove leaves and cut out a core
2. Add 1 cup water to Ninja Food, transfer florets to steamer basket and place it on a trivet in your Ninja Foodi. Lock lid and cook on HIGH pressure for 5 minutes
3. Mash steamed cauliflower and dry them, add shredded cheese, eggs, chili, salt and pepper
4. Mix well and shape into flat patties
5. Heat up oil in your Ninja Foodi and set to Saute mode, shallow fry patties until crisp on both sides. Serve and enjoy!

Kale And Almonds Mix

(Prepping time: 10 minutes \ Cooking time: 4 minutes |For 4 servings)

Ingredients

- 1 cup of water
- 1 big kale bunch, chopped
- 1 tablespoon balsamic vinegar
- 1/3 cup toasted almonds
- 3 garlic cloves, minced
- 1 small yellow onion, chopped
- 2 tablespoons olive oil

Directions

1. Set your Ninja Foodi on Saute mode and add oil, let it heat up
2. Stir in onion and cook for 3 minutes. Add garlic, water, kale, and stir

3. Lock lid and cook on HIGH pressure for 4 minutes. Quick release pressure
4. Add salt, pepper, vinegar, almonds and toss well. Serve and enjoy!

Simple Treat Of Garlic
(Prepping time: 10 minutes \ Cooking time: 5 minutes |For 4 servings)

Ingredients

- 1 tablespoon extra-virgin olive oil
- 2 garlic cloves, minced
- 2 large-sized Belgian endive, halved lengthwise
- ½ cup apple cider vinegar
- ½ cup broth
- Salt and pepper to taste
- 1 teaspoon cayenne pepper

Directions

1. Set your Ninja Foodi to Saute mode and add oil, let the oil heat up
2. Add garlic and cook for 30 seconds unto browned
3. Add endive, vinegar, broth, salt, pepper, and cayenne
4. Lock lid and cook on LOW pressure for 2 minutes. Quick release pressure and serve. Enjoy!

Buttered Up Garlic And Fennel
(Prepping time: 10 minutes \ Cooking time: 5 minutes |For 4 servings)

Ingredients

- ½ stick butter
- 2 garlic cloves, sliced
- ½ teaspoon salt
- 1 and ½ pounds fennel bulbs, cut into wedges
- ¼ teaspoon ground black pepper
- ½ teaspoon cayenne
- ¼ teaspoon dried dill weed
- 1/3 cup dry white wine
- 2/3 cup stock

Directions

1. Set your Ninja Foodi to Saute mode and add butter, let it heat up
2. Add garlic and cook for 30 seconds. Add rest of the ingredients
3. Lock lid and cook on LOW pressure for 3 minutes. Remove lid and serve. Enjoy!

Obvious Paprika And Cabbage
(Prepping time: 10 minutes \ Cooking time: 4 minutes |For 4 servings)

Ingredients

- 1 and ½ pounds green cabbage, shredded
- Salt and pepper to taste
- 3 tablespoon ghee
- 1 cup vegetable stock
- ¼ teaspoon sweet paprika

Directions

1. Set your Ninja Foodi to Saute mode and add ghee, let it melt
2. Add cabbage, salt, pepper, and stock, stir well
3. Lock lid and cook on HIGH pressure for 7 minutes. Quick release pressure
4. Add paprika and toss well. Divide between plates and serve. Enjoy!

Authentic Western Omelet
(Prepping time: 5 minutes\ Cooking time: 34 minutes |For 2 servings)

Ingredients

- 3 eggs, whisked
- 3 ounces chorizo, chopped

- 1-ounces Feta cheese, crumbled
- 5 tablespoons almond milk
- ¾ teaspoon chili flakes
- ¼ teaspoon salt
- 1 green pepper, chopped

Directions

1. Add all the ingredients and mix them well. Stir it gently. Take an omelet pan and pour the mixture into it. Preheat your Ninja Foodi at "Roast/Bake" mode at 320 F.
2. Cook for 4 minutes. After that, transfer the pan with an omelet in Ninja Foodi
3. Cook for 30 minutes more at the same mode. Serve hot and enjoy!

Bowl Full Of Broccoli Salad

(Prepping time: 10 minutes \ Cooking time: 5 minutes |For 4 servings)

Ingredients

- 1 pound broccoli, cut into florets
- 2 tablespoons balsamic vinegar
- 2 garlic cloves, minced
- 1 teaspoon mustard seeds
- 1 teaspoon cumin seeds
- Salt and pepper to taste
- 1 cup cottage cheese, crumbled

Directions

4. Add 1 cup water to your Ninja Foodi. Place steamer basket
5. Place broccoli in basket and lock lid, cook on HIGH pressure for 5 minutes
6. Quick release pressure and remove lid. Toss broccoli with other ingredients and serve. Enjoy!

Rise And Shine Breakfast Casserole

(Prepping time: 10 minutes\ Cooking time: 10 minutes |For 6 servings)

Ingredients

- 4 whole eggs
- 1 tablespoons milk
- 1 cup ham, cooked and chopped
- ½ cup cheddar cheese, shredded
- ¼ teaspoon salt
- ¼ teaspoon ground black pepper

Directions

1. Take a baking pan (small enough to fit into your Ninja Foodi) bowl, and grease it well with butter. Take a medium bowl and whisk in eggs, milk, salt, pepper and add ham, cheese, and stir. Pour mixture into baking pan and lower the pan into your Ninja Foodi
2. Set your Ninja Foodi Air Crisp mode and Air Crisp for 325 degrees F for 7 minutes
3. Remove pan from eggs and enjoy!

Cauliflower And Egg Dish

(Prepping time: 10 minutes \ Cooking time: 4 minutes |For 4 servings)

Ingredients

- 21 ounces cauliflower, separated into florets
- 1 cup red onion, chopped
- 1 cup celery, chopped
- ½ cup of water
- Salt and pepper to taste
- 2 tablespoons balsamic vinegar
- 1 teaspoon stevia
- 4 boiled eggs, chopped
- 1 cup Keto Friendly mayonnaise

Directions

1. Add water to Ninja Foodi
2. Add steamer basket and add cauliflower, lock lid and cook on High Pressure for 5 minutes
3. Quick release pressure. Transfer cauliflower to bowl and add eggs, celery, onion and toss

4. Take another bowl and mix in mayo, salt, pepper, vinegar, stevia and whisk well
5. Add a salad, toss well. Divide into salad bowls and serve. Enjoy!

Just A Simple Egg Frittata
(Prepping time: 10 minutes \ Cooking time: 15 minutes |For 4 servings)

Ingredients

- 5 whole eggs
- ¾ teaspoon mixed herbs
- 1 cup spinach
- ¼ cup shredded cheddar cheese

- ½ cup mushrooms
- Salt and pepper to taste
  ¾ cup half and half
  2 tablespoons butter

Directions

1. Dice mushrooms, chop spinach finely
2. Set your Ninja Foodi to Saute mode and add spinach, mushrooms
3. Whisk eggs, milk, cream cheese, herbs, and Sautéed vegetables in a bowl and mix well
4. Take a 6-inch baking pan and grease it well
5. Pour mixture and transfer to your Ninja Foodie (on a trivet)
6. Cook on HIGH pressure for 2 minutes. Quick release pressure. Serve and enjoy!

Ultimate Cheese Dredged Cauliflower Snack
(Prepping time: 10 minutes\ Cooking time: 30 minutes |For 4 servings)

Ingredients

- 1 tablespoon mustard
- 1 head cauliflower
- 1 teaspoon avocado mayonnaise

- ½ cup parmesan cheese, grated
- ¼ cup butter, cut into small pieces

Directions

1. Set your Ninja Foodi to Saute mode and add butter and cauliflower
2. Saute for 3 minutes. Add remaining ingredients and stir
3. Lock lid and cook on HIGH pressure for 30 minutes. Release pressure naturally over 10 minutes
4. Serve and enjoy!

The Great Mediterranean Spinach
(Prepping time: 10 minutes\ Cooking time: 15 minutes |For 4 servings)

Ingredients

- 4 tablespoons butter
- 2 pounds spinach, chopped and boiled
- Salt and pepper to taste

- 2/3 cup Kalamata olives, halved and pitted
- 1 and ½ cups feta cheese, grated
- 4 teaspoons fresh lemon zest, grated

Directions

1. Take a bowl and mix in spinach, butter, salt, pepper and mix well
2. Transfer to Ninja Foodi the seasoned spinach
3. Lock Air Crisper and Air Crisp for 15 minutes at 350 degrees F. Serve and enjoy!

Quick Turkey Cutlets
(Prepping time: 10 minutes\ Cooking time: 22 minutes |For 4 servings)

Ingredients

- 1 teaspoon Greek seasoning
- 1 pound turkey cutlets
- 2 tablespoons olive oil
- 1 teaspoon turmeric powder
- ½ cup almond flour

Directions

1. Add Greek seasoning, turmeric powder, almond flour to a bowl
2. Dredge turkey cutlets in it and keep it on the side for 30 minutes
3. Set your Foodi to Saute mode and add oil and cutlets, Saute for 2 minutes
4. Lock lid and cook on LOW-MEDIUM pressure for 20 minutes
5. Quick release pressure. Serve and enjoy!

Veggies Dredged In Cheese
(Prepping time: 10 minutes\ Cooking time: 30 minutes |For 4 servings)

Ingredients
- 2 onions, sliced
- 2 tomatoes, sliced
- 2 zucchinis, sliced
- 2 teaspoons olive oil
- 2 cups cheddar cheese, grated
- 2 teaspoons mixed dried herbs
- Salt and pepper to taste

Directions

Arrange all the listed ingredients to your Ninja Foodi. Top with olive oil, herbs, cheddar, salt and pepper. Lock lid and Air Crisp for 30 minutes at 350 degrees F. Serve and enjoy!

Egg Dredged Casserole
(Prepping time: 10 minutes\ Cooking time: 5 minutes |For 6 servings)

Ingredients

- 4 whole eggs
- 1 tablespoons milk
- 1 tomato, diced
- ½ cup spinach
- ¼ teaspoon salt
- ¼ teaspoon ground black pepper

Directions

1. Take a baking pan (small enough to fit Ninja Foodi) and grease it with butter
2. Take a medium bowl and whisk in eggs, milk, salt, pepper, add veggies to the bowl and stir
3. Pour egg mixture into the baking pan and lower the pan into the Ninja Foodi
4. Close Air Crisping lid and Air Crisp for 325 degrees for 7 minutes
5. Remove the pan from eggs and enjoy hot!

Excellent Bacon And Cheddar Frittata
(Prepping time: 10 minutes\ Cooking time: 10 minutes |For 6 servings)

Ingredients

- 6 whole eggs
- 2 tablespoons milk
- ½ cup bacon, cooked and chopped
- 1 cup broccoli, cooked
- ½ cup shredded cheddar cheese
- ¼ teaspoon salt
- ¼ teaspoon ground black pepper

Directions

1. Take a baking pan (small enough to fit into your Ninja Foodi) bowl, and grease it well with butter. Take a medium sized bowl and add eggs, milk, salt, pepper, bacon, broccoli, and cheese. Stir well. Pour mixture into your prepared baking pan and lower pan into your Foodi, close Air Crisping lid. Air Crisp for 7 minutes at 375 degrees F. Remove pan and enjoy!

Pork Packed Jalapeno

(Prepping time: 10 minutes\ Cooking time: 10 minutes |For 6 servings)

Ingredients

- 2 pounds pork sausage, ground
- 2 cups parmesan cheese, shredded
- 2 pounds large sized jalapeno peppers sliced lengthwise and seeded
- 2 (8 ounces packages), cream cheese, softened
- 2 (8 ounces) bottles, ranch dressing

Directions

1. Take a bowl and add pork sausage, cream cheese, ranch dressing and mix well
2. Slice jalapeno in half, remove seeds and clean them
3. Stuff sliced jalapeno pieces with pork mixture
4. Place peppers in crisping basket and transfer basket to your Ninja Foodi
5. Lock Air Crisping lid and cook on Air Crisp mode for 10 minutes at 350 degrees F
6. Cook in batches if needed, serve and enjoy!

Juicy Garlic Chicken Livers

(Prepping time: 10 minutes\ Cooking time: 8 hours |For 6 servings)

Ingredients

- 1 pound chicken livers
- 8 garlic cloves, minced
- 8 ounces cremini mushrooms, quartered
- 4 slices uncooked bacon, chopped
- 1 onion, chopped
- 1 cup bone broth
- 1 teaspoon dried thyme
- 1 teaspoon dried rosemary
- 1 teaspoon salt
- 1 teaspoon freshly ground black pepper
- ¼ cup fresh parsley, chopped

Directions

1. Add livers, bacon, garlic, mushrooms, onion, thyme, broth, rosemary to Ninja Foodi
2. Season with salt and pepper. Place lid and cook on SLOW COOK Mode (LOW) for 8 hours
3. Remove lid and stir in parsley. Serve and enjoy!

The Original Zucchini Gratin

(Prepping time: 10 minutes\ Cooking time: 15 minutes |For 4 servings)

Ingredients

- 2 zucchinis
- 1 tablespoon fresh parsley, chopped
- 2 tablespoons bread crumbs
- 4 tablespoons parmesan cheese, grated
- 1 tablespoon vegetable oil
- Salt and pepper to taste

Directions

1. Pre-heat your Ninja Foodi to 300 degrees F for 3 minutes
2. Slice zucchini lengthwise to get about 8 equal sizes pieces
3. Arrange pieces in your Crisping Basket (skin side down)
4. Top each with parsley, bread crumbs, cheese, oil, salt, and pepper
5. Return basket Ninja Foodi basket and cook for 15 minutes at 360 degrees F
6. Once done, serve with sauce. Enjoy!

Quick Bite Zucchini Fries

(Prepping time: 10 minutes\ Cooking time: 10 minutes |For 4 servings)

Ingredients

- 1-2 pounds of zucchini, sliced into 2 and ½ inch sticks
- Salt to taste
- 1 cup cream cheese
- 2 tablespoons olive oil

Directions

1. Add zucchini in a colander and season with salt, add cream cheese and mix
2. Add oil into your Ninja Foodie's pot and add Zucchini
3. Lock Air Crisping Lid and set the temperature to 365 degrees F and timer to 10 minutes
4. Let it cook for 10 minutes and take the dish out once done, enjoy!

Pickled Up Green Chili

(Prepping time: 5 minutes\ Cooking time: 11 minutes |For 4 servings)

Ingredients

- 1 pound green chilies
- 1 and ½ cups apple cider vinegar
- 1 teaspoon pickling salt
- 1 and ½ teaspoon sugar
- ¼ teaspoon garlic powder

Directions

1. Add the listed ingredients to your pot. Lock up the lid and cook on HIGH pressure for 11 minutes. Release the pressure naturally
2. Spoon the mixture into jars and cover the slices with cooking liquid, making sure to completely submerge the chilies. Serve!

Spaghetti Squash And Chicken Parmesan

(Prepping time: 10 minutes\ Cooking time: 20 minutes |For 4 servings)

Ingredients

- 1 spaghetti squash
- 1 cup marinara sauce (Keto Friendly)
- 1 pound chicken, cooked and cubed
- 16 ounces mozzarella

Directions

1. Split up the squash in halves and remove the seeds
2. Add 1 cup of water to the Ninja Foodi and place a trivet on top
3. Add the squash halves on the trivet. Lock up the lid and cook for 20 minutes at HIGH pressure
4. Do a quick release. Remove the squashes and shred them using a fork into spaghetti portions
5. Pour sauce over the squash and give it a nice mix
6. Top them up with the cubed up chicken and top with mozzarella
7. Broil for 1-2 minutes and broil until the cheese has melted

Spice Lover's Jar Of Chili

(Prepping time: 10 minutes\ Cooking time: 11 minutes |For 4 servings)

Ingredients

- 1 pound green chilies
- 1 and ½ cups apple cider vinegar
- 1 teaspoon pickling salt
- 1 and ½ teaspoons date paste
- ¼ teaspoon garlic powder

Directions

1. Add the above-mentioned ingredients to the Ninja Foodi
2. Lock up the lid and cook on HIGH pressure for 10 minutes
3. Release the pressure naturally
4. Spoon the mix into washed jars and cover the slices with a bit of cooking liquid
5. Add vinegar to submerge the chilly. Enjoy!

Easy To Swallow Beet Chips
(Prepping time: 10 minutes\ Cooking time: 8 hours |For 8 servings)

Ingredients

- ½ beet, peeled and cut into 1/8 inch slices

Directions

Arrange beet slices in single layer in the Cook and Crisp baske. Place the basket in the pot and close the crisping lid. Press the Dehydrate button and let it dehydrate for 8 hours at 135 degrees F. Once the dehydrating is done, remove the basket from pot and transfer slices to your Air Tight container, serve and enjoy!

Bacon Samba Bok Choy
(Prepping time: 10 minutes\ Cooking time:3 minutes |For 4 servings)

Ingredients

- ½ tablespoons fresh lemon juice
- 1 medium ripe avocado, peeled and pitted, chopped
- 6 organic eggs, boiled, peeled and cut half
- Salt to taste
- ½ cup fresh watercress, trimmed

Directions

1. Place a steamer basket at the bottom of your Ninja Foodi
2. Add water and put watercress on the basket, lock lid and pressure cook for 3 minutes
3. Quick release pressure. Remove egg yolk and transfer to a bowl
4. Add watercress, avocado, lemon juice, salt, and mash well
5. Place egg whites in serving the dish and fill whites with watercress, mix well and enjoy!

Sour Cream Mushroom Appetizer
(Prepping time: 10 minutes\ Cooking time: 20 minutes |For 6 servings)

Ingredients

- 24 mushrooms, caps and stems diced
- 1 cup cheddar cheese, shredded
- ½ orange bell pepper, diced
- ½ onion, diced
- 4 bacon slices, diced
- ½ cup sour cream

Directions

1. Set your Ninja Foodie to Saute mode and add mushroom stems, onion, bacon, bell pepper and Saute for 5 minutes. Add 1 cup cheese, sour cream and cook for 2 minutes more
2. Stuff mushrooms with cheese and vegetable mixture and top with cheddar cheese
3. Transfer them to your Crisping Basket and lock Air Crisping lid
4. Air Crisp for 8 minutes at 350 degrees F. Serve and enjoy!

Tasty Brussels
(Prepping time: 10 minutes\ Cooking time: 3 minutes |For 4 servings)

Ingredients

- 1 pound Brussels sprouts
- ¼ cup pine nuts
- 1 tablespoon extra virgin olive oil
- 1 pomegranate
- ½ teaspoon salt
- 1 pepper, grated

Directions

1. Remove outer leaves and trim the stems off the washed Brussels sprouts
2. Cut the largest ones in uniform halves
3. Add 1 cup of water to the Ninja Foodi
4. Place steamer basket and add sprouts in the basket
5. Lock up the lid and cook on HIGH pressure for 3 minutes
6. Release the pressure naturally
7. Transfer the sprouts to serving dish and dress with olive oil, pepper, and salt
8. Sprinkle toasted pine nuts and pomegranate seeds! Serve warm and enjoy!

Visible Citrus And Cauli Salad

(Prepping time: 10 minutes\ Cooking time: 10 minutes |For 4 servings)

Ingredients

- 1 small sized cauliflower with the florets divided
- 1 Romanesco cauliflower with the florets divided
- 1 pound of broccoli florets
- 2 seedless oranges peeled up and sliced thinly

For vinaigrette ingredients

- 1 zested and squeezed orange
- 4 anchovies
- 1 hot pepper sliced up and chopped
- 1 tablespoon of capers
- 4 tablespoon of extra virgin olive oil
- Salt as needed
- Pepper as needed

Directions

1. Add broccoli, cauliflower florets to your Ninja Foodi
2. Lock up the lid and cook on HIGH pressure for 7 minutes
3. Make the vinaigrette by combining the hot pepper, anchovies, olive oil, capers, pepper, salt and mix well. Quick release the pressure
4. Strain the veggies out and mix with vinaigrette and the orange slices. Enjoy!

Faithful Roasted Garlic

(Prepping time: 10 minutes\ Cooking time: 20 minutes |For 4 servings)

Ingredients

- 3 large garlic bulbs
- 1 cup of water

Directions

1. Slice off ¼ of the garlic bulb from the top, keeping the bulb intact
2. Add water to your Ninja Foodi and a steamer trivet
3. Transfer garlic bulb on rack and lock lid, cook on HIGH pressure for 5-6 minutes
4. Naturally, release the pressure over 10 minutes
5. Transfer the soft garlic to grill rack in your oven and roast for 5 minutes. Serve and enjoy!

Feisty Chicken Thighs

(Prepping time: 5 minutes\ Cooking time:6-8 hours |For 6 servings)

Ingredients

- 3 pounds boneless chicken thighs, skinless
- 2 tablespoons apple cider vinegar
- ½ cup agave nectar
- 2 teaspoon garlic powder
- 2 teaspoon paprika
- 1 teaspoon chili powder
- 1 teaspoon red pepper flakes
- 1 teaspoon black pepper
- 2 teaspoon salt

Directions

1. Take a bowl and add garlic pepper, paprika, chili powder, red pepper flakes, salt, and pepper. Take another bowl and mix in agave nectar, vinegar and keep the mix on the side
2. Use the seasoning mix to properly coat the chicken thigh
3. Pour nectar, vinegar mix over chicken. Transfer the mix to Ninja Foodi
4. Lock lid and cook on SLOW COOK MODE (LOW) for 6-8 hours
5. Once done, unlock the lid. Drizzle the glaze on top and serve. Enjoy!

Garlic And Tomato "Herbed" Chicken Thighs

(Prepping time: 10 minutes\ Cooking time: 5-7 hours |For 4 servings)

Ingredients

- 3 pounds boneless, skinless chicken thighs
- ½ cup low-sodium chicken broth
- 2 cups cherry tomatoes, halved
- 4 garlic cloves, minced
- 2 teaspoons garlic salt
- ¼ teaspoon ground white pepper
- 2 tablespoons fresh basil, chopped
- 2 tablespoons fresh oregano, chopped

Directions

1. Add listed ingredients to your Ninja Foodi and gently stir. Lock lid and cook on SLOW COOK mode for 5-7 hours. Serve and enjoy!

The Kool Poblano Cheese Frittata

(Prepping time: 10 minutes\ Cooking time: 25 minutes |For 4 servings)

Ingredients

- 4 whole eggs
- 1 cup half and half
- 10 ounces canned green chilies
- ½ -1 teaspoon salt
- ½ teaspoon ground cumin
- 1 cup Mexican blend shredded cheese
- ¼ cup cilantro, chopped

Directions

1. Take a bowl and beat eggs and a half and half
2. Add diced green chilis, salt, cumin and ½ cup of shredded cheese
3. Pour the mixture into 6 inches greased metal pan and cover with foil
4. Add 2 cups of water to the Ninja Foodi. Place trivet in the pot and place the pan in the trivet
5. Lock up the lid and cook on HIGH pressure for 20 minutes
6. Release the pressure naturally over 10 minutes
7. Scatter half cup of the cheese on top of your quiche and broil for a while until the cheese has melted. Enjoy!

The Divine Fudge Meal

(Prepping time: 10 minute + chill times\ Cooking time: 10-20 minutes |For 20 servings)

Ingredients

- ½ teaspoon organic vanilla extract
- 1 cup heavy whip cream
- 2 ounces butter, soft
- 2 ounces 70% dark chocolate, finely chopped

Directions

6. Set your Ninja Foodi to Saute mode and add vanilla, heavy cream. Saute for 5 minutes
7. Add butter and chocolate and Saute for 2 minutes. Transfer to serving the dish
8. Chill for few hours and enjoy!

The Original Braised Kale And Carrot Salad

(Prepping time: 5 minutes\ Cooking time: 30 minutes |For 4 servings)

Ingredients

- 10 ounces kale, roughly chopped
- 1 tablespoon ghee
- 1 medium onion, sliced
- 3 medium carrots, cut into half inch pieces
- 5 garlic clove, peeled and chopped
- ½ cup chicken broth
- Fresh ground pepper
- Vinegar as needed
- ½ teaspoon red pepper flakes

Directions

1. Set your pot to Saute mode and add ghee, allow the ghee to melt
2. Add chopped onion and carrots and Saute for a while
3. Add garlic and Saute for a while. Pile the kale on top
4. Pour chicken broth and season with pepper
5. Lock up the lid and cook on HIGH pressure for 8 minutes
6. Release the pressure naturally over 10 minutes. Open and give it a nice stir
7. Add vinegar and sprinkle a bit more pepper flakes. Enjoy!

Delicious Bacon- Wrapped Drumsticks

(Prepping time: 10 minutes\ Cooking time: 8 hours |For 6 servings)

Ingredients

- 12 chicken drumsticks
- 12 slices thin cut bacon

Directions

1. Wrap each chicken drumsticks in bacon. Place drumsticks in your Ninja Foodi
2. Place lid and cook SLOW COOK mode (LOW) for 8 hours. Serve and enjoy!

Stuffed Chicken Mushrooms

(Prepping time: 10 minutes\ Cooking time: 15 minutes |For 4 servings)

Ingredients

- 12 large fresh mushrooms, stems removed

Stuffing

- 1 cup chicken meat, cubed
- ½ pound, imitation crabmeat, flaked
- 2 cups butter
- Garlic powder to taste
- 2 garlic cloves, peeled and minced

Directions

1. Take a non-stick skillet and place it over medium heat, add butter and let it heat up
2. Stir in chicken and Saute for 5 minutes. Add ingredients for stuffing and cook for 5 minutes
3. Remove heat and let the chicken cool down. Divide filling into mushroom caps

4. Place stuffed mushroom caps in your Crisping basket and transfer basket to Foodi
5. Lock Crisping Lid and Air Crisp for 10 minutes at 375 degrees F. Serve and enjoy!

A Hot Buffalo Wing Platter
(Prepping time: 10 minutes\ Cooking time: 6 hours |For 4 servings)

Ingredients

- 1 bottle of (12 ounces) hot pepper sauce
- ½ cup melted ghee
- 1 tablespoons dried oregano
- 2 teaspoons garlic powder
- 1 teaspoon onion powder
- 5 pounds chicken wing sections

Directions

Take a large bowl and mix in hot sauce, ghee, garlic powder, oregano, onion powder and mix well. Add chicken wings and toss to coat. Pour mix into Ninja Foodi and cook on LOW for 6 hours. Serve and enjoy!

Garlic And Mushroom Crunchies
(Prepping time: 10 minutes\ Cooking time: 8 hours |For 4 servings)

Ingredients

- ¼ cup vegetable stock
- 2 tablespoons extra virgin olive oil
- 1 tablespoon Dijon mustard
- 1 teaspoon dried thyme
- 1 teaspoon of sea salt
- ½ teaspoon dried rosemary
- ¼ teaspoon fresh ground black pepper
- 2 pounds cremini mushrooms, cleaned
- 6 garlic cloves, minced
- ¼ cup fresh parsley, chopped

Directions

4. Take a small bowl and whisk in vegetable stock, mustard, olive oil, salt, thyme, pepper and rosemary. Add mushrooms, garlic and stock mix to your Ninja Foodi
5. Close lid and cook on SLOW COOK Mode (LOW) for 8 hours
6. Open the lid and stir in parsley. Serve and enjoy!

Delicious Cocoa Almond Bites
(Prepping time: 10 minutes\ Cooking time: 2 hours |For 6 servings)

Ingredients

- 3 cups of raw almonds
- 3 tablespoons coconut oil, melted
- Kosher salt
- ¼ cup Erythritol
- 1 tablespoon unsweetened cocoa powder
- 1 tablespoon ground cinnamon

Directions

5. Add almonds coconut oil to the Ninja Foodi and stir until coated
6. Season with salt. Mix in Erythritol, cocoa powder, cinnamon, and cover
7. Cook on SLOW COOK MODE(HIGH) for 2 hours, making sure to stir every 30 minutes
8. Transfer nuts to a large baking sheet and spread them out to cool. Serve and enjoy!

Chicken Crescent Wraps
(Prepping time: 10 minutes\ Cooking time: 15 minutes |For 4 servings)

Ingredients

- 3 (10 ounces0 cans, almond flour crescent roll dough

- 6 tablespoons butter
- 2 cooked chicken breast, skinless boneless, cubed
- 3 tablespoons onion, chopped
- ¾ (8 ounces) package cream cheese
- 3 garlic cloves, peeled and minced

Directions

1. Take a skillet to place it over medium heat, add oil and let it heat up
2. Add onion and garlic ad Saute until tender
3. Add chicken, cream cheese, butter, onion garlic to food processor and blend until smooth Spread dough over a flat surface and slice into 12 equal sized rectangles
4. Spoon chicken blend at the center of each dough piece
5. Roll piece while wrapping inner filling completely
6. Place wrapped balls in Crisping basket
7. Insert basket to your ninja Foodi and lock Air Crisp Lid, Air Crisp for 15 minutes at 360 degrees F. Serve and enjoy!

Diced And Spiced Up Paprika Eggs
(Prepping time: 10 minutes\ Cooking time: 5 minutes |For 4 servings)

Ingredients

- ½ teaspoon paprika
- 6 whole eggs
- ¼ teaspoon salt
- Pinch of pepper
- 1 and ½ cups of water

Directions

1. Add water to Ninja Foodi. Crack an egg into a baking dish
2. Cover dish with foil and place on a rack, place the rack in Ninja Foodie
3. Lock lid and cook on HIGH pressure for 4 minutes
4. Quick release pressure. Remove loaf of eggs and finely dice
5. Stir in spices and serve. Enjoy!

Faux Daikon Noodles
(Prepping time: 10 minutes\ Cooking time: 15 minutes |For 6 servings)

Ingredients

- 2 tablespoons coconut oil
- 1 pound boneless and skinless chicken thigh
- 1 cup celery, diced
- 1 cup carrots, diced
- ¾ cup green onion, chopped
- 6 cups chicken stock
- ½ teaspoon dried basil
- 1 teaspoon salt
- 1/6 teaspoon fresh ground pepper
- 2 cups daikon noodles, spiralized

Directions

1. Set the Ninja Foodi to Saute mode and add coconut oil, allow the oil to warm up
2. Add chicken thigh and Saute for about 10 minutes
3. Take the chicken out and shred it up
4. Add carrots, onions to the pot and cook for 2 minutes
5. Add the rest of the ingredients and lock up the lid (make sure to return the chicken as well)
6. Cook for 15 minutes on HIGh pressure
7. Do a quick release carefully. Enjoy your "Faux" noodles!

Simple Vegetable Stock

(Prepping time: 10 minutes\ Cooking time: 30 minutes |For 4 servings)

Ingredients

- 1-2 onions, chopped
- 2-3 celery ribs, chopped
- 2 carrots, chopped
- 1 leek, green parts only, rinsed and chopped
- 1-2 garlic cloves, chopped
- 3-4 sprigs parsley
- 1-2 sprigs rosemary
- 1-3 sprigs thyme
- 2 bay leaves
- 1 teaspoon black peppercorn
- 12 cups water

Directions

1. Add the listed ingredients to your Ninja Foodi
2. Lock up the lid and cook on HIGH pressure for 30 minutes
3. Release the pressure naturally
4. Strain the stock through a strainer
5. Use immediately when needed or store in fridges

Conclusion

I am extremely glad and happy that you were able to go through the whole book. I sincerely hope that you enjoyed the contents of the book and found it useful.

The next step from here is to explore even further and find your own culinary footing! Learn the basics from this recipes, and come up with your very own awesome Ninja Foodi Friendly recipes and make your ultimate meal plan!

I wish you luck in your future ventures and hope that you stay safe and healthy.

Appendix: Measurement Conversion Table

Volume Equivalents (Liquid)

US Standard	US Standard (Ounces)	Metric (Approximate)
2 tablespoons	1 fl. oz.	30 mL
¼ cup	2 fl. oz.	60mL
½ cup	4 fl. oz.	120mL
1 cup	8 fl. oz.	240 mL
1 and ½ cups	12 fl. oz.	355 mL
2 cups/1 pint	16 fl. oz.	475 mL
4 cups/ 1 quart	32 fl. oz.	1 L
1 gallon	128 fl. oz.	4L

Volume Equivalents (Dry)

US Standard	Metric (Approximate)
1/8 teaspoon	0.5 mL
¼ teaspoon	1 mL
½ teaspoon	2 mL
¾ teaspoon	4 mL
1 teaspoon	5 mL
1 tablespoon	15 mL
¼ cup	59 mL
1/3 cup	79 mL
½ cup	118 mL
2/3 cup	156 mL
¾ cup	177 mL
1 cup	235 mL
2 cups	475 mL
3 cups	700 mL
4 cups	1 L

Oven Temperatures

Fahrenheit (F)	Celsius (C) (Approximate)
250°	120°
300°	150°
325°	165°
350°	180°
375°	190°
400°	200°
425°	220°
450°	230°

Weight Equivalents

US Standard	Metric (Approximate)
½ ounce	15 g
1 ounce	30 g
2 ounces	60 g
4 ounces	115 g
8 ounces	225 g
12 ounces	340 g
16 ounces/1 pound	455 g

Made in the USA
Coppell, TX
27 December 2020